Baden Powell's Fighting Police – The SAC

Baden Powell's Fighting Police – The SAC

The Boer War unit that inspired the Scouts

Hamish Ross

Pen & Sword
MILITARY
AN IMPRINT OF PEN & SWORD BOOKS LTD.
YORKSHIRE – PHILADELPHIA

First published in Great Britain in 2022
and reprinted in this format in 2024
by
Pen & Sword Military
An imprint of
Pen & Sword Books Ltd
Yorkshire - Philadelphia
Copyright © Hamish Ross, 2022, 2024

ISBN 978 1 39908 366 9

Printed and bound in England
By CPI (UK) Ltd.

Pen & Sword Books Ltd incorporates the Imprints of Pen & Sword Archaeology,
Atlas, Aviation, Battleground, Discovery, Family History, History, Maritime,
Military, Naval, Politics, Railways, Select, Transport, True Crime, Fiction, Frontline
Books, Leo Cooper, Praetorian Press, Seaforth Publishing, Wharncliffe and White
Owl.

For a complete list of Pen & Sword titles please contact

Pen & Sword Books Limited
47 Church Street, Barnsley, South Yorkshire, S70 2AS, England
E-mail: enquiries@pen-and-sword.co.uk
Website: www.pen-and-sword.co.uk

or

Pen and Sword Books
1950 Lawrence Rd, Havertown, PA 19083, USA
E-mail: uspen-and-sword@casematepublishers.com
Website: www.penandswordbooks.com

MIX
Paper from
responsible sources
FSC
www.fsc.org   FSC® C013604

Contents

Preface

'I used to wear that hat,' my grandfather said to me.

It was a Friday evening back in the day when I wore Scout uniform and was on my way to a troop meeting of the 1st St Duthus Scouts.

That was unusual for him to offer anything about his past. I had been told that he had served in the Boer War and the First World War but he never talked about it – no stories or old soldiers' tales – he was a quiet man. So I asked him when it had been.

'In the South African Constabulary.'

I kept on with the question and asked who had been the commander.

'Baden-Powell.'

That was a surprise. In the Scouts we had been told about some of B-P's exploits and the siege of Mafeking and his holding off the enemy for weeks and weeks, but nothing about his commanding the South African Constabulary.

'Did it have a motto?'

'Be Prepared,' was the reply.

That was our motto!

After flag-break and formal troop inspection that evening I had news to give in my patrol corner that I thought was worth sharing.

From time to time I gleaned a little more from my grandfather: the SAC were better paid than the British army; he had served in it for two years; and he had bought himself out. He also had two or three photos of his time in the SAC, one where he had dismounted from his lovely black horse, another was of a patrol in laager out in the veldt, and he had a copy of Arthur Conan Doyle's book *The Great Boer War*, published in 1903. In time that copy became mine and although it has long been superseded I have included a sentence from it in this work.

Not much has been written in the UK about the SAC. However, interesting research work has been done in South Africa based on the digitisation of the attestation forms completed by all recruits. These were analysed by a team from Stellenbosch University.

This work is not a history of the SAC until its disbandment: it deals with two and a half years in which Baden-Powell created the SAC and commanded it in both war and peace until his return to the UK; and it points to the values and structures he gave it that were a model when he founded the Scouts.

Acknowledgements

I would like to thank the sources I have used: the National Army Museum London, which holds Major-General Baden-Powell's South African Constabulary papers, and here I would like to thank Kirsty Parsons, Curator, Collections Development & Review; the Bruce Peel Special Collections, University of Alberta for Colonel Sam Steele's South African Constabulary diary and here I want to thank Jeff Papineau; the National Archives of South Africa, Pretoria; the National Archives Bloemfontein; the National Library of South Africa, Cape Town; Etna Labuschagne, the Anglo-Boer War Museum Bloemfontein; and Dr Joyce Steele, the Royal Highland Fusiliers Museum.

I am most grateful for the help of: Ewan Ross; John Gordon, former President of Inverness and District Scouts; Mike Strachan, ex Scout Leader of the 21st Vancouver Group; Professor Johan Fourie, Stellenbosch University; Fiona Ross; Alistair Gray; Sandy Thompson; Jim Gray; Heather MacAlister, Ancestors South Africa; Diana Gowans, Rhino Research; Jearóid Harris, Warden Gilwell Scouting Centre, South Africa; Paula Groenewald, Regional Team Co-ordinator, Adult Resources, Gauteng; Andrew Campbell, Gauteng Support Team; Robert Faltermeier; Juba Joubert; Robin Smith; Elizabeth Ross; Andrew Thorp, Media Relations Officer, The Scouts; and Caroline Pantling, Head of Heritage Services, The Scouts.

Part I

Chapter One

Creating the Force

On 30 August 1900, Major-General Baden-Powell boarded the first train from Warmbad to Pretoria. He was responding to a telegram from the Commander-in-Chief Field Marshal Lord Roberts summoning him to his base at Belfast in the eastern Transvaal to discuss the formation of a police force for the two colonies that Britain was about to annexe to its Empire. The Boer War had been fought for a year and after initial humiliations in battle the British Empire forces under Roberts' command had bombarded a Boer force under the command of General Louis Botha into large-scale retreat at the Battle of Bergendal.

When Baden-Powell met him next day, Lord Roberts outlined his thinking: the capitals of the two Boer Republics, the South African Republic and the Orange Free State were in British hands; the Boers were no longer capable of mustering armies in the field – their commandos might keep guerrilla activity going but burning farm houses and a scorched earth policy would effectively put an end to that. What Lord Roberts wanted was a mounted force that would have the capability of dealing with any local outbreaks of rebellion in the former republics and at the same time act as a reassuring presence to the Boer community. Baden-Powell was 43, he had been promoted to Major-General after proving his organisational capability during the long siege at Mafeking.

However, the idea did not spring from Roberts, the source was the British high commissioner of South Africa, Sir Alfred Milner. It surfaced in a confidential letter from Milner to Roberts in early May – before Johannesburg was in British hands. Milner wanted the Rand gold mines and the mining district operating as quickly as possible, and thought Johannesburg would have to be policed in a very different way from the rest of the country which should be entrusted to 'mounted marksmen of the Cape Mounted Rifles or Cape Mounted Police type'. He gave it more thought and a month later, on 21 June, Milner wrote again to Roberts about his thinking in filling certain key roles when the war finished:

There is another post which will need a very good man though not quite of the same rank. I mean the command of the Military Police, on which as far as the Transvaal and the ORC are concerned, I should be disposed to rely very much even for military protection. This will be a work requiring energy, organisation, a knowledge of the country and a power of getting on with its people.

Baden-Powell is the sort of man who naturally occurs to one. I think the large and fine force which I have in mind would not be beneath the dignity of a Major-General at any rate to create, especially if he has the whole of the local defence forces – such as volunteers under him.[1]

Lord Roberts agreed, 'Baden-Powell is far and away the best man I know', for heading-up a police force, 'he possesses in quite an unusual degree the qualities you specify.'[2] At their meeting in Belfast, Roberts instructed Baden-Powell to call on the high commissioner and suggest to him a scheme for policing the Transvaal and the Orange River Colony (ORC). Next day, 1 September, Lord Roberts issued a proclamation on the annexation of the South African Republic, the first paragraph of which read:

Whereas certain territories in South Africa hitherto known as the South African Republic have been conquered by Her Majesty's Forces, and it has seemed expedient to Her Majesty that the said Territories should be annexed to and should hence forth form part of Her Majesty's Dominions, and that I should provisionally and until Her Majesty's pleasure is more fully known be appointed Administrator of the said Territories with power to take all such measures and to make and enforce such Laws as I may deem necessary for the peace, order and good Government of the said Territories.[3]

Two days later, however, Roberts was out-proclaimed by President Paul Kruger of the South African Republic who issued a counter proclamation declaring that Lord Roberts' proclamation was not valid according to international law; and he refused to submit to British rule. Hostilities would continue – Kruger was in hiding in his own country and in contact with members of his government and the commando leaders. Their determination to continue the war to the bitter end, but using different tactics, was described by a young burgher, Deneys Reitz, son of a former president of the South African Republic and a soldier in General Louis Botha's army. At the Battle of Bergendal after the Boer army had been bombarded from the battlefield and retreated into the hills,

> General Botha now got everything ready. Surplus guns were destroyed or thrown into the Crocodile River, and the sick and wounded were sent over the Portuguese border, while such stores as had been accumulated were distributed among the men or else burnt. Then, on a morning early in September he led the way into the uncharted bush to begin a new phase of the war.[4]

Complying with Roberts' instructions to meet the high commissioner, Baden-Powell travelled to Cape Town. The train journey was punctuated with long delays because of war-damaged bridges and sections of the line being renewed and deviations were in place. It was a good opportunity to draft out notes of his scheme for he had already a conception of the areas he would work within and he made several pages of notes. He had given himself a time limit, and he had assured Roberts that he would have the force fully operational by the end of June.

Then something interrupted his planning – word had passed down the line that he was on the train, and in his own words he later described what happened.

> On the journey down country I met with a wonderful experience. At several places where the train stopped there were large lines of communication camps, and the men crowded around the train to cheer. At one place they swarmed into the carriage itself to shake hands . . .

> A sudden mania seemed to break out among the crowd and every man seemed to want to give me something as a memento. It might be a pipe or a matchbox, an old knife . . .[5]

This was a manifestation of the halo effect that stayed with him since the reporting of the Mafeking siege in the newspapers. It burst out again as the train pulled into Cape Town station: 'The platform was a swaying mass of humanity, overflowing on to the roofs of neighbouring trains, all cheering and waving.'

We shall see other examples of the way his name had caught public attention when it comes to recruiting for the force in the UK.

As far as discussion with Sir Alfred Milner was concerned it was a case of Baden-Powell laying out what he had already drafted, responding to Milner's questions and being made aware that from the outset the commander of the new corps would be answerable to two powers, the military and the civil authority – and the two would not always be in accord. There was no indication in Baden-Powell's notes that Milner had known him from the past – though Milner had said to Roberts that he was 'the sort of man who naturally occurs to one'. So it was on reputation that he had been offered the post. Milner was satisfied with the scheme he was presented with and approved it.

However, Baden-Powell relished the remit he had been given. He later acknowledged that when he had served in the country earlier he had made friendships with South African Dutch speakers and he looked forward to having a role in stabilizing the country after the war.

In all he spent about three weeks in Cape Town mostly junketing at civic receptions to which he was invited. Then he returned to Pretoria overnight by train on 30 September, and later that day he met General Maxwell, who had been appointed military governor of Pretoria, and General Kelly and eventually Lord Roberts. At one point Colonel Maxse, Coldstream Guards, who had been in command of provisional police in Pretoria, joined them. They went through the details of Baden-Powell's scheme. They agreed on the principles and made some small additions. Roberts, however, considered the force too small at around 6,000: it should be between 8,000 and 10,000 for its first year. This was the first major difference to arise between the civil authority and the military. The underlying cause of tension over the overall complement of the force lay in who would pick up the tab. The two new colonies were expected to be the source of funding raised through taxation, and Milner had estimated a force of around 6,000.

Meanwhile, the military situation on the ground was undermining Britain's claim of conquest – the Boer commandos were increasing guerrilla activities over a huge area; they were highly mobile, hitting the British army columns and then disappearing into the hills and fragmenting and reforming miles away.

Against this kind of warfare the senior military planners understood that a mounted police force with a military capability whose area of operations was the whole of the Boer republics had to have a substantial number.

The military officers also felt Baden-Powell's pay scales were too low for an expensive country, they suggested a colonel should be paid between £1,200 and £1,500, a major £900 (instead of the £700 Baden-Powell proposed), and Troopers should get 7 shillings to 10 shillings per day – 'to get good men'. But Baden-Powell thought such a premium rate might spoil the market for other South African corps and he proposed 5 shillings and upwards, but to give an allowance of 2 shillings as 'compensation for expensive market rates here' and 'all found'.

After the meeting Baden-Powell telegraphed the suggested amendments to the high commissioner and included his view (and that of Lord Roberts) that the force be styled the South African Mounted Constabulary. Then he and Colonel Maxse went for a look around Pretoria for suitable offices for the new corps. They did not come up with a wide choice. There was the STAATS Artillery [*Transvaalse Staatsartillerie*] Barracks, but it was occupied by small contingents of Royal Artillery and Royal Engineers, and there was a hospital in part of a former girls' school that had been acquired for government use.

The barracks would have suited ideally, and Baden-Powell wrote to Lord Roberts requesting it. On 2 October, Lord Roberts agreed, twenty-four hours later he went back on it – the barracks could not be spared after all. He suggested instead the Palace of Justice, at present though it housed the Irish Hospital. As a temporary measure, until the Irish Hospital was moved to other accommodation, Baden-Powell hired offices in Pretoria.

Then he had his first meeting with some personnel who might be taken on to the new force. When the British invaded Pretoria and Johannesburg they set up a Provisional Constabulary, its role was to prevent minor crime and the looting that follows in the wake of war. The republics' police had been mobilized for active service on the Boer side when war broke out, and were involved throughout the fighting. Indeed during the last major battle of massed armies, the Johannesburg Police, for example, acquitted themselves very well at the Battle of Bergendal: when their section of the Boer line was under tremendous fire they twice threw back the British Empire infantry and held on determinedly until they were all but wiped out.

The Provisional Constabulary, which Maxse commanded, comprised British and Colonial troops who had volunteered for a short engagement. A small increment had been added to the pay of the volunteers; they were required to serve in that capacity for up to six months. Maxse took Baden-Powell on a tour of inspection of the quarters that his force had taken over from the Pretoria Police.

There were about 200 men on parade. He toured the barracks, headquarters offices and he inspected the stables. He found it 'all very satisfactory and creditable to Colonel Maxse'. Then he turned to an area he was very interested in – animal welfare. He wrote that he

inspected the Veterinary Hospital under Veterinary-Surgeon Captain Sanderson – well improvised establishment. Visited the Veterinary Laboratory under Prof. Theiler working in conjunction with Vet. Hospital.

In view of the wide prevalence of glanders, redwater, horsesickness, pleuropneumonia, scab, tsetse and other sicknesses throughout the Transvaal – and our present ignorance as to their origin and treatment, such a laboratory is a most valuable institution. The medical officers here are a little anxious to take it under their wing for research (there is already a separate medical laboratory in the place).

Prof. Theiler is an enthusiast at his own job, and does not want to come under the RAMC or any other head of department!

I want (with him) to work the laboratory for practical ends – in stamping out the present decimating animal diseases. To this end I would make stock inspection part of the Constabulary duty – training men at the laboratory for the purpose.

The Constabulary would be the only people able to enforce C D [Corridor Disease] among the indifferent and benighted Boers.

I therefore propose to take the laboratory into the Police department.[6]

The expert that he wanted was Swiss-born Arnold Theiler, who would go on in time to become known as the father of Veterinary Science in South Africa, be appointed the first Dean of the Faculty of Veterinary Science at the University of Pretoria and gain a knighthood.

Two days after Baden-Powell had telegraphed the gist of his discussion with the generals to the high commissioner, Milner responded saying that he was unable to sanction a force of 8,000 nor the higher pay for officers and the allowances for men, and he decided that the force should be styled the South African Constabulary (SAC) – Baden-Powell's title Inspector General.

Next day, 5 October, Lord Roberts sent for Baden-Powell and told him that a strength of 10,000 was really necessary. Baden-Powell batted that back to Milner, arguing that the increased number would pay for itself in a more rapid disarmament of the Boers and settlement of the country. Roberts too put it to Milner, 'The [settlement] of the Transvaal and the ORC depends much more on police than military arrangements. This was my experience in Burmah & I hope you will agree with me.' [7]

Milner, however, was unmoved. Under the hard-line veneer he had an experienced bureaucrat's pragmatism when it came to total numbers and costs. In a letter to Joseph Chamberlain, the colonial secretary, he wrote:

> Over the Constabulary, I have, as you will see from the telegrams, had a considerable fight ... It is not that I want to limit their numbers. Whatever the cost we must have enough of them to stamp out the present guerrilla warfare. But they cannot be got together in a week.

Then he goes on, 'If we ask for 6,000 we may want 12,000. Plenty of time to call for the second when we have got the first.' He took the same approach with his apparently inflexible stance on how much a trooper should be paid: 'It is the same with the pay. We must raise it, if five shillings a day does not get us the men we want.'[8]

The first tranche of recruits was expected to come from men serving in the campaign. Lord Roberts agreed that up to 20 per cent of the army could be drawn on for service in the SAC and he sanctioned that men being discharged from the Rhodesian and Protectorate Regiments could be taken on. It soon became clear though that 20 per cent of the army as a recruiting pool was too optimistic. Men who had served in the campaign and were due to be discharged were war-weary, they had been paid and wanted a furlough before signing on for another short-term engagement.

The standing order of the conditions of service for the force, however, did arouse a lot of interest; not all of it was fruitful. By 10 October, 2,000 applications came in for commissions in the SAC, but Baden-Powell noted, 'young fellows – useless for organising'. One or two commanding officers became interested in the SAC as an opportunity for either their unit or some of its men. Colonel Woolls-Sampson of the Imperial Light Horse (ILH) came up with a proposal that his unit could be integrated into the SAC. The ILH was comprised to a large extent of *Uitlanders* (Afrikaans for outsiders or incomers), but Baden-Powell thought that from an organisational point of view it would be messy. However, he suggested that the ILH, on disbandment, could be a reserve unit and liable to do ten days' training a year with the SAC. Next Lord Lovat, who had raised the Lovat Scouts for the Boer War, came to see him to talk over the possibility of 100 of his men being taken on, but there were conditions to their interest: only if it were for less than 9 months – they intended settling in the country.

There were other men in that frame of mind too, so the inspector general drafted a short service engagement for men who had been serving in the field: one year engagement, the possibility of transferring to 'the Reserve' within that year if they could produce a written guarantee from an employer that he would give 'them 6 months situation at no less pay than they receive in the Constabulary'. For a time the inspector general thought he might have to start enlisting civilians from the coastal towns as so few of the serving troops seemed to come forward.

However, for an imperial force the recruitment field had to include Britain and the Colonies, and Secretary of State Joseph Chamberlain began the process when on 8 October he telegraphed Baden-Powell to ask if men should be enlisted in the United Kingdom. With the ceiling still set at 6,000 men Baden-Powell was cautious and suggested up to 1,000.

Then on 11 October, Baden-Powell met Lord Roberts and his Chief of Staff Lord Kitchener to discuss the conditions of service that he had drafted for the SAC. The draft was agreed and would be promulgated along with Roberts' Proclamation. It was at this meeting that it was suggested that the title for its leader should not be Commandant General but Inspector General.

In mid-October High Commissioner Milner came to Pretoria on a visit without ceremony or fuss. He and Baden-Powell met several times. On their first meeting they talked over a range of things to do with the SAC, from uniform – the cowboy hat with green and yellow facings (the national colours of the Transvaal and the Orange Free State) was agreed; and the rest of the uniform, it was decided, they would purchase from the army stores but as soon as possible they would find their own contractors. They also discussed the necessity of barracks, the separate roles of urban police and CID and the annual cost of the force. Milner asked if the officers could be given the rank of police officers – they mulled over options such as: colonels to be commissioners; majors – district commissioners; captains – sub-commissioners. They talked it over but eventually decided that the officers should have their military rank.

The starting date for the SAC, Baden-Powell considered to be 22 October, the date of Lord Roberts's Proclamation.

The structure that Baden-Powell worked out for the force was implicit in Proclamation No. 24 which Lord Roberts published from Pretoria on 22 October 1900. After the Proclamation's preamble, the first three numbered paragraphs read:

1. An armed and mounted force shall be established in the Transvaal and Orange River Colony, and known as the 'South African Constabulary'.

2. The members of the said force shall be sworn before a Justice of the Peace, or officer empowered by the Inspector General to administer the oath, to act as a police in and throughout the Transvaal and Orange River Colony for preserving the peace and preventing crimes, and apprehending offenders against the peace; and also as a military force for the defence of the Colonies. In addition to their ordinary duties in the Transvaal or Orange River Colony, the members of the force may be called up to serve as a military or police force in any part of South Africa.

3. The said force shall be under the command of Field Officers, to be styled Lieutenant Colonel, and other Officers to be styled Major, Captain, and Lieutenant respectively, to be from time to time appointed as hereinafter provided; and all such Officers shall be subject to the orders and command of the Inspector-General of the said Constabulary . . .

Enclosed with the Proclamation were the conditions of service Baden-Powell had drafted for Lord Roberts. Re-emphasising that it will act 'as District Mounted Police in times of peace, and as a Military Force in times of war' it laid out the terms of engagement at three years and 'The rates of pay will be liberal, so that a superior class of men will find it worthwhile to engage.'

It was to be Lord Roberts, however, who would seize the political moment to get an increased strength for the force. Such was the degree of interest back home in the SAC that on the first day the recruiting office opened in London '1,800 men had come up for enlistment into the Constabulary' – and on the back of that Roberts urged the home government 'to make the force at least 10,000 strong'. He then advised Baden-Powell 'to cable for 4,000 more now from home'; and Baden-Powell drafted a telegram to Milner asking for that number to be cabled for 'while the iron is hot'.[9]

The moment had come and so in the House of Commons, in response to a question from a back-bencher to the Secretary of State on numbers of officers and men enlisted for 'the new police for service in South Africa', Chamberlain replied,

> I am not aware how many officers have been appointed. Their appointment is in the hands of Sir A. Milner and General Baden-Powell. The number of officers proposed for a force of 6,000 men was 200. It has subsequently been decided to recruit up to 10,000.[10]

Early on Baden-Powell worked out a divisional structure of five Divisions (Milner reduced the number to three but conceded five when the government agreed to the increased complement): three Divisions for the Transvaal, one for the Orange River Colony, and one Depot.

> A division would be divided into Troops;
> A Troop would have about 110 men under a captain and a lieutenant;
> Each Troop to be sub-divided into 3 Sections, each under a sergeant;
> Each Section divided into 3 or 4 Squads, under a corporal.

The structure of troops and squads prefigured the structure he would propose seven years later for another organisation (though squad would become patrol) – when he created the Scout movement.

For medical support, he proposed two small hospitals at Divisional HQ in the west and the east Transvaal; he anticipated military hospitals at Bloemfontein and Pretoria would be available. For artillery, instead of organising it into a battery he proposed it should be a Section under a lieutenant.

He had taken steps well before Proclamation No. 24 was promulgated to sound out officers he wanted as divisional commanders. Among the first he offered an appointment to was Lieutenant Colonel A.H.M. Edwards, 5th Dragoon Guards.

Then Lieutenant Colonel J.S. Nicholson arrived from Bulawayo. He was well-qualified for the SAC as he had commanded the British South African Police in Bulawayo and Baden-Powell saw him as the man to be his Chief Staff Officer (CSO), and there was Colonel H.J. Pilkington, West Australians.

Then there was a man he wanted to meet and size up – Colonel Sam Steele, Strathcona's Horse. Strathcona's Horse was a Canadian mounted unit raised by Lord Strathcona, a wealthy Canadian. Once in South Africa it was funded by the UK government. It was commanded by Colonel Sam Steele who had served in the Canadian North West Mounted Police in the Yukon. On 3 October Sam Steele wrote to his wife, 'Major General Baden-Powell asked Col Biggar if I could be induced to stay in South Africa.' [11] The two of them met on 19 October and clinched it for Baden-Powell because he offered him the command of a Division, and was willing to wait until Strathcona's Horse completed their period of engagement in January.[12] On 16 November Baden-Powell proposed to Milner that Steele be appointed to the division in the Northern Transvaal, and Milner approved and followed it up a few weeks later by agreeing that Steele could enlist 1,000 Canadians. Sam Steele accepted the appointment and on 24 November Baden-Powell wrote,

My Dear Steele

I am delighted to get the promise of your service – and the High Commissioner has telegraphed full approval of my taking you.

I wanted also to take a troop of your men now, but on asking Lord Kitchener yesterday he says that even 20% of your strength cannot at present be spared from the field. This is very disappointing to me, as he had promised a while back that I might take up to 20%.

I hope it will not put your men off coming to us in the end. I mean to keep a place open . . .[13]

These men were Baden-Powell's selection along with Major Wilberforce, Queen's Bays, to command the depot. In addition, Lord Roberts suggested Colonel C.P. Ridley, Northumberland Fusiliers, who was then an acting brigadier general, as a suitable man to command a Division; and Baden-Powell agreed. However, when

Milner suggested that Ridley might be Deputy Inspector General, Baden-Powell was cautious with a protégé of Roberts and proposed 'waiting until we know more of him before appointing D. I. G.'

Major Beevor was asked to be the SAC's Chief Medical Officer; and Captain Sanderson, a New Zealander, to be their Chief Veterinary Officer; and Major R.S. Curtis to be Director of Works, responsible for organising a military works section and contracting for construction of barracks and forts.[14]

So in a situation like that, the old adage applied: 'those who appoint can also disappoint'. On 7 October, Milner approved Nicholson over Maxse as CSO, and on 9 October Baden-Powell 'informed Maxse I should not require him'. Baden-Powell notes 'Maxse went to England.'

However, there were competing interests for some of these men – and perhaps a degree of resentment that a new corps was receiving a lot of attention. For example, General Paget turned up – Baden-Powell was out of his office looking round a hospital – and ordered Colonel Nicholson to return to his command the following Monday. Baden-Powell protested; he wrote to Lord Roberts' secretary pointing out that General Paget already had two colonels acting as brigadiers in a small unit. Then he went to see Roberts about it, but Roberts told him in the present situation troops in the field were the priority and police considerations would have to give way for about three weeks, he thought, before Nicholson could be released. Then the Guards refused to release Major Beevor right away.

These factors were impedimenta along the way, to be expected and to be worked round. More important was the cultivation of a culture with a tone and explicit values that would imbue a devolved force that was further sub-divided into small working units; and in this regard Baden-Powell seems to have been the right man to create it for he was not thirled to army learning by rote and doing it by numbers. He was not in favour of drill for drill's sake, there were only two elements he wanted instilled into each man: horsemanship and musketry. Each individual was important and would be relied upon to use his intelligence. The first thing, therefore, was in the selection of men at all levels.

Chapter Two

Recruiting

W hat captured the attention of those 1,800 applicants who, according to Lord Roberts, registered an interest in joining the new force on the first day the recruiting office opened in London?

The newspapers in Britain picked up very quickly on the mounted force that was being established under Baden-Powell; not just the national dailies but the regional papers. Up and down the country variations of the same theme were sounded, and almost all of them led with the name of the man in charge of the SAC.

This was the man whose name was forever linked with the siege of Mafeking because the newspapers had made it, as Raymond Sibbald writes, 'the great success story of the war'. *The Times* correspondent was in Mafeking at the time of the siege and telegraphed the up-to-date account of happenings, but that was not what the editor in London wanted: 'the reports that appeared in *The Times* represented the *Boy's Own* school of journalism, rather than the truth.'[15]

What the reader was presented with in one report described Colonel Baden-Powell 'the Defender of Mafeking' in the following way:

> Every passing townsman regards him with curiosity not unmixed with awe. Every servant in the hotel watches him, and he, as a consequence, seldom speaks without preternatural deliberation . . . His espionage excursions to the Boer lines have gained him an intimate and accurate idea of the value of the opposing forces and a mass of data by which he can immediately counteract the enemy's attack. He loves the night, and after his return from the hollows in the veldt, where he has kept so many anxious vigils, he lies awake hour after hour upon his camp mattress in the verandah, tracing out, in his mind, the various means and agencies by which he can forestall their move, which, unknown to them, he has personally watched. He is a silent man. In the noisy day he yearns for the noiseless night, in which he can slip into the vistas of the

veldt, an unobtrusive spectator of the mystic communion of tree with tree, of twilight with darkness, of land with water, of early morn with fading night, with the music of the journeying winds to speak to him and to lull his thoughts.

Baden-Powell, though, did not look on the defence of Mafeking as a one-man show and as we shall see later he put forward others for recognition. Thanks to the newspapers, however, his became the name with resonance.

The *Shields Daily News* reported on Saturday, 10 November 1900; the *Glasgow Herald* the same day. The *Glasgow Herald* headline was 'Recruits Wanted for Baden-Powell's Police.' By the third week of December the *Tyrone Courier* carried the notice and the Aberdeen-based *Press and Journal* announced that there was such interest it 'has already resulted in 17,000 applications'.

Candidates for the force, according to Baden-Powell's Conditions of Service, were to be between 20 and 35 years of age. 'Men must as far as possible be good riders and good shots, strictly sober, and actually recommended by their COs or Employers and medically fit.'

The most northerly recruiting centre in the UK for candidates was Cameron Barracks Inverness. By the end of February, the *Press and Journal* reported:

Baden-Powell's Force
Brisk Recruiting in Inverness

There has been brisk recruiting in the northern district for Baden-Powell's Police and up till yesterday 75 applications were received at the Cameron Barracks Inverness. Captain Wymer, the recruiting officer, has had a busy time during the past ten days passing recruits and giving the necessary information to applicants. Some of the applicants are well-built young men who have no difficulty in passing the shooting test, as they are almost all from country districts.

One of them, as an exemplar of the requirements necessary for attestation, was the author's grandfather (who was referred to in the Preface). When the recruiting announcements appeared he was under the minimum age for the SAC, but on 28 January 1901 he had his 20th birthday; and a week later, on Thursday 7 February, he had his completed application form witnessed by a justice of the peace; and he had done it, so family lore had it, without telling his parents – his father had a tailor's business on the High Street in the small town and the son was apprenticed to the trade. But the coming of the railway to the far north meant city-made suits were available, so the business of bespoke tailoring was on the downward slide.

The whole process up to the signing the 'Articles of Agreement' in front of Captain Wymer took him two weeks – 21 February 1901.

> And in consideration of the undertaking hereby given by the said Recruit the said Recruiting officer on behalf of the governments of the Transvaal and Orange River Colony hereby undertake and agree to provide the said Recruit with a free passage from a port in this country to a port in British South Africa together with messing during the passage.

During the two weeks though the 'said Recruit' had provided evidence of being able to ride and shoot and to his being of sound character ('to steadiness and sobriety' as the application form had it). There were letters from the captain of 'A' Coy 1st Volunteer Battalion Seaforth Highlanders in which Lachlan Gray had served for two years, and one from Sergeant Mackay of the same battalion, who knew him

> since his boyhood. He is a steady intelligent young fellow, he is a good rider and very fond of horses, he is also a good shot with the rifle, I have shot alongside him on the Tain ranges often, he can hold his own with anyone of his own age and experience in the Tain Coy.

There was also one from Donald Fowler, Provost of Tain who wrote of him, 'I have known him since his youth. He is of respectable parents and I can with confidence recommend him as being fitted for active service. He is a good horseman and has had varied experience in connection with same.'

The final piece of documentation was the Attestation Paper signed by the recruit and the attesting office in South Africa, dated 6 April, certifying that Lachlan Gray's service with the South African Constabulary for three years (written in manuscript) was from 31 March 1901. A typed section appears after the sentence that the recruit would be entitled to receive pay at not less than 5 shillings a day 'also to a free passage home on the completion of five years continuous service'. He was posted to A Division and allocated to No. 9 Troop.

Following this same kind of process, in the first three months of 1901 a steady stream of recruits left Britain for South Africa. The War Office telegraphed on 28 February that 1,700 for SAC were due in South Africa before 16 March; 2,000 before 31 March; and that 1,300 were being prepared for embarkation by May.

On the basis of that, Baden-Powell set out the distribution for the divisions.[16]

	Strength	en route	arrive 16	arrive 31	prep.	Canada
A	353	200	300	400	100	300
B	–	–	–	300	400	300
C	346	120	200	537	200	300
D	–	–	500	500	600	300
E	662	500	600	138	–	–
Depot	275	100	100	125	–	–
					Total:	8,756

Paragraph 28 of Baden-Powell's Conditions of Service stated that where 'a number of men join from one corps or place, they will be squadded as far as possible together in the South African Constabulary'. A distribution of 300 Canadians to 4 Divisions would still accommodate the squadding small group structure he had in mind.

However, the Canadian contingent's progression to the SAC did not follow the UK recruiting pattern but became subject to slip-shod selection and political intervention which, overall, did not work to the good. The process started off in a professional way. In November, High Commissioner Milner agreed to Colonel Sam Steele of Strathcona's Horse being given command of B Division in the northern Transvaal; and three weeks later approved of Sam Steele enlisting 1,000 Canadians – Baden-Powell suggested making it 2,000 if necessary.

In mid-December the Canadian Government wanted to know if the force would take officers and men. Baden-Powell channelled the response that the SAC would give ten captains and fifteen subalterns commissions to nominees of the Canadian Government and would take 1,000 to be sent for attestation.

At about that point Milner's range of experience of government departments alerted him to possible problems with the arrangement and, on 8 January 1901, he telegraphed Baden-Powell that he feared there might be jobbery in the selection of officers for the twenty-five posts on offer to Canadians.

On 12 January Baden-Powell met Sam Steele who was on his way home to Canada with Strathcona's Horse. He told him about the Canadian Government's agreement to send 25 officers and 1,000 men and that he had sent Captain Fall (who had been in Strathcona's Horse but joined the SAC) and Captain Ogilvy with full instructions for enlisting men. Steele was anxious to oversee the recruiting and said he would utilise Fall and Ogilvy to assist. There and then he gave Baden-Powell the names of three officers he recommended for commissioning: Colonel Gordon, Captain White-Fraser and Captain Boyd. Baden-Powell told him that he 'would agree to any recommendation by him'. Steele then asked whether commissions might be reserved for men nominated by him and Baden-Powell said, 'certainly under the conditions we had sent to the Canadian Government namely that the commissions should by preference be given to officers who had already served as such in the Campaign.' Baden-Powell also told him that on his return from Canada his posting would be as Commandant of the Northern Transvaal at a salary of £1,200 a year.

During the following week Baden-Powell was told that White-Fraser, one of the Canadians recommended by Sam Steele, had a drink problem. Baden-Powell telegraphed Steele to confirm if it was true and before he left for Canada on 21 January, Steele telegraphed to say 'the report of White-Fraser being addicted to drink is not true.'

All well and good, but when Sam Steele got to Canada he found that Lord Minto the governor general had already 'appointed half of the officers and decided who he wanted for the rest'. Steele became combative at this and 'demanded that his nominees (the three names he had given Baden-Powell) be accepted and that Fall be removed'. Rod Macleod, Sam Steele's biographer, writes 'Minto rejected all Steele's nominations except Jarvis.' Steele knew though that Minto's instructions from the Colonial Office 'only allowed him to recommend appointments',[17] but he also knew – if he pushed it and took it to the wire – what was the judgement of a Canadian Colonel against that of a grandee of the Empire?

Lord Minto registered a frisson of disquiet though, and it stayed with him, because a few months later in a letter to Baden-Powell he passed the buck to

Captain Fall. It was 6 June 1901. Baden-Powell, nearing the end of the deadline he had given to Lord Roberts for a functioning SAC, wrote the draft of his reply in the staff diary:

> Having received a letter from Lord Minto saying that Col Steele seemed disappointed at arriving late in Canada for recruiting, but he (Lord Minto) was not therefore disposed to consider Fall had done badly in the recruiting – recommending Capt Scarth and Trooper Barnes. I replied (1st June) 'I quite agree Fall has done very well.'

The inspector general went on:

> I must get rid of Vaux inefficient as medical officer and of Critchley who drinks. I have not accepted Col Steele's offer to bring 1,000 more Canadians as I fear it might embarrass him with the Canadian Government. Thank Cols Otter, Drury and Evans – and Ministry for Militia, and self for kind help.[18]

Disappointed is not the term to describe Sam Steele's reaction to the *fait accompli* he was presented with: on 16 March he wrote to his wife Marie from Ottawa,

> There are as yet no more recruits to be got and a good thing too. They are as a body a disgrace to Canada. I may have to stay and see them off. The officers are fools as a rule and the lot not to be compared to any that went before them (in any shape or form).[19]

Sam Steele was in Montreal on leave and recovering from bronchitis during April and May and he left Montreal for South Africa on 8 June. Meanwhile, the Canadian contingent arrived in South Africa. Captain Fall gave his report on the raising and despatch of the contingent: 18 officers and 1,209 men had left Canada; sickness broke out on the ship and 6 men died. Baden-Powell congratulated him on his work but then challenged him with Sam Steele's charge that Fall had borrowed money from one of his men. Fall's response to that was that it 'was correct in a way'. Fall discovered on a journey up country that he had no petty cash; a man in Strathcona's Horse had a lot of money on him and Fall borrowed £5 from him. 'But it was really an ordinary transaction of emergency on a railway journey.'

The Canadian contingent was to be the largest to come from the Colonies. As early as 6 December Secretary of State Chamberlain disapproved of a recruiting campaign in Australia – due to political considerations regarding the Australian State governments. It was at this time that the Secretary of State confirmed the number to be raised in the UK would be 4,700 'if the right class available'. He also proposed that a high percentage of them should be married. Milner, however, considered that 20 per cent should be the maximum for married men, and preferably 10 per cent. The idea of encouraging married men was in the hope that after their period of service they might settle in South Africa. Baden-Powell agreed that ideally 10 per cent should be the upper limit for married men, due to the additional costs 'in building suitable quarters, schools, hospital, and 3 shilling allowances etc'.

The mantra iterated by Baden-Powell, Milner and Chamberlain about getting the right class of recruits for the SAC can be put to the test now thanks to research carried out by a group based at Stellenbosch University. Their analysis of the composition of the SAC is fascinating because it is based on the digitised attestation forms and delistment records for over 10,000 recruits.[20]

The top year for enlistment was 1901 with 5,413 recruits; the following year the number dropped to just over 2,000. Most recruits came from – England 57.76 per cent; Scotland 13.17 per cent; Ireland 10.77 per cent; Canada 6.19 per cent; Transvaal 2.88 per cent; Australia 2.42 per cent. Their average age was 24 years and less than 1 per cent were married.

Two tables of the research appear as follows.

Table 4. Proportion of occupations by year of enrolment

Class	1900	1901	1902	1903	1904	1905	1906	Total
	%	%	%	%	%	%	%	%
Farmers	6.1	13.1	20.0	11.9	7.8	7.9	6.9	13.7
White collar	65.4	63.4	57.2	64.7	60.8	52.6	59.6	61.5
Blue collar	28.5	23.5	22.8	23.4	31.3	39.5	33.5	24.8

Although the bulk of the recruits came from Britain, overall recruits came from far afield, and the researchers looked at the occupations.

Table 5. Proportion of Occupations by Region of Birth

	Farmers		
	Upper Class (%)	Middle Class (%)	Lower Class (%)
Americas	23.55	54.44	22.01
Asia	9.52	40.48	50.00
Australasia	15.16	59.02	25.82
Boer Republics	64.53	30.07	5.41
England	8.99	65.60	25.40
Europe	15.63	65.63	18.75
Ireland	17.19	49.26	33.54
Scotland	10.79	70.32	18.90
Southern Africa	25.46	43.17	31.37
Wales	9.68	66.94	23.39
Total	13.67	61.56	24.78

What of the burghers of the two republics that Britain was in the process of annexing, were they to be policed entirely by *Uitlanders* or was it anticipated that some burghers would enlist? In later years Baden-Powell would say that he had wanted to give Boer commando leaders divisional commands in the force.

While the process of enlistment in the UK and Canada was underway in January 1901, Baden-Powell was in Bloemfontein. Here he proceeded cautiously: he recorded that there were 60 local burghers working in the Constabulary 'doing very useful work in scouting, intelligence and holding posts and carrying out arrests'. Most of them were loyal farmers of the district who were 'engaged on short indefinite periods of service'. On 29 January he returned to Bloemfontein from Thaba 'Nchu where he had been inspecting the police buildings. He noted in the staff diary that he inspected the Mounted Burgher Police, praised them for their good work 'and promised I would do my best to have them compensated for loss of property by the war'.

Then he made a bolder move and went privately, and at an early hour, to meet one of the Boer commando leaders whose name was branded traitor. On 29 July 1900, Commandant Marthinus Prinsloo had surrendered unconditionally to the British. The young Deneys Reitz, who was on commando, wrote of him,

Prinsloo (the same who surrendered so ignominiously with three thousand men a few months later) had telegraphed General Botha at the last moment to say that he and his officers were attending a cattle sale at Harrismith on the day set for the attack, and were therefore unable to be present.[21]

General Christiaan Rudolf De Wet, one of the most prominent Boer commando leaders of the war, and who was in the same engagement with the British but successfully led his commando to safety, delivered a harsher view of Prinsloo: 'The circumstances of his surrender were so suspicious that it is hard to acquit the man who was responsible for it of a definite act of treachery.' [22]

Whatever the truth of it there were two polarised positions in the Boer community, there were the 'bitterenders' and there were the 'hands-uppers' or 'joiners' and Prinsloo was certainly in the latter category.

In the diary for 30 January 1991, Baden-Powell recorded, 'I visited Commandant Prinsloo, privately, 7am and had a long talk over the situation. He thinks it a good thing utilising Burghers (sic) as police and suggests extending it further.'

However, from the evidence of the attestation forms analysed by the group from Stellenbosch University it failed to have the effect that Baden-Powell hoped for:

Baden-Powell's idea was that the inclusion of Boer recruits would create links between the Boer population and the British, but the plan backfired because the collaborators were disowned by their people, and the policy of enlisting the 'joiners' caused the Boers' hostility towards them to rebound on the SAC.[23]

The numbers – 254 recruits (2.88 per cent) from the Transvaal, and 44 (0.50 per cent) from the Orange River Colony[24] – show burghers were reluctant to join; and those who did, on average, served for 416 days.

An example of the situation that 'hands-uppers' could find themselves in comes from Baden-Powell's diary of 30 January, the day he met Prinsloo. It was believed that General De Wet's commando was in the Orange River Colony and moving south. Baden-Powell offered to send out scouts to the north-west to reconnoitre 'which was accepted by Gen Tucker'. He sent '20 burghers out and a few native scouts to watch drifts in the Modder'.

The war went on, and the effect of the British military tactic of targeting non-combatants worked against recruiting burghers into the SAC. That policy began with Lord Roberts, who had his government's support for it, and it continued under Kitchener. Elizabeth Van Heyningen writes:

> Roberts burnt farms as an act of intimidation, to drive the Boers into surrender during the conventional phase of the war. Kitchener's work, on the other hand, was less punitive; it was part of his strategy to deprive the roving commandos of substance and support.[25]

Baden-Powell was well-intentioned in trying to recruit more burghers but the odds against him were too great.

As for the long trek of the indigenous African peoples to the goal of equality – that still stretched far beyond the horizon at this stage; and when he came to formulate a new distribution and establishment Baden-Powell proposed 97 Troops of 101 men and 9 native Troops of 50.

Chapter Three

Bricks without Straw

Before the year 1900 was out the SAC had new headquarters – not a former barracks nor a palace of justice but a dynamite factory; and one that was very much in production with about 100 employees. It was about 11 miles north-east of Johannesburg near Zuurfontein – now Modderfontein – and was on a branch line of the railway network. Permission to use the factory had required the express agreement of the commander-in-chief. The choice of a dynamite factory came about in this fashion.

On 20 November the inspector general wrote to Colonel Nicholson:

Dear Nick,

I enclose HE's letter of 11th in which he does not agree to our having the Palace of Justice.

It reached me on my return from visiting the dynamite factory. This place is very nearly <u>perfect</u> for our purposes – if they will only turn out the Hollanders – but I don't see how they can do so. There is enormous manufacturing plant there and the employees are still living there in some number. But if we can have it temporarily or in part it would do us well.

Ideal married quarters, offices, carpenters and smiths' shops, a splendid officers' mess, excellent hospital, storehouses, engine sheds for stables etc. Electric light and water laid on. All on high ground – with any amount of land – and three big dams (one a lake), on its own railway. Eleven miles from here.

I have tel. to HE asking if we can use it.

It adjoins the farm Waterval which we were offered by Gibson to rent.[26]

The Nobel Trust had established the company *Zuid-Afrikaansche Maatschappy van Ontplofbare Stoffen* to provide explosives for the goldmines of the Witwatersrand in the early days of the gold rush. The factory's product would have been of use to the republic's military during the conventional phase of the war, and dynamite would certainly be a useful commodity for the Boer commandos – and there was a lot of it in the factory.

On the same day that Baden-Powell had written to Nicholson he telegraphed Milner with the information that Kitchener was unable to supply the SAC with many men, saddlery or equipment, and he suggested increasing recruiting in the UK to 4,000 men in addition to the 1,000 from Canada. He also requested Milner that Crown Agents or the Colonial Office should be asked to send saddlery and bandoliers and the War Office to send 6,000 'new pattern short rifle with loading clip'.

He sought and received the same day the chief of staff's permission to use the dynamite factory 'temporarily as a depot for recruits and remounts'. Having heard that Roberts had gone south he also wrote to him. Next day Baden-Powell sent Captain Williams with explanatory letters to the governor of Johannesburg and the manager of the dynamite factory saying that they would take up occupation of the factory on Thursday, 29 November.

Colonel Nicholson, in the interim released from the army, moved in first with about eighty all ranks; Baden-Powell arrived the following day and found that they had constructed good defensive works.

A meeting with Mr Phillips the factory manager was arranged for 5 December. It comprised Baden-Powell, Colonel Nicholson, Mr Phillips and Mr Thomas HM Inspector of Explosives. The negotiations were crisply handled: Phillips was anxious to hand over charge of the dynamite to somebody, but as Baden-Powell put it, 'we headed him off.' It was then agreed that 'the company remains responsible for the care and safety of all explosives.' The role of Mr Thomas was to watch in the interests of HM Government that 'none is made away with to unauthorised people', and the SAC 'have nothing to say to it beyond patrolling and keeping the Boers at a distance in the ordinary course of duty'. Sixty employees would remain at work in the factory, the others would be sent on leave; the company would provide water and electricity at a charge, to be determined later; and the SAC could use any building they liked; and since the factory was on a branch line of the railway they could have the use of the company's locomotive.

Not only was there a locomotive, though, there was also a coach. Having earlier applied to the railway network for a permanent pass to travel by rail on his inspections, he was not thrown by the response from Sir Percy Girouard, Director of Imperial Military Railways, saying he had no objection but if it was also granted to the inspector general's chief of staff and ADC it would be 'a loss of money to the government'. However, he was willing to provide a travelling coach.

Baden-Powell replied that he could get 'the shell of a coach here which I could get fitted up for living in. Also there is an engine here which only requires 2 days' work by a fitter to be of use.' He ended by asking Girouard if he could lend the SAC a fitter.

Next day, 7 December, he asked Mr Phillips the manager of the dynamite factory for the loan of the coach: 'I propose to fit it with lavatory etc. for inspection duties.'[27] With access to the railway network of a vast country the inspector general could use the coach as an office that could be shunted on to a siding overnight and it could double as hotel accommodation and enable him to have easier contact with his far-flung imperial force.

On the cost-effectiveness of the force the Controller, when he drew up his estimate of expenses in ordnance and other supplies for Milner, found that the cost of equipping an SAC constable was 'close on £20 about £4 less than the British soldier'.

Before the end of January Surgeon Major Beevor arrived at Zuurfontein and took over the duties of Chief Medical Officer. Baden-Powell gave him the outline of the number of medical staff he had drafted, and he suggested to him that medical officers be allowed private practice 'with limitations. In this way I think we may get more fully in touch with the people in the district.' It was an astute tactic that was less likely to alienate the Boers.

So at this point the SAC had 89 officers, 1,046 men and 1,311 horses; they had a base, an infrastructure was being put in place with medical, dental and veterinary support. A private company, Dickeson, was to manage messes for NCOs and clubs for men with refreshment rooms, shops, and reading rooms at Bloemfontein, Zuurfontein, Heidelberg, Danielskuil, Thaba 'Nchu and Krugersdorp and there were recruits galore on course.

Preparations for training the gathering force meant SAC manuals, not army manuals, and Baden-Powell drafted a set of proposed Regulations for Drill and Manoeuvre of SAC but he wanted it edited and Colonel Pilkington prepared a small manual of it.

It was also time to get the rest of the key personnel the inspector general wanted and he asked Milner to cable the War Office for Major J.H. Fair from England.

However, the blow had fallen earlier; and it happened abruptly. The army's change of policy came about in November – Kitchener, chief of staff to Lord Roberts, suggested to Baden-Powell that recruits coming out from the UK to join the constabulary should be equipped and armed 'at home'. Following that suggestion, the same day, Baden-Powell met him and Kitchener made it clear that the SAC could not have all the men who wished to join from the forces in the field – the men could not be spared; nor could Kitchener promise saddlery and equipment such as bandoliers for the SAC. It was a dire situation for the new force. Baden-Powell later blamed the army 'for first telling us we should be police and should be "found" by Army, and then without warning telling us to be soldiers and to find ourselves'.[28]

The knock-on effect went further than men and equipment. In early December a supply of clothing for a first issue to the force had been available; Baden-Powell had put in an order for 4,000. Two weeks later Colonel Nicholson, SAC chief of staff, went to army stores to finalise details and delivery and arrangements but reported to Baden-Powell that the army could not supply any clothing as they had undertaken. As a result the inspector general had to go about getting estimates from leading merchants in South Africa for immediate supply. With the establishment of the force now set at 10,000 – the largest imperial force in South Africa – delays in the supply chain would be inevitable.

Then came a change of commanding officer: Roberts left South Africa on 12 December to be replaced as C-in-C by Kitchener. However, there was to be no change of policy. Describing the SAC's predicament Baden-Powell used the biblical analogy of making bricks without straw. Versatility had to be the order of the day.

The first batches of recruits from the UK would be arriving in February, and Baden-Powell asked Milner to cable the War Office to have clothing and necessaries sufficient for each batch sent out with it from England.

Another option was to by-pass the army's supply structure in South Africa and order from the army in the UK, but that had to be done through the chief ordnance officer. He was responsive and ordered 6,500 sets of clothing from the UK; he also promised to get the SAC the services of a master armourer. As a temporary measure Baden-Powell, on 10 January 1901, asked Lord Kitchener

for 9 million rounds of ammunition and 5,000 rifles 'on loan'. Eight days later
Kitchener came back to him asking for an explanation of the 'demands for rifles or
carbines'. Baden-Powell replied that he wanted rifles or carbines on loan pending
the SAC's own supply of 9,000 rifles coming from the UK.

Until clothing for the force arrived it was very much a case of making-do.
Night patrols on the high veldt – with no greatcoats for the men – required
adaptations; and Baden-Powell gave directions, in orders, on how to make a cloak
out of a second blanket with a string at the neck and a belt round the waist.

Word got about, and the matter was raised in the House of Commons. On 18
February a member asked if the recruits for the SAC were embarked on the SS
Aurania 'without arms and uniform, and totally undrilled'.

This brought the expedient response from Chamberlain:

> These 900 men of the South African Constabulary, like other
> detachments of the force sent from this country, will be attested on
> arrival, and will then be provided with arms and uniform, and will be
> trained under the personal superintendence of Major–General Baden-
> Powell. A certain number of them have already served in the Army and
> Militia. These, and all arrangements in connection with this force, have
> been made in strict accordance with General Baden-Powell's wishes
> and requirements.[29]

Meanwhile, Baden-Powell telegraphed Milner suggesting that since the army
could not supply them with rifles Milner should ask the Secretary of State to
arrange for drafts of recruits to bring the new pattern rifle with them. The force
also required twelve tripod Maxims for pack mules, and these should be passed
by government inspection before being despatched.

As a result, in a matter of weeks Baden-Powell received from Maxim-Vickers
drawings of pairs of their QF gun. He wrote to the company asking its range
and whether it was adaptable for mule transport. Then he wrote privately to Sir
Hiram Maxim 'to ask that the cost be kept low'.

For much of the other equipment a mounted force needed, there were
alternative avenues to going through the War Office. Saddles, Colonial pattern,
for the military were £5 and with bit and bridle an additional 18 shillings and
6 pence. The Canadian Government suggested that they supply saddles similar

to those used by Strathcona's Horse, but Baden-Powell contacted Sam Steele and he agreed that the saddles were 'far too heavy for ordinary horses'. However, the inspector general of Cavalry telegraphed Baden-Powell and told him a new light cavalry saddle was being adopted in India. Baden-Powell requested twenty-five samples. He also directed the controller not to indent for rifle buckets – he thought they were unnecessary and caused sore backs – at a saving of about £2,400 on the original estimate.

Then he contacted Cooper Allen of Cawnpore, India. The firm had a thriving business providing saddles and leather goods for the British Army; its representative, Mr Allen, was in South Africa in early January 1901 and Baden-Powell met him. Mr Allen had brought samples of leather equipment with him. Baden-Powell selected the Elliot saddle as the most comfortable. It sold at about £6 16s but Baden-Powell thought it could be pared down and by cutting out 'various useless details' the price was reduced to £4 13s complete except the bit. Baden-Powell showed him the Boer pattern of bandolier and waist belt – the company could replicate it. From the company's inventory Baden-Powell selected the Royal Artillery brown boots and mountain battery gaiters; and to round it off 'gymnasium shoes for sale to the men'.

Months later, though, on 7 May, the steam ship *Tantallon Castle* ran aground on Robben Island in Table Bay and 1,490 saddles from India for the SAC ended up in Davy Jones's locker. On 30 May Baden-Powell was in Pretoria to meet Lord Kitchener and told him 'the great obstacle to our progress is want of boots/ clothing etc.' As a result the Inspector General of the SAC was allowed 'to take 200 boots'.

Not only short of horses and clothing for recruits, who were due in large numbers, the SAC lacked experienced police NCOs. Anticipating that most of the recruits would be young and inexperienced, on 11 February Baden-Powell wrote privately to the Inspector General of the Royal Irish Constabulary (RIC) asking whether any of his men could be spared to be transferred to the SAC:

It would be a great help to us since we are not allowed to take trained NCOs from the army, and we must have a leaven of trained men. Also it would be a good thing for this country to get that class of Irishmen into it – and it would be a good step in the present course of emancipating the Irish from their old bad influence.

Today this would seem a case of the SAC's IG showing a bit of attitude – then there was a context that is now little known about. Donal Lowry, University of York, tells us that during the Boer war,

> Ireland was in the grip of 'Boer fever' as advanced nationalists rallied to the support of the Transvaal Republic and the Orange Free State in their struggle against the British Empire. Obscured by the passage of time and the international campaign against *apartheid*, South Africa ranks alongside France and the United States of America as a major external ideological influence on the development of modern Irish nationalism.[30]

The Royal Irish Constabulary's inspector general came back to his SAC counterpart on a development of the idea. It also looks as though he had had communication from the secretary of state because according to Baden-Powell's note on 17 March the RIC's inspector general wondered if the SAC would take any of their officers 'in their present ranks'; but the terms offered by the secretary of state were not of interest to the men of the RIC.

However, the shortage of fit horses was to continue a problem for the SAC throughout the remainder of the war. As early as mid-October 1900, before Lord Roberts's Proclamation establishing the SAC, the director of Remounts told Baden-Powell that his department could not supply horses in the numbers required for the force. Kitchener, however, wanted at least a token presence of police in the field and he was under the impression that the SAC was being resupplied by the Remount Department. The follow up to Kitchener's enquiry had the director of Remount Department coming back and offering 300 horses – on purchase – to the Provisional Police. Baden-Powell then asked the Remount department to order 1,000 from England – 14 to 14.5 hands – and he proposed going for 1,000 from Basutoland and 3,000 from Australia; and in his notes of the day he wrote that Western Australia was 'most promising as it is not drained by the Indian market'.

On 20 October Baden-Powell went to the Remount Department to look over the promised 300 horses. There were 260, and he found that only 80 were good enough for a long day's work. This was to be a recurring topic in the staff diary. He drew up a list of five countries and the cost of a horse and its transportation: top of the league was the UK at £30 per horse and £35 for transporting it; Australia £12 for the animal and £25 for transportation. Cheapest was Argentina at £8 and £12 respectively. The officer commanding Remounts was concerned that the freight costs were high but was unsure about it so Baden-Powell made his own enquiries.

Part of the problem, however, was the long sea voyage for horses. Sandra Swart of the University of Stellenbosch carried out a study on the role of horses in the war and explored it 'through the lens of their mortality'.[31] Some horses 'had come from another hemisphere and needed weeks to grow or shed their winter coats, depending on when they arrived in South Africa'.

We shall later read the graphic description of the horse deck when Baden-Powell went on board ship to see their conditions. The horses would have to be given time for acclimatization after they arrived in South Africa and that meant being sent up-country to pasture and stables to adapt and to put on muscle mass before they could be put to work.

However severe the shortages the new force suffered, the work had to go on and in one area – training – Baden-Powell did not give much detail of their methodology in the staff diary but he wrote about it later in his memoir *Lessons from the 'Varsity of Life*. It was carried out at the depot at Modderfontein; it was certainly not a method of training that was in the army tradition. Baden-Powell wrote:

> It was done by putting it to the men to train themselves to a very large extent, and the spirit in which they responded, and the results which followed, was a real eye-opener to most of us.

> Decentralised responsibility was the secret, to every man from Divisional Commandant down to the last corporal in charge of a group responsibility was given and praise or blame accorded on the results of his work.

> Discipline was bred from within instead of being imposed from without. It is true that our method of training was criticised by many military disciplinarians, especially as I had said I did not want old soldiers for the Constabulary. I wanted intelligent young fellows who could use their wits and who had not been drilled into being soulless machines only able to act under direct orders.[32]

The validity of their training regime would have to be tested in action and results will speak for themselves.

Part II

Chapter Four

Tenderfoot Corps

T he recently appointed inspector general, who had been a soldier all his adult life, had clear ideas on how to manage a force that was to have a distinctive profile and purpose across the two republics. He had been given the go-ahead for a divisional structure: each division would be an independent unit and administration would be decentralised. His rationale was empowerment of the unit and the individual. The job of the inspector general, as he saw it, was to monitor and inspect that 'proper system and efficiency is maintained'.

Having created a force that would take months to reach its complement, the inspector general's task was to project a tone that would allow a certain culture to form, because there were some men in this fledgling force who, released from army thinking and the large formations they had been part of, responded well in the small groups in which they now operated.

A key method he used to do this was to communicate in writing to every member of the force and he did it in the form of a written document, a booklet entitled 'Notes and Instructions for the South African Constabulary'. Each member of the SAC was to have a copy so it was a huge job that required a commercial printer – in this case T. Maskew Miller, Bookseller and Publisher of Capetown and Bulawayo – to undertake.

Baden-Powell addressed it to all ranks and declared:

> I publish the following instructions in this form so that every member of the Force may be in possession of a copy.

> It is only fair that every one of you should know what is expected of him.

> I look to you therefore not only to read through these Instructions, but to study them so that you do not forget them.

> And I shall expect you honourably to act upon them – each to the best of your ability and loyalty.[33]

He dated his preface 22 October. The contents were comprehensive amounting to over 100 pages and there were appendices. (Part of it appears in the Appendix to this work.)

He was forthright from the outset:

> I should like to point out to everybody, both officers and men, that service in the SAC is very different from that in the Army. You get, here, three or four times the pay of the Army and a great deal more work is expected of you. You will get here less of drill and of useless work than the soldier, but you will get more of responsible duties and of useful work than they do; for this reason you receive additional pay.

The reality to begin with, however, was a make-shift arrangement pending the dissolution of the Provisional Police and absorption of recruits for the SAC, the vast majority of whom were to come from overseas and who were expected to be of the right calibre. Some of the Provisional Police would no doubt join the new force and be very suitable; others would not.

Another constraint was the system the inspector general had to work within – however much he had broken free from the trammels of military thinking he had to answer to two masters.

When the British occupied Pretoria and Bloemfontein they set up military structures to control civil affairs. Major-General Maxwell was made military governor of Pretoria and Major-General Pretyman's bailiwick, with his base at Bloemfontein, was the military governorship of the Free State. Below them were twelve districts headed by a district commissioner in the Free State, and fifteen in the Transvaal. Eventually this military management would cede to civil control.

If the British civil service of that time were thought of as a good example of an ideal type bureaucracy – based on specialisation, professionalism and impersonal relations rather than nepotism and cronyism – then an experienced politician/bureaucrat like Milner would have noticed contrasts with another hierarchical organisation, the army, and in that vein he wrote to Chamberlain:[34]

> In the upper ranks of the army there is nothing like sufficient ability to manage their own business, much less to do other people's. Lord Roberts, who is head and shoulders above all the others, in his tact in dealing with non soldiers as well as his professional ability, has not got

the men under him, or owing to the rotten system of selection or no selection which has so long prevailed, would not be able to find the men to administer properly. With few exceptions wherever soldiers are now doing civilian work things go badly.

Milner's imperial secretary, G.V. Fiddes, became the commander-in-chief's civil adviser and he saw at first hand the military administration of the former Free State at Bloemfontein; he described it as 'chaos pure and simple'.

Therefore, the SAC inspector general had to step lightly, dealing with the army acting as civil authority, the army's commander-in-chief – who had a tendency to adhocery – and the civil authority, the high commissioner. In early October, before the vesting date for the SAC, he met Maxwell, military governor at Pretoria and they agreed that the Provisional Police would come under Maxwell. In the former Free State, though, there was a different arrangement; the police were to be under the military governor in matters relating to civil administration and under the inspector general of the SAC for discipline and the maintenance and efficiency of the force. Then in Baden-Powell's discussions with Milner they agreed that the urban police and the CID would be 'totally distinct' from the SAC.

Meanwhile, one of the SAC's first actions as a military force was in Ridley's E Division and took place on 16 November about 30 miles west of Bloemfontein when a Constabulary post under Captain Tucker and Lieutenant Molyneux was attacked by a commando under General Hertzog. The enemy were beaten off but at the cost of five killed and four wounded; the enemy losses were six killed and ten wounded. Among their dead, Baden-Powell wrote in the staff diary, was Commandant Brand.

As part of good practice Baden-Powell followed this up with a general order to all Divisions commending the good work of Tucker's troop in beating off Hertzog's commando but stressed in his order to all ranks the necessity for entrenching because 'once this is done the smallest post can hold its own for weeks if necessary and it is what we want the enemy to discover by experience'. When he telegraphed his congratulations to Tucker's post, however, he asked for a report on why their losses, which included sixty horses killed, were so heavy and why their post was not entrenched as had been ordered. The answer was that their small post had been attacked at dawn the day after they arrived and they had had no time to prepare cover for their horses.

Later in November a neat SAC small-group initiative took place. Lieutenant Malcolm and eleven men were on a two-night patrol, about 40 miles south of Bloemfontein, when they surprised an enemy commando that had split into two laagers for the night. The Constabulary patrol quietly tethered their horses in a declivity, positioned themselves between the two and opened fire on both, and lay low while each Boer laager fired at the other. From the report of the Africans who buried the dead next day, the Boers lost ten killed. Malcolm's patrol had no casualties and extracted without being detected. They went northward and surprised another Boer commando, on the move this time; they laid an ambush for the commando's advance guard and captured 'the point' of eight men, and brought them to the nearest army post on the railway, pursued all the way by the main body of the commando. When the inspector general met Malcolm on his return, he 'complimented him on his work'.

Another small-scale action, was led by Lieutenant Saunders with a detachment of SAC, including eleven NCOs and men and six Basuto scouts, was reported by Captain Vaughan as having done 'excellent work'. The NCOs came in for special mention – Sergeant Major Donkin in particular, who over several skirmishes had had four horses shot under him. The reward, Vaughan proposed for these men, was 'confirmation in their rank'.

The first Hague convention on the custom of war was signed by a number of countries, including Britain in 1899, shortly before the outbreak of hostilities. The South African Republic and the Free State were not signatories – because they had not been invited to the signing: the two governments issuing invitations to the signing, Russia and the Netherlands, had scruples about alienating Britain if the two Boer republics were invited.

Nonetheless, President Marthinus Steyn of the Free State, at the beginning of the war, issued a plea to the burghers of the republic: 'to let the deeds of none of you be such as to disgrace a Christian, a burgher and the Free State'.[35] Not all of the Free State commandos observed his plea: on 23 November Lieutenant Neumeyer, a member of the Constabulary, was captured by Boers near Aliwal North on the Orange River. They bound him by the arms and shot him in the head with pistol fire. Baden-Powell wrote of him that he had proved himself a first-rate officer.

Some already proved they could do good work but some were not up to it and were returned to unit. This was the fate of a batch of newcomers. Earlier, Baden-Powell had instructed Major the Hon. Hanbury-Tracy, who had been intelligence officer and press censor on his staff during the siege of Mafeking, to obtain some recruits for the SAC in the Cape. For whatever reason there were issues there – Hanbury-Tracy carried out his instructions but then telegraphed that he had applied to rejoin his regiment and been accepted. According to Baden-Powell, that was contrary to his instructions to him, and in a meeting with the military secretary he reported Hanbury-Tracy as having gone AWOL, and he wrote to Lord Roberts modifying any commendations he had made of him 'owing to his having done bad work lately and gone home without leave'. In a follow-up, on 30 November, Baden-Powell wrote in the staff diary, '25 of the men sent up by Major Tracy from Cape have been sent back as useless otherwise everything very satisfactory.'

Over the two days Baden-Powell spent inspecting E Division he covered a wide range of areas. As far as training was concerned, he directed Ridley that it should at first be mainly in musketry and that riding and drill under troop arrangements follow later. He told him to clear a barrack room to make it into a supper room and rest room for the men. Then they talked over the question of structure of the force – Ridley had been an acting brigadier general and Roberts' nominee as a divisional commander. E Division was covering all of the former Free State; would it be better to have a north and a south division? Ridley did not see any necessity for it. However, Baden-Powell felt, if the enemy had any successes towards the south, it might become necessary. His information was that the enemy were collecting in some force and the general direction of their actions was southward.

Next day their inspector general had a parade of the SAC, he inspected the men and congratulated them on 'the very good start' they had made. He spoke to the officers individually. Some of them raised the possibility of a housing allowance or increase of pay – they were all being paid on the lowest pay rung for their rank. It was very much a case of listening and finding out about the snags that came up for self-contained devolved units; it was a contrast to leading a column in the veldt. For example, the military's acquisition of the civil authority structure caused a problem for Major Pack-Beresford. He complained that he had been brought to Bloemfontein to be district commissioner and found that the position was already held by Captain Hume and that he had lost his previous position as second-in-command of Kitchener's Horse. Baden-Powell took it up with Milner and the solution he came up with was to have Hume appointed revenue officer and Pack-Beresford district commissioner. Milner also wanted suitably qualified district commissioners appointed police majors.

Before he left Bloemfontein, Baden-Powell saw Kitchener who asked him to post 3 Troops to the west and south-west of the city. Baden-Powell agreed –as soon as Kitchener could 'let me have saddles'. Such was the paucity of the SAC's equipment at the beginning of December.

He also inspected the emerging A Division under Colonel Edwards in temporary headquarters at Krugersdorp in the western Transvaal. Baden-Powell found that Edwards's arrangements were very satisfactory. At this time there were only 3 Troops, and they were suitably deployed. The Divisional HQ was sited in the former police offices. There were also police barracks and stables, a deserted hotel was being turned into a men's club, and a house adjoining was to be the officers' mess. The buildings were clustered in a group well away from the town and on good camping ground close to water.

Baden-Powell rode out to inspect No. 2 Troop. The post they had established was in a good position on a rocky ridge overlooking Roodepoort; the men were making a strong structure to hold it. A Boer commando attacked the post just after dawn for two and a half hours some days earlier. The defenders acquitted themselves well and beat them off killing two, wounding some and capturing six of their horses. The inspector general complimented the Troop on defeating their attackers but warned them against wasting ammunition – let the enemy come into close range.

For their part the men had their moans: overworked; no canteen. Baden-Powell emphasized, though, the necessity of establishing the post in quick time and then the pressure would be off. He also told them that canteens were to be supplied, and he reminded them that they were being paid extra.

A paragraph in 'Notes and Instructions for the SAC' summed up the inspector general's thinking in about three sentences; but the print run was not yet complete – the different context of the formal inspection would have had to do to be going on with.

The inspector general summarized his findings of inspecting Nos. 1, 2 and 3 Troops: their camping and defence arrangements were good; the condition of their horses was improving but they needed more care; that overall the men of the Provisional Police were unsatisfactory. In addition, however, he thought that stationing the SAC 'among the Boers – especially when a few attacks have been made on them unsuccessfully – promises to be most effective'.

A major hindrance for the new force, however, was senior army officers pulling rank and commandeering a Troop of the SAC from their post. The district commissioner at Krugersdorp telegraphed Baden-Powell alerting him that General French had ordered an SAC Troop to operate under the command of Major Gosset commanding a section of the railway near them; French also redeployed No. 3 Troop to another location. In response Baden-Powell wrote to General French saying that such use of the SAC was not in accord with the ideas of the chief of staff who wanted the inspector general to be working them. In Baden-Powell's estimation the Troop that French had redeployed was of poor quality 'wasters borrowed from the Provisional Police' and he, Baden-Powell, had not wanted to station them alone until No. 1 Troop could be relieved from its present position to support them.

Then, when General Barton asked Baden-Powell if the SAC would guard the railway in the Elandsfontein area, Baden-Powell replied, 'quite impossible'.

In early December Lord Roberts was recalled to the UK and was succeeded by Lord Kitchener. Before the hand-over took place, Baden-Powell wrote to Roberts again recommending Mr Frank Whiteley, the mayor of Mafeking during the siege, for an award. In his official report on the siege, Baden-Powell had highlighted,

> This gentleman's services were invaluable during the siege. In a most public-spirited manner he took up, at my request, the difficult task of arranging for the feeding and housing of all the women and children, and carried out their management with marked success throughout the siege, devoting himself to the task without any return whatever.[36]

During the long siege, however, it would seem that there were different agenda among the military, the mayor and the town council, because three months after Baden-Powell wrote to Roberts he received a telegram from the town council of Mafeking saying that with reference to his mention in despatches of their former mayor they did not agree to the praise and 'would not accept any honour to him as an honour to them!' With a shrug of the shoulders Baden-Powell wrote, 'They will have to go without honour.'

Apart from being mentioned in despatches, Frank Whiteley was awarded the CMG (Companion of the Order of St Michael and St George). He was an Englishman, had worked in business in South Africa before becoming mayor of Mafeking, and quite soon after the war returned to England and made his home in Ilkley. Thirty-three years after the siege, Baden-Powell, on an official tour for the Scouts, visited him at his home a few months before Frank Whiteley's death.[37]

Another echo from Mafeking sounded in early December 1900 when Baden-Powell went to Cape Town and met Milner. They discussed a number of areas including medical provision, a headquarters hospital and its location plus a small hospital per Division. They discussed the overall budget and matters of administration. While he was there Mrs Heal, the widow of the jailer at Mafeking came to see him; and she asked him what he could do about a pension for her. In his official report of the siege, Baden-Powell had drawn specific attention to the work of Mr Heal: 'Mr Heal, the jailer, carried out most arduous and difficult duties most loyally and efficiently. In addition to ordinary prisoners, he had in his charge military offenders, and also a large number of Dutch suspects, spies and Irish traitors.'

While at his post and carrying out his duties, Mr Heal had been killed by shellfire. Baden-Powell had already taken action on Mrs Heal's behalf and when she met him he told her that it had now gone out of his hands into those of the government. If she left her address her pension would be forwarded to her.

His reference, in his official report on the siege, to Dutch suspects and Irish traitors was in the context of the significant number of foreign volunteers who joined the Boer cause; the Netherlands contingent was the largest. And we saw in Donal Lowry's article the reference 'Boer fever'[38] – it resulted in the recruitment of two Irish contingents: the Irish Transvaal Brigade commanded by John MacBride, who was given the rank of Major by the South African Republic; and there was also the Second Irish Brigade.

On New Year's Day, as a token of what the year held, a Boer commando came within 5 miles of Zuurfontein bearing no good will and attacked a four-man patrol of the SAC. As a result of the attack Trooper John Mercer died of his wounds and Corporal C.F. Jack and Trooper Maples were severely wounded. When he returned to HQ on 3 January, Baden-Powell visited the wounded men in hospital. However, he did put in orders that 'the men had brought their misfortune on themselves by not taking proper precautions.'

Ridley reported from E Division in the Free State that Captain Saunders' patrol had done good work near Thaba 'Nchu. They attacked a Boer picket, killing one and wounding two. However, the engagement alerted a large group of Boers who came after them. They got away, Saunders carrying a wounded Boer on his horse as a prisoner. In a separate initiative Sergeant Major Donkin and Sergeant Rogers 'again distinguished' themselves by following De Wet's commando and killing two men and capturing twenty-two horses. They were pursued but got away with twelve horses.

Sergeant Rogers went on to distinguish himself further a few months later – he became the first member of the SAC to be awarded the Victoria Cross. An Australian, who had opted for the few months' service in the Provisional Police and then joined the SAC, he won the VC for gallantry during a skirmish at Hout Nek near Thaba 'Nchu on 15 June. Lieutenant Dickinson, Sergeant Rogers and six men of the SAC were the rear-guard of a column when they were

> suddenly attacked by about 60 Boers. Lieutenant Dickinson's horse having been shot, that officer was compelled to follow his men on foot. Sergeant Rogers seeing this, rode back firing as he did so, took Lieutenant Dickinson up behind him, and carried him for half-a-mile on his horse. The Sergeant then returned to within 400 yards of the enemy, and carried away, one after the other, two men who had lost their horses, after which he caught the horses of two other men, and helped the men to mount. All this was done under a very heavy rifle fire. The Boers were near enough to Sergeant Rogers to call upon him to surrender; his only answer was to continue firing.[39]

However, that lay a few months ahead. On the first Sunday of the year an SAC church parade was held at Zuurfontein. After the service the inspector general addressed the officers and men. He warned them against carelessness when they were scouting; he described the progress in the organisation of the force and again went over the duties that were expected of them.

He had drafted what he thought had to be provided for the creature comforts of officers and men; and that same day, at a general meeting of the officers, an officers' mess was founded. All officers would belong to it; all would contribute three days' pay to the General Fund and there would be a monthly subscription of half a day's pay; the General Fund would be administered by a committee representing every division and by a secretary. Each Division would have its own mess and manage its own accounts by its officers. General rules were passed regulating expenses, preventing gambling and 'excessive mess entertainments'.

He proposed that each division would have sergeants' messes and troop clubs, which would include canteen, recreation and supper rooms, indoor entertainments, and come under a management committee of NCOs and men. A civilian catering firm, Messrs Dickesons, was given the contract to run them, and a funding scheme was arranged to provide the facilities that he had specified. The troop clubs would be a cashless environment, coupons were to be used instead of cash and this would avoid large sums of cash being held. As for the scene the clubs should set, a few months after drafts of recruits arrived, the inspector general sent a circular letter to each divisional commander which pointed out that they had 'a large number of gentlemen in our ranks and we must make their surroundings more like what they are accustomed to, than let them come down to the usual barrack room standard'. They must be clean and have good feeding arrangements, have 'reading and writing rooms, decent latrines, baths etc.'

The style he cultivated as inspector general of this new force was to be supportive and give praise when merited but, equally, to hand out criticism when it was deserved. He knew what he wanted of the force and of its officers and men. However, there was a huge frustration, the army held the strings that constrained him, both in resourcing and, in the short term, in manpower. The inspector general was responsible for the Provisional Police but the soldiers who comprised it were due to finish their term of service at the end of the month and the high command seemed to have been given no thought to this problem. Baden-Powell warned Kitchener in the first week of January that he had no men to replace them.

Three days later Baden-Powell went to meet Kitchener at Pretoria and stressed that the men holding the posts in the Gatsrand were 'borrowed' from the Provisional Transvaal Police whose time expired at the end of the month. Due to the state of the guerrilla war at the time or lack of a long-term view on his part, the commander-in-chief's decisions were guided by short-termism. He pronounced that the Provisional Police 'must remain on at present'. When Baden-Powell asked if he could have some of the 900 men serving in the army who still had their names registered for the SAC, the response was 'impossible at present'. Then Kitchener turned the focus on to what was Baden-Powell's plan of 'proposed disposition of police posts?'

Although he was constrained by the army's grip, his job was to oversee and shape the corps such as it was.

However, there was one assignment he followed up alone. On 17 January he wrote in the staff diary that he had gone to Johannesburg to locate a certain Von Dalweg about his allegations of the abuse of Boer women at Derdepoort, but failed to find him. Two days later, however, he sent the military governor at Pretoria the papers he had on it. The case concerned the alleged abuse of Boer women in Derdepoort early in the war, and the papers he sent were the evidence of a Mr Surmon and some Africans he had questioned, both to the effect that there had been no abuse. He said that Von Dalweg was a prisoner on parole at Johannesburg who was reported to have written in the German press that there had been 'violation of Boer women by natives under the direction of British forces'; that the women were supposed to have reported the case to the *Landdrost* [chief town official] of Rustenburg and that some went to the local hospital with venereal disease. Kroondal, in the Rustenburg area, had (and still has) a small German community. Baden-Powell questioned the officers, the *Landdrost* and the hospital doctors as to the truth of the allegations – 'they denied all knowledge of them. I suggest Von Dalweg be called to account.'

As inspector general of the SAC, he picked up incompetence in the management of accounts in Ridley's E Division as early as 11 January: pay lists were carelessly made out; vouchers were not signed; expenses were incurred without preliminary sanction; and too many native police were employed – all Ridley needed were three Troops of twenty-five each, under a lieutenant to act as scouts. He put those points in writing to Ridley and included another that Ridley was showing too many 1st class troopers; and he reminded him that 'all must be 3rd class until they pass the tests laid down in orders'.

A week later Baden-Powell went to Bloemfontein and saw Ridley, who was on the sick list suffering from dysentery. Ridley told him he was having continual small difficulties with the military governor and the military as regards the SAC. He tried to combat them but it was all uphill going. For example, he had received a consignment of 500 mules the previous week and General Hunter, the Bloemfontein garrison commander, took 250 of them away for military work. Hunter also took two Troops of SAC and they were stuck out at Wepener and unable to get back.

Shortly after their meeting Ridley telegraphed that two of his Troops had been taken to form part of a military column despite his remonstrance. Baden-Powell reacted firmly to that and reported to the chief of staff that these Troops were to have been reformed into five Troops that week at Bloemfontein and they had been taken out of the district altogether; and he gave notice, 'I cannot now undertake to organise the Constabulary, as I had promised Lord Roberts, by June.' He also reported it to Milner.

Milner supported him and agreed that military commanding officers should not take control or commandeer units of the SAC except in emergency. On

7 February Baden-Powell went to Pretoria to meet Kitchener. On his agenda was the misuse of SAC by the military. Kitchener agreed to publish a memorandum to commanding officers not to use the SAC as troops, he also agreed with Baden-Powell's proposed deployment of Constabulary posts in the Orange River Colony (as the Free State was now called).

Kitchener's agreement to publish a memorandum to commanding officers was followed by the adjutant general who wrote to Baden-Powell asking him to submit a draft memorandum defining the relation between the army and the SAC. Baden-Powell drafted the following:

> The SAC, now in course of formation, have specific duties of their own to perform, and are therefore not to be made use of for military duties by officers commanding troops without previous reference to the Adjt Gen or to the I. G. SAC.

> This applies also to their transport and other property. Exceptions to this order may be made only in cases of emergency <u>where the enemy is present in force</u>.

> In such cases the Constabulary will come temporarily under the command of the OC troops (if he is senior to the OC commanding detachment of SAC) on the spot.

> The SAC have, however, instructions to offer their assistance to the troops on all occasions where compatible with their police duties.

January also brought a good omen for the future of the force: a draft of recruits from England arrived. They formed up for inspection. Baden-Powell found them 'a very satisfactory lot, able to ride and to shoot'. It must have been a moment for them too, being inspected by the man whose name had headlined the newspaper calls that they had responded to. He addressed them on their duties: the difference between them and soldiers; care of self and care of the horse; hints about attack, defence and patrolling in the veldt; and in addition he briefed them about what the SAC provided by way of savings bank, institutes and procedures for raising complaints. He also touched on opportunities for promotion and civil employment on their discharge.

Three weeks later another batch of recruits from the UK arrived. Baden-Powell inspected them. He found them 'a very promising lot. Half have already been in regular or volunteer forces.' However, three had deserted at Cape Town. He got a letter from Major Hoare, who was in charge of recruiting in the UK, to say that in early February 1,200 had already enlisted and the next draft of about 500 would be sent off. Earlier, though, Major Hoare had had concerns: he wrote to Baden-Powell that the War Office was recruiting for the SAC in England and he was afraid that they would not get the right class of men. At that Baden-Powell telegraphed Milner to make representations about that in the UK. Milner moved on that one and telegraphed the inspector general to say that the secretary of state has 'impressed on the War Office that the maintenance of a high standard of recruits for SAC is of first importance'.[40]

There was some way to go, however, in making sure all of the force were up to scratch – early in the year two instances of indiscipline in the force were brought to Baden-Powell's attention. A court martial had awarded Trooper Norwood 28 days detention for refusing to go on sentry duty. The trooper's excuse was that he was so overworked in the day that he felt he would fall asleep on sentry. Baden-Powell commented on it in orders, he said the sentence was very light, that the man had no excuse, and that it was up to the NCO putting him on duty to decide if he was fit for it and his business was to obey. Then Baden-Powell went on that they must expect to be hard-worked, they were paid extra for it – 'that they must not consider this force like the army in that respect. That so-called fatigues are just as much duty as any other work.'

The other incident was reported by Ridley and had a much more serious side to it. An SAC patrol under Superintendent MacDonnell had come across a strong party of Boers and had to retire. One man was slightly wounded, a horse was killed and a rifle, bandolier and saddle were lost. MacDonnell who was slightly wounded rescued the severely wounded Trooper Teitz under heavy fire. Several other men also performed well. Baden-Powell put in orders 'a complimentary notice' but he 'declined to commend' the OC to Milner 'as there had been defective scouting. Also a few men appear to have bolted. Shooting such men would have been justifiable.' Later, after Baden-Powell had been given 'the full evidence' for MacDonnell's rescue of Trooper Teitz in action he judged that 'although the act was a meritorious one it scarcely justifies an application for a D S Medal' [Distinguished Service Medal].

About 20 miles south-west of Bloemfontein on 5 February Lieutenant Malcolm and twenty SAC under his command encountered a number of Boers, roughly about the same number as themselves, under Van Aswegen and drove them off. In the firing one of the commando, Van der Walt, was wounded and another, Remsberg, was captured. The SAC section suffered no loss.

In the field E Division was shaping up, but at HQ level slip-shod administration had taken hold. Baden-Powell kept confronting Ridley with his carelessness: not having kept a record of the number of horses he had bought; and apparently handing over 100 riding mules to the Remount Department – 'when we want all the riding mules to help for pack purposes with guns etc.' He had also requisitioned building materials which the inspector general would not sanction, having instructed Divisions to search and acquire materials locally. In this instance Ridley seems not to have adjusted his thinking from traditional military supply practices. The SAC was to establish a number of strong points, or small forts, manned by small groups, triangulating down from the Modder River and deep inside Boer commando territory, and Baden-Powell instructed that 'all forts must be made of material available locally – and there is any amount of it to be got just for the asking from the railway people: broken rails, sleepers etc.'

It seemed to have little effect. Some days later Baden-Powell wrote in the staff diary, 'Warned Col Ridley that indents and vouchers etc. must be signed by him only or the temporary commander of the Division.' He told him too that he must be particular that Troop commanders studied 'our type of fort before going out to occupy detached positions.'

Having had Milner's approval for five divisions, Baden-Powell sounded out Colonel Pulteney, Scots Guards, to see if he would be interested in commanding a division of the SAC. He also telegraphed General Pretyman, for his opinion of Colonel Long, Royal Artillery, regarding his suitability for a divisional command. Pretyman came back to him first, via Ridley, with his assessment of Long: 'a good officer – disciplinarian – but without any give and take.' When Pulteney replied it was to say that he could not take up an appointment with the SAC until he found out whether he was to be asked to command his battalion.

Intakes of recruits would continue to arrive and Colonel Steele plus the Canadian contingent were due in a couple of months when another Division would be deployed to the northern Transvaal so the inspector general would have extensive travelling for his inspections. The rail coach Baden-Powell had on loan from the dynamite factory had by now been adapted to his specifications, and he would have to pay the IMR [Imperial Military Railway] for running his travelling coach on the network – the charge was to be 7½ pence per mile. He complained to the Director of the company, Sir Percy Girouard, who replied that it would cost him less in the long term – that for a general to travel on the network in the normal way the cost would work out at two staff officers at 3 pence per mile plus two servants at 2 pence a mile, making the charge 10 pence a mile.

Baden-Powell had no objections; in the staff diary of 18 February he wrote a little more detail of the budgetary benefits – perhaps for Milner's scrutiny of expenses – 'I can take all these in the coach and have my office working and can be shunted into sidings convenient to my work and living in my coach will save hotel expenses.'[41]

This was the coach that in fifty years' time would be given by the factory to the Scouts at Modderfontein and they restored it. A photo of the coach and another of the Scout patrol that worked on it appear in this book.

However, one division for the ORC then would continue, but it required a lot of monitoring. Ridley went his own way in acquiring district commissioners. In January Milner had appointed Goold-Adams, a former soldier and commissioner of the protectorate of Bechuanaland, to the position of deputy administrator of the Orange River Colony. Baden-Powell knew him from the siege of Mafeking and had officially praised him for his work and advice. On 22 February Goold-Adams contacted Baden-Powell saying that at Ridley's request he was handing over to him, as district commissioner, five officers. Baden-Powell replied:

> But it ought not to be 'handing over' – we share them . . . these D.C.s work under your orders but they are in the pay of the SAC and exercise general supervision of the duties and the efficiency of the Constabulary in their District. Each captain commanding a Troop commands a sub district of the country and is responsible to the D.C. for the good order of his sub district.

He went on to say that was his understanding of Milner's ideas, that he thought, 'it would work I think on those lines in the Orange River Colony and the Transvaal – provided that we, the civil department and the Constabulary pull together as one – as you and I shall do.'

A pattern of casual oversight and lack of attention to detail had been set and continued in E Division. SAC chief of staff, Colonel Nicholson, on an inspection, found a great deal of unauthorized expenditure in the administration of the division; and the 'model defence work' had never been completed and what had been done was along bad lines. He arranged for Captain Collins to go down to the division and manage the work of the partly completed construction.

When it came to standards of behaviour for officers, the inspector general made clear what was unacceptable. In February he had Captain Boyd-Wilson up in front of him. Earlier, he had reprimanded him for failing to have his post adequately fortified; and to add that he 'now shows signs of drinking. Have told him to resign his commission from the force.'

Early on was when to set standards of discipline, it was also the time to encourage professional development for the force's medical support. Major Beevor, the principal medical officer, agreed with Baden-Powell's idea of allowing private practice for the MOs – so did Milner. Baden-Powell put it thus:

> It will bring police more in touch with the local people and will oust the undesirable doctors, who are mostly Hollanders or drunkards, and encourage our MOs to keep up their knowledge of medical science as in practising among the better classes they will be in competition with other medical men.

Beevor explained to him how too much waste went on in the military surgeries because the Colonial Office used the Crown Agents to obtain supplies and instruments. This was an area in which the inspector general would have been interested, for economy and budgetary awareness were very much part of his managing the force from the start. However well Baden-Powell might have performed had he been given command of an army, he appeared to have mastery of the fine detail in specifying the Constabulary's requirements.

With recruits from the UK arriving and more promised, Baden-Powell established another Division in the east of the Transvaal, C Division under Colonel Pilkington. Its headquarters were at Heidelberg. It was a good site on a plateau with spring water and it overlooked the town. Baden-Powell visited the SAC camp where there were the nuclei of two Troops, and the 'two very good forts made by them are a pattern for the rest of the garrison.'

As early as 20 February, a group of forty of the new Division were in action for the first time; and they got off to a good start. A Boer commando had partially derailed and fired into a train near Heidelberg. In response, a military mounted force under Major Vallentin went to relieve it; along with them, working as an integral unit, were forty SAC under Captain Capell. While the main military component attacked the commando from its flank, Capell was ordered to advance against the enemy front to try to make contact with the train. This the SAC did under fire; they advanced in extended order until they reached a donga [gully] about 1,500 yards from the train. There they tethered their horses and crept forward, led by Capell, till they gained a stone kraal [old enclosure] perhaps 700 yards from the enemy and kept up a heavy fire on them while Capell and Sergeant Major Ogilvy ran across the open area and got on to the train. The exchange of fire continued until an armoured train with troops steamed up. The enemy withdrew leaving five dead. The British casualties were seven wounded, but none among the SAC.

The officer commanding the combined force commended the SAC saying,

> the men behaved splendidly, particularly as many of them had never been under fire before. Their scouting was good; the way in which they skirmished, concealing themselves from the sharp-eyed Boers not more than 700 yards away was worthy of old soldiers and their fire discipline was good.

As for the development of the SAC, though, some of the planning did not achieve fruition. For example, the Veterinary Laboratory that Mr Theiler was to have been part of did not materialise. Theiler was based in a laboratory at Pretoria, he had been carrying out a study of horse sickness and was closely liaising with the SAC. Baden-Powell wrote, for a second time it would seem, to General Maxwell, the governor of Pretoria, asking for the services of Theiler as a veterinary chemist at Zuurfontein.

Care of the horse came next to care of self in Baden-Powell's guidelines to the SAC, and horse sickness was a devastating viral disease in southern Africa. The frequency of comments in the staff diary about the condition of their horses is evidence of the concern: the horse was vital to them. It was the same on the Boer side, and along with man's dependency, in the words of Deneys Reitz, came that strange bonding that can develop between man and the horse that faced the same rifle fire that he faced – his comrade and fellow mortal.[42]

> I now suffered the loss of my dear old roan horse. One morning he came staggering and swaying up to me from the grazing-ground, and I saw at once from his caving flanks and glassy eyes that he was stricken with the dreaded horse sickness, from which scarcely one animal in a hundred recovers. Nosing against me he seemed to appeal for help, but he was beyond hope, and in less than an hour, with a final plunge, he fell dead at my feet. This was a great sorrow, for a close bond had grown up between us in the long months since the war started, during which he had carried me so well.

Milner had telegraphed Baden-Powell in mid-January to ask whether Theiler and his laboratory were moving in. The reply was affirmative: 'he is attached to the SAC and we want him as soon as he can be spared by Gov. Pretoria. Horse sickness bad here and some poisoning.' Ten days later Milner wired that the SAC could have Theiler but his laboratory was required by the Health Officer of Pretoria. Baden-Powell's response was that the Health Officer already had one laboratory 'and wants Theiler as well – probably to make a vaccine which is a paying concern'.

On 7 February in Pretoria, Baden-Powell had what he described as 'a joint interview' with General Maxwell, Dr Turner, principal health officer and Theiler as to starting a veterinary bacteriological institute. They agreed that human and veterinary bacteriological research be carried out in the same institution. Furthermore, as the police vets and cattle inspectors would require training the site for it would be more suitable in Zuurfontein than Pretoria, and so it was left at that stage subject to Milner's approval. Next day Turner visited the Zuurfontein site and agreed it was more suitable than the one at Pretoria. Three days later, however, Baden-Powell wrote to Milner to say that he was sending Colonel Nicholson to him with the SAC estimates; then he wrote four cryptic sentences, 'questions of medical department, veterinary and cattle disease, dynamite factory complicity in the war, Dr T. unsuitable for head of department'.

On 15 February Baden-Powell had a letter from General Maxwell, Governor of Pretoria, enclosing one from Dr Turner on the possible use of the dynamite factory for a bacteriological institute. Turner agreed that it was the better site but it required alterations 'which are not desirable till we know for certain the future of the factory'. Baden-Powell responded that while he agreed he thought a temporary veterinary laboratory is 'immediately necessary as we are losing 3 to 5 horses a day through horse sickness, poison and today glanders. And I want Theiler for this work.' He copied his letter to Milner and added a note,

> I do not see why – though Dr Turner wishes eventually to be head of
> a general Bacteriological Institute for the country he should not in the
> meantime allow us the use of instruments and Dr Theiler to try and
> save some of the horses.

One week later, in reply to this request, Maxwell sent Baden-Powell an application from, in Baden-Powell's word, 'a loafer who undertakes to cure horse sickness at 3 shillings a head and considers this "will solve the matter."' Such was the solution from the military governor to a serious problem – a snake-oil quack at cut-price rates.

Milner, however, had long-term considerations in mind, including his own role when the military governorships fell into desuetude. On the first day of March he was travelling through the country, and he sent a brief telegraph to Baden-Powell saying that he did not 'think it necessary for us to utilise Theiler at present'. His second short text, however, was supportive in a different area: he considered that the military must not use the SAC 'and will fight the question if necessary'.

Although the idea of a veterinary institute ultimately fell into the coils of petty politics, it perhaps mattered little where it was sited or under whose aegis it operated so long as Theiler's scientific work went ahead.

Milner saw Baden-Powell on his trip to the former republics. The force was building up, returns from London showed that 789 recruits had left the UK before February and another 2,446 by the end of the month. So the summer months seemed to be on target, and Milner sanctioned the granting of the honorary rank of Lieutenant Colonel to the principal medical officer, Major Beevor; to the controller, Captain Anderson; and the director of military works, Major Curtis.

On a matter of policy Milner had earlier telegraphed Baden-Powell telling him that after the war was over the protectorate of Swaziland – currently a protectorate of the Republic of South Africa – would not be policed by the SAC but by a special police. This followed Baden-Powell writing in the staff diary his assumption that since the British troops were clearing the country down to the Swazi border – and there was report that Steinaecker's Horse were in the area – discussion about policing that country would arise. At this stage he was thinking in terms of allocating three Troops of white Constabulary and three of black; but it would be necessary 'to consult the future Civil Officers of Swaziland' and so he invited Mr Smuts '(late HM Agent to Swaziland)' to come and see him.

A conference took place in late February with four in attendance: Mr Smuts, the SAC IG, Colonel Nicholson and Colonel Pilkington C Division's CO. This Mr Smuts is not to be confused with the distinguished Boer leader, General Jan Christian Smuts who played an important part in the field and on the political scene as a figure for his country – this figure was Johannes Smuts who had secured a position as a spokesman for British interest in Swaziland. At this meeting in February, he outlined a proposed policy development: Swaziland being run as a protectorate independent of the Transvaal would require a different kind of police who would be under the control of the Administrator of Swaziland, and they would need to be special men able to speak Dutch and Zulu. Baden-Powell held a different view. However, Mr Smuts did not expect to settle the country without some extra force, and he thought the SAC would be available for that role rather than troops. It was left in the air at that and, as we shall see later, the SAC IG would investigate the frontier positions.

However, that was future planning, but in the present combatants on both sides in irregular warfare had to be prepared for the unexpected. There were alleged cases of Boers wearing captured British army uniform to lure their enemy. A train in the Transvaal was captured and plundered by Boers. In one of its wagons there was a consignment of hats for the SAC that had been imported from the USA. Baden-Powell issued an alert to the OC A Division to warn his outlying posts not to be deceived by men wearing SAC hats. At administrative level also the inspector general had to deal with the unexpected: in E Division Ridley proposed taking on some officers on probation without first submitting their names to HQ – this had to be rectified.

A few weeks later, on 6 March, in the eastern Transvaal, at night, a patrol of C Division in a Cossack Post [small site for outpost duty] was guarding a small culvert on the railway near Heidelberg when they heard mounted men approaching. They let the Boers get to about 30 yards before challenging them – in case 'it was a mounted patrol of our own people' and then they opened fire. The Boers galloped off, returning fire, but did not continue the engagement.

Abuse of showing the white flag was also alleged during this war. Baden-Powell, dealing with the army in their purely military role, sent copies of his order regarding defence posts. He reported that General Wynne and General Kelly highly approved. He then put in orders that

1. We are not obliged to cease firing because enemy put up white flag.
2. We are not bound to cease firing because an unauthorised person on our side puts it up.[43]

The SAC was given the responsibility for providing the bodyguard for the high commissioner now that Milner was to take up residence in Johannesburg. On 14 March Baden-Powell rode over and inspected the grounds round the house where Milner would stay. He was satisfied with what he saw from the viewpoint of guarding the building. When he returned to Zuurfontein, he addressed the group who had been selected for guarding the high commissioner. They were under the command of Captain Wilcox. He stressed the importance of their task, the personal safety of the high commissioner was committed to their care.

The following day Milner visited the dynamite factory at SAC HQ and the heads of departments were introduced to him and he lunched at the mess. Before he left, Baden-Powell discussed with him some thoughts he had on the appointment of district commissioners as majors. Milner was amenable to good ideas that had the effect of reducing the budget. The inspector general could substitute inspecting staff. Milner agreed, but only for the Transvaal; he thought that those who had been appointed to the role of district commissioner in the Orange River Colony should continue. This was followed up later in the month at a joint meeting in Bloemfontein of Milner, Baden-Powell, Ridley and Goold-Adams where it was decided that one division would be sufficient for the Orange River Colony and there would be eight districts.

From early in the year, when he privately met the surrendered former Commandant Prinsloo, whose name was vilified by the 'bitterenders', there were sixty burghers working for the force. Their duties at that time were restricted to scouting, intelligence gathering, holding posts and carrying out arrests. Most of them were loyal farmers and they were engaged on short periods of service. However, by the end of March Baden-Powell hoped that the contingent was going to be increased to 500 and if it worked out the total could go up to 1,000. As we now know from research carried out by Stellenbosch University, that number of burghers in the SAC was never attained.

However, during the early months of the year their number increased somewhat and Baden-Powell monitored them. He inspected two burgher Troops. One was well sited and the men, their supplies and the horses were 'in very good order' and the Troop had its own farrier. The other Troop post was at Boschkop and was commanded by Sergeant Scott. The area had been a gathering place for Boer commandos, but they had moved away. Next Baden-Powell rode to Abrams Kraal where there were 2 Troops as well as 200 men of the Royal Irish Rifles in a very good position.

In addition to those burghers who joined the SAC there was a local corps raised in January in the Bloemfontein district who were known as the Burgher Police (later the name was changed to Farmers' Guard) and they were attached to the SAC.[44] On 27 March Baden-Powell arranged with Ridley to post four burgher and three SAC posts in a circle of about 30 or 40 miles diameter around Bloemfontein in the following ten days. He suggested to Ridley that burghers should be enlisted for fixed periods of two or three months; alternatively, they be paid a month in arrears, 'so that the officers have some hold on them'. He also recommended that the burghers be divided among the Troops; he suggested two squads to each Troop to act as scouts, patrol leaders or interpreters. He was keen to have burghers in the force or attached to it, but there was a question mark perhaps about the extent of the loyalty of some. Milner, after the war, made the statement, 'I know that a great many of them ['joiners'] were men of a low type, actuated by base motives, though I do not for a moment admit that this is universally true.'[45] Both Milner and Baden-Powell would have been aware that it required a high degree of commitment for burghers to face their own people in warfare: if they were captured they were likely to be shot as war-traitors.

As the force built up with the inflow of recruits from overseas, newcomers were sometimes soon in action, and in this kind of warfare there were instances of individuals showing great determination. At Abrams Kraal, for example, there were three wounded men in hospital, 'comfortable and cheery'. One of the trio had been captured by the enemy. Now the Boer commandos had little enough by way of medical care for themselves when they were on commando; and it was not at all unusual for them, under a white flag, to hand a captured wounded enemy back. The man had been captured after his horse had been killed and he himself wounded in two places, but he carried on firing till he could not go on, then he threw away the bolt from his rifle and hid what rounds of ammunition he had left so that the enemy would get nothing.

On 28 March Baden-Powell issued an order expressing 'His Excellency the High Commissioner's satisfaction at the appearance and progress of the SAC.'

When the SS *Canada* docked at Cape Town early in April with drafts of 900 recruits Baden-Powell inspected them at the dockside, observing the disembarking and equipping arrangements; he went over the accommodation of the *Canada* and found it very satisfactory. It was also a time for contacting civilian suppliers: he interviewed representatives of White, Ryan and Co about wagons and harnesses from the USA and also Stetson's agent about hats for the SAC. Then, on a gracious note, he thanked Mrs Hayne who ran 'Tommy's Welcome' for the refreshments and presents that were given to the SAC men who were travelling up-country.

On 14 April Baden-Powell went to Bloemfontein and arranged with Ridley to be prepared to have eleven Troops in position around Petrusburg by 25 April if the military could occupy the place and give the SAC support. He inspected the SAC camp at Lydenham, 6 miles south-east of Bloemfontein. They were relatively well equipped except for hats, but the horses sent from the Queenstown district by Captain Spriggs were unsatisfactory, they were too small and light and most of them were in poor condition.

Two days later he was in Johannesburg discussing with Milner the distribution of posts in the Orange River Colony. The idea was to set up a belt of posts across the former state from Bloemfontein to Jacobsdal with the intention of enclosing tracts of land, which, when pacified, could be protected. Baden-Powell also alluded briefly to the administrative problems in E Division. When he returned to Zuurfontein there was a memo from Milner regarding the disposition of posts.

The detail of Baden-Powell's reply gives some idea of the extent the SAC's development was thwarted by the army. He first reminded Milner that he had not promised to have the SAC 'effective until June even at the time the army was to have helped me with trained men and with transport'. The army still owed them remounts and saddles, and he pointed out that their contracts for overseas supplies would not arrive for weeks. Of the 4,000 recruits they now had, over half were untrained. That was not the problem, however, he could get them to work, he wrote, 'if the army will help us by letting our horses come up (900 waiting in

Natal and 1,100 to follow) and by giving us ox transport 60 wagons, harness for 25 spans, hospital tents 9, ammunition 1,500,000 rounds, horseshoes and guns.'

Serving both masters, the next day he went to see Kitchener in Pretoria and gave him a copy of his memo to Milner. Kitchener had a reputation for not delegating authority, for keeping decision-making to himself, and he wanted to go over the details himself and asked Baden-Powell to come back the following day. When Baden-Powell returned to SAC HQ there was a note from Milner with some simple queries about the estimates; but, in the background, as Milner told him, someone had been going to him with tales about the SAC being extravagant. Baden-Powell wrote a note 'this is not exactly in accord with the facts'.

Zuurfontein was a suitable site for a barracks for Baden-Powell and he met Sir Percy Girouard and Major Twiss to discuss the idea. They were not enthusiastic about it, they advised a careful search for water before deciding on Zuurfontein; they thought that Rietfontein was probably a better site as it would eventually come within the reach of Johannesburg water supply and it was also at a higher elevation.

The idea of enclosing tracts of land meshed well with Kitchener's idea of pinning down the enemy to let the army columns engage them – the blockhouse line. As Thomas Pakenham put it:

> Kitchener, the sapper, had spotted a new possible use for the blockhouses, originally built to defend the railway lines. What about a gigantic grid-mesh of blockhouses lines: barbed wire, alternating with blockhouses, each miniature fort within rifle-range of each other? Wouldn't this create just the steel net into which the columns could drive their quarry?[46]

Having had time to study Baden-Powell's proposed distribution of an entanglement of posts across the Orange Free State, Kitchener thought they were too widely diffused in Baden-Powell's sketch; and he 'suggests drawing them in a bit and not attempting to take up the whole line at first, but only as far west as Emmaus and Paardeberg'. He said that he would send a column of 300 men and two artillery pieces to hold Petrusburg so that eight SAC Troops could start their posts on 28 April, and Baden-Powell promised that a fortnight later he would have another six Troops occupy the western part of the country.

When the system was more extensively developed the correspondent of *The Times* described it and included a sketch map:

> On the accompanying map lines of blockhouses and South African Constabulary posts are marked with small crosses. It is not necessary to make any distinction on the map between the two, but where reference is made in the text to constabulary posts they will be so designated. The main difference between these posts and blockhouses, is that while the latter are purely lines of defence, the former are provided to a varying extent with a striking arm. No hard and fast rule or type is adhered to in either case, but, generally speaking, constabulary are established at intervals of five or six miles with occasional blockhouses between them.[47]

Out of the blue the gods decreed a windfall – Captain Acherly contacted Baden-Powell saying that there were large stocks of ordnance stores intended for the Boer commandos lying at Delagoa Bay. They included great coats, suits of cord cloth, '27 ½ tons of horseshoes at 2 shillings and 6 pence per hundred weight . . . and 2, 400 boots at 8 shillings and 6 pence'. There were different opinions on who had legal entitlement, but someone called Erhorn had power of attorney; there was an agent and Baden-Powell got Kitchener's authority to send an officer to bring the goods that they wanted up by train.

The beneficence continued with Kitchener agreeing that the SAC could retain for their own use the vehicles they had captured – provided that a return was rendered. Kitchener also agree to the SAC having 9 EP tents, 6 hospital tongas [light 2-wheeled vehicle used for bringing wounded from the field], 25 sets of harness and 1,500,000 rounds of ammunition – 'if they can be spared'. After all that largesse, on a plaintive note, Baden-Powell asked him 'to let us have back 240 horses and 270 mules still owing to us by Remount Department'.

Provision had to be made for casualties in the operation that was to follow; and on 22 April Milner rode over from Johannesburg to SAC HQ to discuss the proposed distribution of posts and consequences for the financial estimates. He agreed to the cost of twelve tents for casualties, some extra staff and sanctioned taking on twelve doctors. As a result of Milner easing the budget restrictions, the SAC, by the end of May, had six hospitals of 50-70 beds established.

According to plan, and dovetailing with Kitchener's orders, on 27 April Ridley reported that his force would be ready to move with the convoy next day to establish a post at Abrams Kraal, then one at Surrey and on to Petrusburg. The sequence of moves, travelling at about 12 miles a day, would take about a week. Then the remaining posts would be established.

Almost every day throughout May the SAC were in action with the enemy. On the first of the month, in the Orange River Colony, Major Apthorpe with seven Troops occupied Abrams Kraal with only slight opposition; and Lieutenant Malcolm patrolled to near Poplar Grove. In these moves the enemy lost four killed and eleven captured. The next day, though, the enemy took the initiative and attacked a satellite outpost that had been set up from the SAC post at Koppies Kraal, driving the men into the main post. In that engagement the SAC had one man wounded and four of their burghers were captured. Given the deficiency of resources that were vital to them, it is not at all surprising that in the record of the death and wounding of comrades there should be included among their losses: '10 horses killed and 11 rifles lost'.

On 3 May Major Apthorpe had a skirmish with Boers near Surrey Dam and drove them out of their position at Driefontein. As the enemy retreated they ran into an ambush set for them by the SAC – several of the enemy were reported hit but none killed. However, two SAC men were wounded.

In A Division the Boers did the attacking in the first few days of May, and these engagements varied: there was a small scale attack where two SAC were wounded on a night patrol near Zuurfontein; and on 4 May Captain Fowler with a patrol of thirty men was attacked in the Gatsrand, but he managed to withdraw with one man wounded and two men captured – their horses had been shot.

In E Division a patrol near Abrams Kraal was attacked and two men whose horses had been shot were captured – but the two fired all their ammunition then buried their rifle bolts and disabled their rifles before they gave in.

Ridley reported that 3 Troops went to Kuil Put, encountering only light opposition; and the burgher Troop engaged a number of Boers north of the Modder and killed four, wounded and captured six, one of whom was Field Cornet Diedric of Boshof.

In A Division a patrol of recruits undergoing training at night captured five members of a Boer commando asleep. A few days later, Edwards reported that a party of twenty Boers crossed the Vaal heading northward; Captain Reynolds attacked their laager with twenty men, leaving another ten to hold the drift on their line of retreat so that the enemy came in for double fire. The party got away with difficulty, and, it was assumed, with some losses. A few days later Captain Reynolds was told by a doctor that a party of Boers had rounded up large flocks of sheep. The doctor gave their route and Reynolds followed it, ambushed them and brought back over 1,000 sheep. The patrol suffered no losses in these engagements.

Sometimes the odds against a small group of SAC were just too great: on 4 May Captain Fowler of A Division and a patrol of 30 men were attacked by about 180 to 200 Boers in the Gatsrand. Fowler got his patrol out with the loss of one man wounded and two captured owing to their horses being shot.

Throughout these small-scale actions the new corps was learning and becoming responsive to situation and terrain. There were times too when it acted as part of a combined force with army support. This happened, for example, on 7 May. Baden-Powell went out with 3 Troops of SAC and army units from Katsdoorn to Petrusburg against a force of Boers. He summarized the action:

Marched at dawn with whole force on convoy from Katsdoorn for Petrusburg leaving 2 Troops under Capt Tucker to hold Katsdoorn.

About 6 miles out of Petrusburg found enemy about 120 strong (counted by me) holding Koppies. Shelled them while SAC 3 Troops attacked. Enemy retreated at once to second position just outside Petrusburg, where same operation continued. Enemy retreated southwards in two parties.

SAC were excellently handled by their officers and men were faultless in their working. We had one man wounded and 2 horses killed.

Camped 2 miles south of the village, Petrusburg being deserted except 1 German doctor and about half a dozen sick men, women and children.

The doctor said of one of the men (Pretonius) that he had never been on commando but was a member of the Provincial Mounted Police. We afterwards found he had been on commando. The doctor seems 'undesirable'.

That night, after moonrise, Baden-Powell with Ridley and escort rode to Katsdoorn, having telegraphed that they were coming. However, the telegram was never received and as they approached the post they were fired on by an outlying group in ambush and had one horse killed.

On 8 May, in the Transvaal, Captain Chamney of A Division and a patrol of 17 men plus the Potchefstroom Town Guard had been following a group of Boer cattle rustlers when they were attacked by a force of about 100 Boers. Chamney got his men into a kraal where they fought the enemy for several hours before driving them off. In that engagement they lost two killed, five wounded and nine horses killed. Among the wounded was Lieutenant Worrell. Several members of that patrol were cited in the *London Gazette*: Captain Chamney 'for bravery and determination in holding a kraal against superior forces and beating them off'; Lt Worrell 'for gallantry on the same occasion' and Trooper Lodewijk was cited for coolness and gallantry in action.

Next day Baden-Powell went by rail in his coach to inspect 5 Troops of the Canadian recruits at Danielskuil. They too had arrived by train that morning. He described them as, 'Fine lot of men but very sickly.' They had been subject to numerous diseases including mumps and measles on the sea journey.

On 11 May Lieutenant Beamish of E Division with a patrol of 32 men near Abrams Kraal was attacked by a sizable force of Boers, estimated at around 100. In the running fight thirteen of the SAC were captured owing to their horses giving out.

As the force increased in size, lack of uniform and equipment became more evident. On 12 May Baden-Powell inspected 6 Troops in the Heidelberg area; he found they were badly in need of boots, hats, mess tins and cloaks; and there was no hospital: they had to go by train to the nearest hospital at Elandsfontein. He rode out to the SAC post at Kliprivier 10 miles west of Heidelberg where there were 2 Troops under the command of Captain Capell. The position was good but the defence was poor; and he issued instructions to substitute the blockhouse design for the open circular works. This would have been the simplified blockhouse using stones, sandbags and corrugated iron.

That same day, about 4 miles south of Petrusburg in the Orange River Colony, a party of around 200 Boers attacked an SAC patrol. The patrol came out of it with one man wounded and seven captured. Three days later the seven were released, but their rifles were taken.

In this guerrilla warfare on the veldt scouts of both sides would often spot groups of the other moving in the distance. Although the SAC would be hard put to emulate the veldt-craft of the Boer commandos, their structuring of Troops sub-divided into Squads gave them scope to rehearse small-group actions. On 15 May a patrol of thirty SAC under Lieutenant Goodair saw an opportunity to put their training to use. The patrol scouts spotted a party of Boers laying an ambush for them: so they had already been seen and their line of approach estimated. The patrol rode on to a site concealed from the enemy's position and well-suited for their purpose; they prepared the ground work; and then they rode towards the Boers' awaiting trap. At the first shot they simulated a disorderly flight in fear. The Boers followed them and fell into the SAC ambush. Although the Boers were able to retreat from it they had at least four men hit.

Throughout May the SAC extended the number of posts across the former republics; they were quickly learning the ropes for when their posts were attacked, their record in beating off the enemy was good. In several actions there were examples of great resolve.

In the Orange River Colony on 16 May, the burgher post at Leeuwkop was attacked by Kolbe's commando but the defenders successfully held them off. Two days later the post at Katsdoorn Put was attacked but the attackers were beaten off; the SAC had one man wounded but they pursued the enemy for 5 miles. Baden-Powell recorded that Boer Koetzee surrendered to the SAC post at Kuil Put 'with valuable information'. A few days later, Lieutenant Malcolm's patrol made a night march of 30 miles and surprised a Boer laager at Paardekraal. They killed one of the enemy, wounded two and captured five. They also captured thirty horses and saddles. They lost one man killed and two wounded; but they established a post at Donkerpoort. The division also established a new post at Van Heerdens Kraal, 20 miles west of Bloemfontein. In the course of a heavy month of expansion and action, Colonel Ridley became ill. Baden-Powell telegraphed Pack-Beresford to be available by 25 May to take over E Division.

This brought results as, according to an early history of the war, under Pack-Beresford's direction the protection of Bloemfontein was soon assured by an almost impenetrable screen of posts manned largely by surrendered farmers.[48]

Kitchener was anxious to have an SAC post at Swartz Kop in the Transvaal and he telegraphed Baden-Powell asking when they could occupy it. Baden-Powell's reply was crisp and short: 'any day if Army will give us transport'.

In his schedule of inspections the inspector general included Potchefstroom; and on the agenda here was police work and relations with the resident magistrate. The magistrate was Mr Duxberry and he wanted clarification on their respective roles. The inspector general explained the high commissioner's instructions that town policing was to be undertaken by the SAC; but their complement would be decided by the magistrate. However, the inspector general would be responsible for their discipline, their clothing, pay and appointment; and the magistrate their orders and duty. Thus explained it seemed a workable system not involving hierarchies.

However, the SAC's military role was dominant in May 1901, and there were four SAC camps established in Krugersdorp by this time; there was already an Institute functioning with a shop and billiard room. On 22 May Baden-Powell rode out from Potchefstroom to inspect Captain Reynold's troop. He found it 'in particularly good order. Horses and men well-cared for, and in good condition. Defence works good.' From there he went on to Loup River and inspected Captain Chamney's post. Both posts could have been held with fewer men; one Troop could have covered them. Then it was on to Captain Plaice's Troop in a fort near the town. It was in good order but they were still without horses or transport. So when he was there – since the army seem not to have confirmed the transport the SAC required – the inspector general 'partially arranged to get 30 ox wagons on hire at 10/ [ten shillings] a day.' Colonel Kekewich commanded the army units in the area and he was anxious for the SAC to be left at Potchefstroom. Baden-Powell told him that he might be able to spare one Troop – but two Troops must be moved away very soon.

As it was coming on for the deadline he had given Roberts for having a full-blown Force in the field, the inspector general wrote to Milner giving him, what he described as, a professional update. Three quarters of the Force was now formed; and he commended the good work of the two recruiting officers in London, Major Hoare and Captain McLaren.

Two days later the inspector general was in action; he took three sections and went on a reconnaissance to Leeuwkop.

> We found Boers in occupation. But they cleared off on our approach – and while a few tried to lead us on to the main party, 45 strong, took position on a *koppie* on our left.

> These sniped us a good deal but harmlessly.

On our withdrawal Lt Jenner with a few men remained behind and volleyed the leading scouts of the Boers as they came up to the Leeuwkop – killing one.

The Boers followed us all the way back as far as Gerth's farm, sniping but doing no damage.

On the same day two Troops of the SAC went to occupy Engelbrechts Drift east of Viljoens Drift on the Vaal and found the position held by about 200 Boers. They attacked by both flanks and drove the enemy out, killing four, wounding several and capturing eight horses and a large amount of mealies. The SAC's casualties were two wounded; one severely and the other dangerously. As a result of that engagement Sergeant Kennedy, Corporal Gobey, Sergeant Downes and Trooper Bowden were specially mentioned.

For the next two days Baden-Powell was 'on the sick list' as he put it; but he wrote up the information that came in daily. On the first day he received a garbled message that the fighting had continued into the following day at Engelbrechts Drift and that the SAC had suffered losses: four men wounded, two missing believed killed. On account of that news, when he was fit enough, he went to the army post at Vereeniging and saw General Cunningham who had sent out reinforcements of an artillery piece and mounted escort – but no attack had been made on the newly established post. Then Baden-Powell saw Trooper Bowden, who brought in a despatcher. The despatcher said that the SAC casualties were men on foot who had been sent out to reinforce the advanced post 2 miles from camp and were attacked by Boers. These men had been vulnerable – lack of horses.

On 28 May, Baden-Powell rode out to Engelbrechts Drift to see it for himself. He went over the ground; on the south bank, where the fighting took place when the SAC occupied it. It was broken up with ridges and dips and a deep river bed '– all in favour of the Boers who knew every inch of it'. Then he wrote, 'Our men had behaved most gallantly and coolly not only in holding their own but in driving the enemy out of positions he had attempted to hold in our flanks. . . The Boers here have helio [heliograph] and lamp signals working and comprise two parties Transvaalers and ORC evidently much disconcerted at being turned out of the drift.'

Colonel Edwards of A Division alerted him that boots were urgently required. Baden-Powell inspected the war loot destined for the Boer commandos that they acquired from the Delagoa Bay stores. His opinion on it was 'cheap but will do for the present'. There were corduroy suits, boots and shirts as well as the horseshoes. The poor quality prompted him to order 10,000 boots and serge coats from London.

Next day he met Kitchener in Pretoria. He told him that a big obstacle hindering their progress was lack of boots and clothing, they had ordered 6,500 sets of them in December and another 4,000 later but all they received so far was about 4,000; and were now told they could have no more. At that Kitchener explained that 'Town Guards etc. have taken the stocks we should have had, and the stuff [that the SAC ordered] is not actually in existence here yet.' It was at this point that the commander in chief graciously allowed the inspector general to take 200 boots. Then Kitchener said he wanted a statement of money expended and liabilities incurred monthly by the SAC. Yet it was Milner who held the purse strings.

Baden-Powell had already discussed with Colonel Wickham, the army's chief transport officer, the SAC's shortage of transport; and Wickham was willing to supply the SAC with transport just like any other troops. Baden-Powell put this to Kitchener who responded with his byword when it came to supplying the SAC – 'not at present'.

This raises the question whether Kitchener was canny about what he put in writing concerning the SAC's shortages, because a few weeks earlier Lord Roberts, in London, replying to a letter from Kitchener, wrote: 'It is curious that Baden Powell should not be acting with more vigour.'[49] Vigour was not what Baden-Powell lacked. As we shall see later, confirmation of Roberts being in the dark about the SAC's lack of horses will appear early in 1902.

The other master the SAC inspector general served was Britain's high commissioner to South Africa, Sir Alfred Milner, who left South Africa in May for a trip to the UK – from which he was to return as Lord Milner. Before he left Cape Town he cabled his 'confidence in the SAC'. From its record on the ground so far, Milner's confidence was not misplaced.

In the early hours of 31 May, in the Transvaal in A Division's sector, a group of Captain Douglas's Troop based at Olifantsfontein did some fine work. Lieutenant Johns was cited 'for good service' in the capture of Commandant Malan and seven men and their supplies including rifles, horses and seventeen mules. Malan had been attempting to cross from east to west to reassemble his own commando.

Throughout the time of their engagements with the enemy Baden-Powell kept track of the good practice that he wanted in the force. In late May he wrote to Colonel Pilkington C Division with instructions to change the design of the loopholes in their forts; they were circular in shape. He told him to change the practice of men parading mounted and 'telling off – all on army bad principles and not according to my "instructions"'.

He also issued notes in general instructions on courts of inquiry held on men who surrendered to the enemy. He had already assessed that on 11 May those men who ran away near Abrams Kraal 'had no excuse'. He ordered that those who ran away but were not captured by the enemy should be tried at the discretion of the officer commanding the division; those who were captured to be tried by court martial for cowardice and made to pay for the arms that were lost; and those who were captured on 14 May near Petrusburg would pay for arms and equipment lost. He drew the attention of all ranks to the 'standing instructions against surrendering'.

Having inspected the divisional hospitals Baden-Powell upbraided Colonel Beevor, the principal medical officer, telling him that they were unsatisfactory. The one at Heidelberg had apparently been established for weeks, yet was not in working order; the hospital at Meyerton had nothing but bare tents. He told Beevor to remain at HQ and direct affairs; to appoint a senior medical officer for each Division; and finally he gave him written instructions on what he was expected to achieve and the funds at his disposal to accomplish it. Then he turned to personnel he wanted rid of, a medical officer who held the rank of captain and one of the nursing sisters: 'The presence of these two is seriously injuring the reputation of the medical staff.'

The visits to hospitals were not only to check on standards but also to visit the SAC sick and wounded. In Elandsfontein, on 3 June, Baden-Powell recorded that 'Capt Blain died of wounds soon after I visited him.' William Blain had served in the army as a sergeant before qualifying for a commission, he had then bought himself out and he became a teacher; but he responded to the call for volunteers for the SAC.

Major Pack-Beresford was by now acting Divisional Commander; Ridley was in hospital and was to be moved to the coast. He would later be sent to England on sick leave; Colonel Pilkington would then take over E Division; and Major Fair would take over C Division. Meanwhile, in his acting role, Pack-Beresford got down to overhauling the administrative system that was very imperfect; he wrote to Baden-Powell that he wanted 'a hand in getting rid of rotters (subject to sanction of I.G.)'. Baden-Powell agreed to what he proposed.

On the last day of May the inspector general wrote up a summary for the month:

Since the beginning of the month A and C Divisions have come into existence in the West and East Transvaal respectively, and a nucleus of the B Division (300 men) has been started for the North Transvaal.

These Divisions have established 10 posts on both sides of the railway line between the Vaal River and Pretoria; and E Division has established 18 out of the required 22 along the Modder River.

6 hospitals of 50 to 70 beds have been established.
900 horses have joined from Australia.
The SAC have been engaged with the enemy 30 times during the month.

Specially commended actions
8 May   Capt Chamney's patrol held a position.
20 ..   Lt Malcolm surprised a Boer laager.
24 ..   Lt Williams' 2 Troops seized and held Engelbrechts Drift.
31 ..   Capt Douglas captured Cmdt Malan.

Unsatisfactory engagements
13 men captured Abrams Kraal   11 May
4 men captured Koppies Kraal   1st May.

SAC casualties for May		Boer casualties
Killed	8	21
Wounded	27	13
Prisoners	17	24
Surrendered	10	
	52	68

Thus the engagements with the enemy continued. On 1 June Baden-Powell went out with 4 Troops of SAC and about 150 Yeomanry on a night move against

Boers at Zevenfontein near Leeuwkop. Two SAC Troops occupied Swartzkop – Kitchener had authorized the support of some artillery and infantry. In the event there was only slight opposition from the occupying Boers. At night on 3 June, Captain Douglas's Troop ambushed a party of about 15 Boers and 200 horses near Olifantsfontein. The SAC group captured fifteen horses and Douglas then sent out a patrol to round up the others, but they stampeded. Later about eighty of them were rounded up by the RPR [Railway Pioneer Regiment]. However, the RPR would not hand them over to the SAC. Baden-Powell wrote to Kitchener asking him to order the RPR to hand them back; and Kitchener – in a rough-and-ready response – ordered that half of the 70-80 horses be handed back to the SAC.

By the first week of June seventy-eight out of the planned ninety-seven Troops were established: Depot 4; A Division 19: C Division 23; and E Division 32. By coincidence, Sam Steele boarded his ship at Montreal on 8 June.[50] When he reported for duty, B Division would be made up to strength.

As their numbers increased so did the posts they created. Those west of Bloemfontein assisted General Bruce Hamilton, working from the south, and General Charles Knox, working from the north with their columns. One-Troop posts were held at Abrams Kraal, Daniels Kuil and Boschkop; there were 5 Troops at Petrusburg and 3 burgher troops and 3 SAC Troops were at Bloemfontein. Then in the process of being set up would be three triangular sections with 7 Troops each under the command of majors Apthorpe, Vaughan and Lyon.

The programme of inspector general's inspections continued: the firing slots in posts in C Division had been improved; in E Division he found that there were about 150 horses though not in good condition; and there was no shelter, no blankets or proper feeding troughs. He ordered that they should be let out in batches to graze and exercise. Lieutenant Randall was in charge of remounts. The inspector general judged 'he does not seem up to it'. Then there was the case of Captain Critchley whose 'propensity to drink' was handled by Pack-Beresford in the form of a letter warning him that if he continued to drink he would be dismissed. The inspector general was not satisfied: it was not fair to men in service under his charge, and if they kept him on it would be bad for the reputation of the corps. He had better send in his resignation; and 'Beresford informed Critchley accordingly.'[51]

Kitchener telegraphed that he wanted SAC posts extended along the Modder before expanding southwards. The following day Baden-Powell met him and asked for transport, 200 ox wagons, or it could not be done. That led to Baden-Powell having to ask head of transport to give a statement to Kitchener 'showing what transport might be spared'.

Lobbying had evidently been going on at Whitehall and Kitchener came under pressure from the War Office for his heavy use of the SAC in the field. He was told:

> The constabulary cannot be utilised to the best advantage if employed merely as mounted troops moving in flying columns from district to district. The aim and duty of the Constabulary – should be to achieve prolonged, continuous and effective occupation of definite areas. With their allocated areas the Constabulary should be perpetually active, familiarising themselves with the inhabitants of the country and rendering it untenable by small bodies of enemies or rebels. Occupied areas should contribute to the pacification of the country.[52]

On 17 June the SAC was well on its way to reaching full establishment and Baden-Powell could take satisfaction from the fact that despite shortages of equipment and horses he was meeting the timescale he had given Lord Roberts. But it had taken a toll on him; he was on the sick list and he remained on it for two weeks. He was burned-out, he needed R & R [rest and recuperation]. A medical board convened on him and recommended his going to England on sick leave.

So by this stage then, Milner had expressed his confidence in the SAC; but in the written and face-to-face exchanges between Kitchener and Baden-Powell nothing by way of an evaluative comment on the force comes through.

On 7 July he sailed from Durban to Southampton; and he continued working at his notes in his cabin as though he was back at HQ. He later conceded that he 'had been pretty hard at it practically day and night'.[53] When they put in at Funchal in Madeira on 23 July he posted the mail he had written on board to Cape Town.

Baden-Powell arrived at Southampton on 27 July; he had not been back in the UK since his name had become popularised and established by its newspapers. By now the halo effect had reached Royalty. Edward VII, as yet uncrowned king, invited Baden-Powell to Balmoral for a week-end. During their conversations the king showed interest in the SAC and asked relevant questions.

Apart from royalty there was the political dimension that had an interest and a need to know about the corps. Months later, in the House of Commons, replying to a member's question on the efficiency of the SAC in the light of its shortage of horses, Chamberlain replied,

> I consulted General Baden-Powell, the Inspector General of the South African Constabulary, on this point when he was on leave, and he informed me that he did not consider that the deficiency in horses impaired the efficiency, a large portion of which is at present employed in garrisoning blockhouses. According to the last monthly slate received, the total number of all ranks was 9,316, and the total number of horses was 5,106 – a rather higher proportion than when I discussed the matter with General Baden-Powell.[54]

When he was on leave, on his initiative, Baden-Powell also went on a work-related jaunt to Dublin to meet his counterpart inspector general of the Royal Irish Constabulary. The details they covered will be seen and become relevant later, when the SAC takes up its policing role.

It was all part of the convalescing process.

Chapter Five

Strict Adherence to Duty

T
he British policy of burning farmhouses began in 1900; Lord Roberts summed up the brutal premise for it in a statement of September: 'Unless the people generally are made to suffer for misdeeds of those in arms against us the war will never end.'[55]

The outcome from that line of thought was soldiers pillaging, burning farms, rounding up or wantonly destroying livestock and removing occupants to concentration camps in which thousands of mainly women and children, white and black, would die.

A scenario of a Boer family's reaction to the news of an army column coming towards their farm to clear it was depicted by one of the most renowned 'of those in arms against us' – Boer commando leader General Christiaan De Wet, whose memoir *Three Years' War* was published in New York in 1902:

> When then a column approached a farm, even at night, in all sorts of weather, many a young daughter had to take hold of the leading rope of the team of oxen, and the mother the whip, or vice versa. Many a smart, well-bred daughter rode on horseback and urged the cattle on, in order to keep out of the hands of the pursuers as long as possible, and not to be carried away to the concentration camps, which the British call Refugee Camps (Camps of Refuge). How incorrect indeed! Could anyone ever have thought before the war that the twentieth century should show such barbarities? No. Any one knows that in war cruelties more horrible than murder can take place, but that such direct and indirect murder should have been committed against defenceless women and children is a thing I should have staked my head could never have happened in a war waged by the civilised English nation. And yet it happened.[56]

After Kitchener took over from Roberts he continued the farm clearance policy: 'Every farm is to them an intelligence agency and a supply depot so . . . I have determined to bring in the women from the more disturbed districts to laagers near the railway and offer the burghers to join them there.'[57]

What part was the SAC to play in the clearances? Baden-Powell dinned in to drafts of new recruits and divisional assemblies of all ranks that they were not soldiers – they had a police role. To be sure they had a military role and thus far that role dominated; but the SAC would have a continuing presence after the hostilities – though not as part of a garrison force – but under civil command. However, it was about more than protecting their post-reputation – in his 'Notes and Instructions for the SAC', the inspector general had described it as being 'the unwritten code of honour, which I shall expect will guide the actions of every officer, NCO and man of the Constabulary.' Then he went on:

> I appeal to the British spirit already ingrained in you, of 'playing the game', that is of doing your duty just as thoroughly when you are away from the eye of authority as when under it – not from fear of punishment for neglect to do it, but simply because it is 'the game' and is expected of you as a man of honour.[58]

The earliest reference to the then fledgling SAC's involvement with 'refugees' appears in Baden-Powell's staff diary as early as 23 January 1901 when SAC HQ was still at Zuurfontein. He wrote that fourteen refugees were imported from East London to work for the SAC as artisans. When they arrived, however, it seemed that they had 'differed in their reading of the agreement' and they declined to work for them; and they were sent back to East London. 'They now wrote complaining of their treatment.' He replied by letter through Milner, Captain Cadogan and the Secretary of the Refugee Committee that the fourteen had signed on as having read the conditions as to pay, service etc. 'Their object was, however, to get to Johannesburg and that this was not dealing fairly with us in our wish to help them.'

This reference may trigger connotations of the kind of refugee camp that De Wet wrote about; but according to Elizabeth Van Heyningen the refugee camp at East London was opened a year later, March 1902.[59] In Thomas Pakenham's full-scale history of the Boer War, he wrote that there were 'two sorts of refugees': those who were removed in the clearances of the farms whom Pakenham felt could more accurately have been called 'internees'; and those families whose menfolk had surrendered to the British and so were vulnerable to reprisal from their own people as a result.[60] From the wording in the staff diary the fourteen seem to have had freedom to choose – and had their own agenda.

Baden-Powell returned to the idea of employing burghers from the camps to do manual work for the SAC. This time it was to employ refugees from the camp at Johannesburg. Colonel Colin Mackenzie was the military governor of Johannesburg; and Baden-Powell met him in late April and came up with the idea of employing some refugees from the camp at Johannesburg to make bricks at Zuurfontein 'in anticipation of our building there'. It looks though as if this may have remained at the level of an idea after Baden-Powell's discussion with Girouard, Director of the railway network, who was less than enthusiastic about Zuurfontein as the site for a barracks.

Kitchener's determination to remove families 'to laagers near the railway' gave rise to severe problems for the military governors. On 25 January Baden-Powell had an interview with General Pretyman, governor of the Orange River Colony. Pretyman wanted to get off his chest the fact that the policy of clearing the country of inhabitants was not working well. The problem of housing and feeding them was very difficult; and their livestock did not have sufficient grazing.

Into the scenario stepped a personality who did so much to bring to the British public the conditions in the concentration camps – Emily Hobhouse. She already had a platform in the UK raising public awareness to the plight of the women and children detained in the camps; and she was back in South Africa in early 1901 and had an interview with Milner:

> Finally, after I had told him many details (and I did not mince matters) and told him how uneasy the English conscience was growing and how desperately sore the Afrikanders felt and how for the Honour of England we ought to mend matters in the camps, then finally he said he would do all in his power to forward my going the round of the camps as representative of the English movement and with me a Dutch lady –

However, there was a 'but' – Milner said he must recommend and urge Kitchener to let the pair visit the camps and take two trucks with clothing and provisions. Afterwards she assessed the man, His Excellency:

We parted very good friends . . . He struck me as amiable and weak, clear-headed and narrow. Everyone says he has no heart, but I think I hit on the atrophied remains of one. It might be developed if he had not, as he says he has, made up his mind to back up the Military in everything.[61]

On 9 February Baden-Powell 'inspected two camps of burgher refugees (over 500) at Heidelberg'. He found that 'they are being well looked after' by the District Commissioner who complained though that he had many masters: the military GOC, the officer commanding the garrison, who was frequently transferred and replaced, and then there was the governor at Pretoria. That was the extent of Baden-Powell's comment on these two camps.

He met General Maxwell governor of the Transvaal at Elandsfontein on 4 March and asked him for some of the hospital tents now that the army hospitals had hutted accommodation. Maxwell was using the tents for Boer families who had been removed from their homes. Baden-Powell suggested to him that these families could be moved to the mining area of the Rand, which was no longer in production because of the war, 'where they could be well housed, on the railway and under protection . . .' Maxwell, though, 'was not inclined to promise much'.

Emily Hobhouse was in South Africa in March 1901 and she came across a train of SAC recruits; and from her description of them they were recruits for the corps recently arrived in South Africa – as the Honourable Member in the House of Commons pointed out (Chapter 3) without uniform or weapons – her perspective on the quality of the men was scathing: on 10 March this is what she wrote in a letter:

One thing more I must say and that is I saw a whole train-load of Baden-Powell's Police and sorrow filled my heart for the unhappy people who are to be policed by them – why, they look as if they needed police for themselves. Where on earth was such a low, rough, almost criminal-looking crew raked together? And such lads! Poor South Africa! Will no nice English people ever come out here?[62]

One of the photos in this book shows a group of SAC recruits without uniforms having recently arrived from England – but after having been issued with rifles – and considering them alongside Emily Hobhouse's impression of the train of recruits that day, they could give the impression of being a bunch of renegades.

From another letter that Emily Hobhouse wrote it may be that while Baden-Powell got little change out of General Maxwell in his desire to move families from tents to hutted accommodation (so that he could get tents for the SAC) Maxwell was on another tack: Emily Hobhouse found that Maxwell's wife, who was an American, 'is appealing to the United States for clothing for Irene camp'.[63]

Milner, months earlier, had voiced his opposition to the army's policy and he wrote to Kitchener, 'I should take all the horses I could lay my hands on, but I should *burn no houses*, except for definite acts of treachery, nor should I attempt to clear the district of food-stuffs or of population.'[64] Milner took that early stance on utilitarian grounds – getting the mining industry working again needed a stable infra-structure and supplies – not for humanitarian reasons. However, that did not deflect the commander-in-chief.

With the god of destruction in the ascendancy there was licence for looting and the wanton slaughtering of animals; and in that context orders to the SAC had to be specific – not critical of the military but assuredly clear and limiting individual action in relation to the civilian population and their property.

On 12 May 1901 Goold Adams wrote to Baden-Powell asking for a copy of the orders he may have given to the SAC regarding their relation with the civilian inhabitants. In response Baden-Powell sent a copy of an extract in Standing Orders p. 18 (no copy in the staff diary) and he included a copy of his 'Notice to Inhabitants as to the duties of the Constabulary'. He also promised to issue an order containing Goold Adams's suggestion 'to forbid men of the SAC to enter a house, loot or take cattle, game etc. without orders from an officer'.

Six days later the order was distributed to the SAC:

> While at present we are doing military duty we must keep in view the fact that our ultimate work is that of policing our districts. Therefore, so soon as each post is safe it must commence to pacify and collect police information regarding farms, inhabitants, stock etc.
>
> No looting or damage of premises, taking of cattle or shooting of game without orders from an officer.

> The best step to pacification is to gain the confidence of the inhabitants
> by strict adherence to duty.

However, while the SAC were doing military duty there were times when farms became a battle area for them. The first was in the last week of February when they were involved in removing occupants of a farm near Van Wyks Rust – it had been the scene of a fire-fight between them and Boer commandos. The SAC had got word that the farm was a nightly rendezvous for commandos. On the strength of the report, late one evening, Superintendent Johns and Corporal McIntyre went out and hid near the farm building. Under cover of darkness a group of Boers arrived, left their horses under a guard, and went into the house. Johns sent McIntyre back to camp for eight reinforcements and he tried to get the Boers' horses. He found the guard had fallen asleep but instead of about six horses as he expected there were about twenty-five. He got three horses away but he was disturbed by one of the group coming out of the house – all he could do was slip the collars off some other horses, hoping they might stampede when the shooting started.

When the eight reinforcements arrived Johns posted them in a semi-circle round the house. However, there were not sufficient men to surround the whole farm and so Johns sent one man back for more. Before the others arrived, however, the Boers came out and went for their horses and the SAC opened fire on them. The enemy scattered and got away leaving one man, Van der Merwe, severely wounded. 'The Constabulary removed the people living in the farm and sent them to Pretoria.'

According to the summary sheet for May another fire-fight at some farms took place on 10 May when Lieutenant McCartney and a group from his post at Koppies Kraal drove Boers out from their haunt in farms 12 miles to the south. In the course of the exchange of fire McCartney and one man were wounded. The wording of the summary reads, 'Brought in the families.'

However, the full gamut of the clearance policy included confiscating crops as well; and Kitchener, on 24 March, specifically approved 'the constabulary destroying or collecting crops beyond military posts to prevent their being used by the enemy.'

This practice continued into the following year. In early February 1902 Baden-Powell was inspecting A Division in the western Transvaal. He wrote that the two Troops at Witpoortje and Buffelsdoorn:

were protecting native refugees coming in to the railway line of camps and have been with their assistance removing large stocks of hidden grain (of which most of the farm houses have stores concealed in double walls of the houses).

The district is now clear of Boers and of all supplies.

Because a Boer commando had to take its own meat supplies with it – on the hoof – there were armed engagements between them and the SAC that ended with the SAC driving away livestock to safe areas. At the end of May a patrol of SAC and Mounted Infantry under the command of Captain Brookesbank SAC cleared the country south of Koppies of 'all supplies and brought away 30 horses and 17 cattle'.

Encounters in the field with the enemy often ended with the SAC rounding up the commandos' livestock. Major Pack-Beresford reported that at Besters Kraal on 24 January 1902 the commando leader Erasmus and about 250–300 men charged one of Pack-Beresford's detachments that was driving off confiscated cattle and captured nineteen SAC. However, there were other detachments of SAC in the area and they reacted quickly and drove off the Boers, released the prisoners and recaptured the stock.

Before long this tactic of war caused over-grazing and contributed to the spread of disease among the herds; this led to detachments of SAC being deployed to guard corralled cattle.[65] We shall see in the next chapter where Boers made a successful raid on one of these safeguarded areas to repossess some of their own side's livestock.

However, in time the land could be restored to give of its bounty; and eventually cattle disease could be cured – but the suffering and loss of human life that was the consequence of burning farm houses and transporting the inhabitants to the concentration camps could never be made good. It had been a military tactic to help win a war. Yet there was another power in the background: could it have done more?

Emily Hobhouse, in her meeting with the High Commissioner in January 1901, assessed him as being 'amiable and weak, clear-headed and narrow'. In Milner's own words, writing to Foreign Secretary Chamberlain in December 1901, he said,

I entirely agree with you in thinking, that while a hundred explanations may be offered and a hundred excuses made, they do not really amount to an adequate defence. I should much prefer to say at once, as far as the Civil authorities are concerned, that we were suddenly confronted with a problem not of our making, with which it was beyond our power properly to grapple. And no doubt its vastness was not realised soon enough. It was not till six weeks or two months ago that it dawned on me personally (I cannot speak for others), that the enormous mortality was not merely incidental to the first formation of the camps and the sudden inrush of thousands of people already sick and starving, but was to continue. The fact that it continues is no doubt a condemnation of the Camp system. The whole thing, I think now, has been a mistake. At the same time a sudden reversal of policy would only make matters worse. At the present moment certainly, everything we know of is being done, both to improve the camps and to reduce the numbers in them. I believe we shall mitigate the evil, but we shall never get rid of it.[66]

Chapter Six

A Seasoned Force

By January 1902 Kitchener had a change of tune for the SAC – his 'not at the present' had been last year's ditty.

When Baden-Powell returned from sick leave he met Kitchener in Johannesburg. Kitchener pronounced himself 'very satisfied with what we have done'. He also published a complimentary order on the SAC.

> Am much pleased to hear of numerous captures by SAC in all directions during past week. Hope you will encourage all to maintain this activity and that there will be no falling off now they have made a good start.

The change in Kitchener was noticeable as early as 8 July 1901 when he wrote to the War Office:

> The South African Constabulary is gradually becoming an effective force.

> They have also required considerable training. Operating from the vicinity of the railway and occupying fortified posts, enclosing large areas, thus denying the passage of the enemy through certain districts they have become lately of considerable value, and have shown commendable spirit and steadiness.[67]

Considering Baden-Powell had assured Roberts that he would have the force up and active by 30 June, the deadline had been met. However, twelve days after Kitchener sent his despatch of 8 July Lord Roberts put him on the spot by asking if there was anyone 'who would do better at the head of the Constabulary? I gather from your reports that you are not altogether satisfied with B.P.'[68] Kitchener was not going to react to that: the SAC were performing impressively in the field.

A month later, he gave an example of that 'spirit and steadiness': he referred to an engagement that took place on 17 August when a joint force of SAC and Morley's Scouts, under the command of Captain Woods SAC, came across a 'greatly superior Boer force' (later reported to have been about 800) that was halted at Middelburg and attacked it, killing twenty-three and capturing eleven men and putting the force to flight. However, when the enemy realised they had been attacked by a much smaller force they rallied, counter-attacked, and after hand-to-hand fighting drove the smaller group back and recovered their eleven prisoners. The cost to the small British force was one man killed and five wounded.[69]

Then in his first despatch of January 1902, Kitchener went into hyperbole commending Pack-Beresford.

> Very excellent work has been done in this north-western portion of the Orange River Colony by Major Pack-Beresford, of the South African Constabulary. At the end of December this officer conducted a well-managed raid upon Bothaville, which led to the capture of 36 prisoners, 80 horses and 29 vehicles, and on 4th January he followed up this success by taking Field Cornet Theron's laager near the junction of the Vet and Zand rivers. Upon this occasion Major Pack-Beresford secured 35 prisoners (including Field Cornet Le Roux), 70 horses, 30 rifles, and the whole of the enemy's transport.[70]

The following day, 9 January, Lieutenant-General Sir Ian Hamilton (who was Kitchener's chief of staff) wrote from army headquarters to Lord Roberts in London:

> The SAC men are doing splendid work at present in clearing the country, and there is no doubt they are a very much finer type of man, and much better suited to act independently, and to cope with the difficulties of new surroundings, than the average soldier of the line. I wish to be very moderate and careful in making any such statement, but I do really think that at the present stage of affairs, one SAC is worth three average soldiers.[71]

Indeed, by the time he wrote those words, the names of thirty-two officers, NCOs and men of the SAC had appeared in the *London Gazette*; and eleven of them were NCOs and Troopers 'for special good service' in Captain Woods' attack on the laager that was referred to a little earlier.

One of the first actions that Baden-Powell published in orders at the start of the year was a brief account of the engagement that took place on 29 November when Captain Kitson and 30 men were surrounded by 200 Boers. The SAC held the enemy off for eleven hours till dark; then, bluffing, they made a feint in one direction with ten men. The result was that all thirty of them got back safely to camp. Specially commended were: Sergeant Hart, Corporal Plant (whom Baden-Powell recommended to the commander-in-chief) and Troopers Smithers and McCallum.

However, it was Colonel Edwards, commanding officer of A Division, who came up with the suggestion that a badge of merit be granted to all ranks of the SAC who distinguished themselves for gallantry; and Baden-Powell approved it and designed it – it became called the Gallantry Badge.

Edwards may have been inspired by what happened when about five squads of his No. 18 Troop were involved in a series of actions at Rooi Kop on 31 December 1901 for which Lieutenant McLeod commended the gallantry of thirty men.

It began when Corporal Slean and two men, scouting for the group, came across ten Boers and in a short fight killed three of them; but the firing summoned a larger group of the enemy – about thirty – who encircled the three. After a long fight, all three men were wounded, Corporal Slean mortally. His wounded comrades were captured. At this point Lieutenant McLeod and the rest of the group rode up and opened fire. The firing attracted a larger number of Boer commandos – McLeod estimated perhaps 100 – who charged towards them. However, the SAC repulsed the charge and the enemy fell back with the loss of nineteen men. Then the Boers changed tactics and encircled them. In response to this the SAC charged and broke through – at the cost of eight men captured and five horses killed.

Baden-Powell recorded that the Boers 'maltreated' their captives for their resistance. He cited no source for that information, but it is the first time such a claim appears in the staff diary. He also noted that Troopers Medway and Wood were recommended for gallantry. Kitchener duly mentioned them in a despatch: Trooper L. Medway for gallantry in action at Rooi Kop; and Trooper M. Wood who, on being told that a native scout had fallen behind and was in danger of capture, went back for him, killed the leading Boer and brought the scout away. In the same despatch Corporal D. Plant is mentioned for gallantry on 29 November, for going out alone to locate the enemy and making a diversion to draw him off while the rest of the SAC group withdrew. The note continues, 'He had been three times previously mentioned.'[72]

As its inspector general, Baden-Powell marked his return to the SAC by issuing an order congratulating all ranks 'on their progress during the past 6 months and informing the corps of the interest taken in it by the King'.

Then Kitchener sent a telegram: 'Very glad to hear of SAC renewed success. Having been away did not get the news before. Tell all that I am much pleased at excellent work.'

By contrast the inspector general's meeting with Milner was low-key. It may have been cordial – as Shakespeare wrote 'One may smile, and smile, and be a villain' – but only a month earlier Milner had put the knife into Baden-Powell in a private memo sent to Chamberlain: he suggested that senior officers of the SAC would be happy if the force continued under Nicholson. No one had said so to him directly – *no names no pack-drill* – which was a characteristic of Milner's man-management style. As Emily Hobhouse assessed him 'amiable and weak, clear-headed and narrow'. We shall see later other examples of Milner's indirect methods. Baden-Powell's biographer, Tim Jeal, makes the point that Milner was hardly disinterested, 'he wanted to secure for himself total control of the SAC'.[73] Giving the knife a twist, Milner went on '. . . he is not a good organiser. He has too many "happy thoughts", he is too constantly changing his plans, and in doing so he worries and fails to gain the confidence of the men under him.'

Now this charge of 'constantly changing' can be put to the test to an extent from the written record. Baden-Powell wrote it up assiduously each day, over long hours – the staff diary is in book form, lined and paginated at source; if he were chopping and changing ideas frequently there would be evidence of it in the record (pages out of sequence, stroking out). To be sure in forming a new force there would have been brain-storming: he was abandoning army traditional structures and he was breaking new ground but he had not sown dragon's teeth which would spring up as the presently structured and motived SAC. Once he set the idea down on paper, though, he stayed with it. As for failing 'to gain the confidence' of those under him Milner had not discussed 'directly' with the divisional commanders; and when we shall see Colonel Steele's diary for B Division it is clear that Steele – who was the most experienced commander in the SAC – had confidence in the judgement and fairness of his inspector general.

However, the fight was in the field not in the office; and the SAC were engaged in military action over a wide area in both the Transvaal and Orange River Colony at this time. Troop Sergeant Major Douglas of No. 19 Troop, A Division was commended in orders for coolness and energy under fire at Rhenosterpoort on 24 December and carrying on his duties after being wounded; in mid-January Captain Cartwright engaged with 250 Boers 22 miles north-east of Bloemfontein; the next day Captain Capell reported that about 70-100 Boers were gathering near his convoy at Syferfontein, and he proposed getting the help of the National Scouts against them.

With ample evidence for the effectiveness of the force, Baden-Powell changed his style of inspections: no longer pep-talks on the difference between them and soldiers; instead he went in for a thorough examination on a Troop by Troop basis; and he began in the northern Transvaal with B Division commanded by Colonel Sam Steele. He had not seen Steele since the year before, when Steele was leaving for Canada. Nor did he yet know the extent of Lord Minto's role in selecting the Canadian officer contingent for the SAC: in his letter to Baden-Powell in June, Lord Minto had passed the buck for it to Captain Fall, but as we shall see later Minto played a dominant part.

After his furlough at home in 1901, Steele had been delayed in Canada through illness and it was not until early August that he reported for duty in Pretoria. His biographer, Rod Macleod, records that Steele had anticipated B Division would consist of the 1,200 Canadian recruits – he was unaware of Baden-Powell's earlier decision to allocate the Canadians among divisions. Until his family came out to join him, Steele was billeted in Pretoria, in the house that belonged to President Paul Kruger of the South African Republic, who was now in exile.

Steele met Kitchener (and came away with a favourable impression); his orders were to extend B Division's line of posts to the north-west. Among his officers was a Canadian, Major Ogilvy, who he hoped would shape up to be his second in command. However, it was not to be: on 19 December, a group of SAC that included Steele encountered a party of Boers driving cattle before them. Ogilvy led a charge on the enemy, but perhaps precipitately without sufficient support, and was mortally wounded.[74] Before Baden-Powell began his tour of inspection, he wrote a letter of sympathy to Ogilvy's father.

B Division's depot and remount establishment was at Knoppieslaagte, 12 miles from Pretoria, and it was under the command of Captain Wilcox. It was here that Baden-Powell began his formal inspection. What they had done with the remount site was impressive: by their own efforts they had put up paddocks, a forge and a pharmacy for 170 horses under the direction of Veterinary-Captain Christy. Baden-Powell estimated that the building and its fittings would have cost the army between £700 and £800 to build.

However, the biggest problem the SAC faced was lack of serviceable horses. Baden-Powell detailed it in the staff diary on 15 January:

> The Remount question is a very urgent one. We are suffering heavy losses partly from horse sickness, partly from debility of horses landed from Australia.
>
> It is necessary for us to have a good remount officer and vet at the coast to approve or reject horses tendered to us. And they can manage a remount farm there to get the horses fit for travelling.
>
> Out of the 1300 remounts last landed not more than 200 are now at work in the field. The majority, especially after a bad voyage as some batches have had (7 weeks), are in the lowest condition on landing and cannot assimilate their food. The change to oats, new kind of grass, war, new climate at this juncture makes their recovery very slow – especially if a railway journey of 5 to 7 days follows, in trucks, at very varying temperature, and most irregular feeding and watering (to a certain extent unavoidable).
>
> The horses have so far been accepted because remounts were urgently necessary and it was hoped that with good feeding and care they would pull up. So, to a certain extent they do – but only after weeks and months of rest and careful management.
>
> The coast depot would be able to prepare all horses for journey upcountry, and would only send first those that are fit for it.
>
> The extra expense of such a depot would be saved in the saving of horseflesh.

The upshot was Milner agreeing to the cost of a remount depot near the coast; Baden-Powell renting a farm from the Dutch Church near Heidelberg for two years, at £72 a year, as an inland remount depot; specific training for SAC transport corporals in the management of horses on the rail journeys upcountry (for example chopping hay to feed to horses in nosebags – otherwise it got trodden under hoof in the trucks); and negotiations with the shipping companies in terms of additional rates for horses arriving in good condition.

Second only to their lack of horses in reducing the corps' effectiveness was the high percentage of sickness affecting officers and men: in January 10 per cent of C Division were on the sick list, and by the first week in February 10 officers and 711 men of the entire force were out of action; and at one point, colonels Nicholson, Ridley and Pilkington were all on the sick list.

Consequently the force's medical provision was a high priority; and Baden-Powell focused first on the SAC hospital in Pretoria; it was under the supervision of Captain Porter assisted by Captains Dawson and Ellis and Sisters Nicholson and Laurence. There were 120 beds and there were 112 patients of B and C Divisions – over 70 of them were typhoid cases.

The medical staff were hard-worked, but there were not enough of them for the typhoid epidemic that was raging. To cope the Deputy Medical Officer wanted fifty more beds; two more nurses; twelve trained orderlies; and eight untrained, at one shilling a day. He also strongly recommended hospital clothing.

There was a marked contrast when it came to the hospital at Naauwpoort under the supervision of Captains Parnell and Newlands. The first evaluative comment Baden-Powell wrote was 'Capt P. wants energy.' The hospital was overcrowded; one marquee was letting in rain and there was no cookhouse. Baden-Powell's summation of it: 'Considering length of time that has elapsed since established it is not an establishment to be proud of.'

Accompanied by Colonel Steele, Baden-Powell inspected B Division's base at Naauwpoort. No. 4 Troop was stationed there. The inspector general gave it a 'Fairly Satisfactory' rating. They had no horses to look after so Captain Pomeroy should have been putting them through rigorous practice in signalling, shooting, theory of defence and police duties.

In all Baden-Powell inspected ten of its thirteen Troops (B Division was not yet up to full strength) and Sam Steele accompanied him on eight inspections. There were also two staff officers. Baden-Powell went over the scrutiny in a rigorous fashion, paying attention to critical points such as the construction of their blockhouses: two of them did not fit the SAC preferred style and one was vulnerable to dropping fire. At Syferfontein, he inspected No. 1 Troop, now commanded by Captain Boyd and Lieutenant Humfrey; he described it as satisfactory. However, he included some received information: 'The Troop was spoiled by Capt Lang Sims. Has now been reorganised with new NCOs etc. and promises well.' No. 5 Troop at Vlakfontein, commanded by Captain Birdwood and Lieutenant Agnew, he assessed as 'Satisfactory' but the blockhouses were not a good type – 'the SAC pattern preferable.' He noted that the Troop savings bank was most satisfactory: it had ninety-six deposits amounting to £2,300. In No. 6 Troop, commanded by Captain Swift and Lieutenant Currie, the inspector general noted that the percentage of sick and minor crime was higher than average; and also of men wanting to leave. Overall he rated it 'Satisfactory'.

However, he observed:

> Only in two or three Troops were the comfort, self-respect, and wellbeing of the men sufficiently considered. It is most necessary for officers to remember the human side of their men – especially those in outlying blockhouses and to supply them with literature, food extras, amusements, instructions etc.

Then, without Steele accompanying him, he inspected No. 8 Troop. The men had done a lot of hard work in building defences and stables. In talking to the men though he 'warned them against the use of bad language'. The following day he went on to inspect No. 12 Troop.

At the end of the divisional inspection, Baden-Powell drew up what he called an order of merit and listed Troops and officers in rank order. No. 2 Troop came first and its commander, Captain Anderson, headed the list of officers. Thereafter, though, the rank order of Troop and commander did not match. He added an asterisk against the first four Troops in his order of merit and similarly against the first five rated officers; then a note beneath saying that the two staff officers put down the same rank order for those marked 'independently of me and of each other' – a most unusually close agreement on nine discrete grades!

Next day, 28 January, Baden-Powell wrote to Sam Steele.

> My Dear Steele
>
> After leaving you I visited both Hussey Walsh's and Bateson's Troops. The former was very satisfactory – under command of Jarvis. Horses looking well but dying of horse sickness.

Bateson had only a portion of this troop at Fort Canada. I think it would be well to let him get in some of his detachment if possible in order to have some supervision over their training as the Troop is a very young one.

Jarvis seems to me quite fit to make a captain.

Lawrence and Sanders will not, I think, be any good to you. It would be best (if you think so too) to advise them that is my opinion – and let them resign.

As Burstall's Troop is under orders to move from Dwarsvlei, I strongly suggest McNaughton's half-troop from Scheerpoort takes his place there, if you think so too.

Scheerpoort is too near in to be of use against Boers; it is infected with horse sickness; and is a long way from the other half of the Troop at Hekpoort. Dwarsvlei misses these disadvantages.

Burstall's Troop has a lot of superfluous stores he could hand over to the relieving troop. This is a common fault in Troops – to have a large excess of QM stores. It should be put a stop to.

A few weeks ago 4 of our Troops in A Division had to burn heaps of useful stores because they had to make a sudden move and had not transport to carry their surplus.

Bateson's Troop has a lot of surplus stuff.

If you want water tanks those iron drums can always be got from the Dynamite Factory at 10 shillings each.

Yours

[signed] R Baden-Powell

Significantly, he did not override Steele's right to man-manage his own Division, but he gave him a way to get rid of two junior officers – 'if you think so too'. This may have struck a chord with Steele because Rod Macleod records that Steele was unhappy with some of his English subalterns who were more interested in sport than in their profession.[75] Nor at this point had Baden-Powell sent Steele his order of merit of the Troop commanders, but later he did; and Steele came back to him in six letters on that order of merit, in which, according to Baden-Powell in the staff diary, 'he gradually comes round to my view of them approximately.'

Dwarsvlei, the site that Baden-Powell recommended, was the scene of a small-scale action the year before in which Captain Hugh Montague Trenchard of the Royal Scots Fusiliers was seriously wounded; but in his long recovery he moved on to a different military path and would eventually become known as the father of the Royal Air Force.

Steele had earlier objected to Major Wilberforce as his second in command. In response Baden-Powell proposed changing Wilberforce from B Division to second in command of E Division, replacing him as second in command of B Division with Stuart, one of the staff officers on the inspection; and he proposed moving Captain Urquhart of C Division to staff officer HQ. Steele had nominated three officers as suitable candidates for the SAC, and Baden-Powell agreed to take them.

However, when it came to the fine detail of managing the SAC, there was little collegiate decision-making. For example, Sergeant Smith of B Division had a grievance, complaining of being unfairly sentenced by a board of officers. Baden-Powell inquired into it and found that the sergeant had been convicted on charges of drunkenness and stealing a bottle of port – 'without sufficient direct evidence to prove either'. He wrote to Sam Steele to censure Captain Boyd, who was president of the board of officers that convicted the sergeant; and he added a rider that the captain had conducted trials irregularly two or three times before. He then issued an order that the board's decision had to be quashed, referring to insufficient evidence that the prisoner had been drunk and no evidence that he was the man who stole the bottle of port; that a fellow sergeant who might have given important evidence was not called. He directed that the prisoner be released and reinstated.

Sometimes, though, it was a clear-cut for disciplinary action when there were witnesses: Captain Wood, Surgeon Captain Shanks, a lieutenant and others alleged that Captain Orde had been drinking heavily. Baden-Powell saw him and told him he wanted his resignation.

Right: Baden-Powell –
Inspector General
of the South African
Constabulary by
J. Matthew. (*Heritage
Services, The Scouts*)

Below: Colonel Sam
Steele outside President
Kruger's former home.
(*Bruce Peel Special
Collections*)

Left: Colonel Sam Steele and Nursing Sisters of the SAC. (Bruce Peel Special Collections)

Below: SAC officers. Baden-Powell 6th from right (back row); Sam Steele on his left. (*Bruce Peel Special Collections*)

Above: SAC farriers shoeing a horse. (*Anglo-Boer War Museum, Bloemfontein*)

Below left: SAC Surgeon-Captain Arthur Martin-Leake VC. (*Robin Smith*)

Below right: SAC Trooper Lachlan Gray, No. 9 Troop A Division. (*Sandy Thompson*)

An SAC camp. (*National Library of South Africa, Cape Town*)

SAC officers. (*National Library of South Africa, Cape Town*)

Above: President Kruger's former house, now occupied by SAC officers. (*National Library of South Africa, Cape Town*)

Below: Baden-Powell SAC inspector general on formal inspection of B Division; Colonel Steele in attendance at Raadsaal, Pretoria. (*National Library of South Africa, Cape Town*)

SAC troopers. (*National Library of South Africa, Cape Town*)

SAC recruits recently arrived from England. (*National Library of South Africa, Cape Town*)

A group of SAC patients. (*National Library of South Africa, Cape Town*)

SAC recruits arrived from England, before being armed. (*National Library of South Africa, Cape Town*)

In the veldt an SAC officer plucks a fowl for dinner. (*National Library of South Africa, Cape Town*)

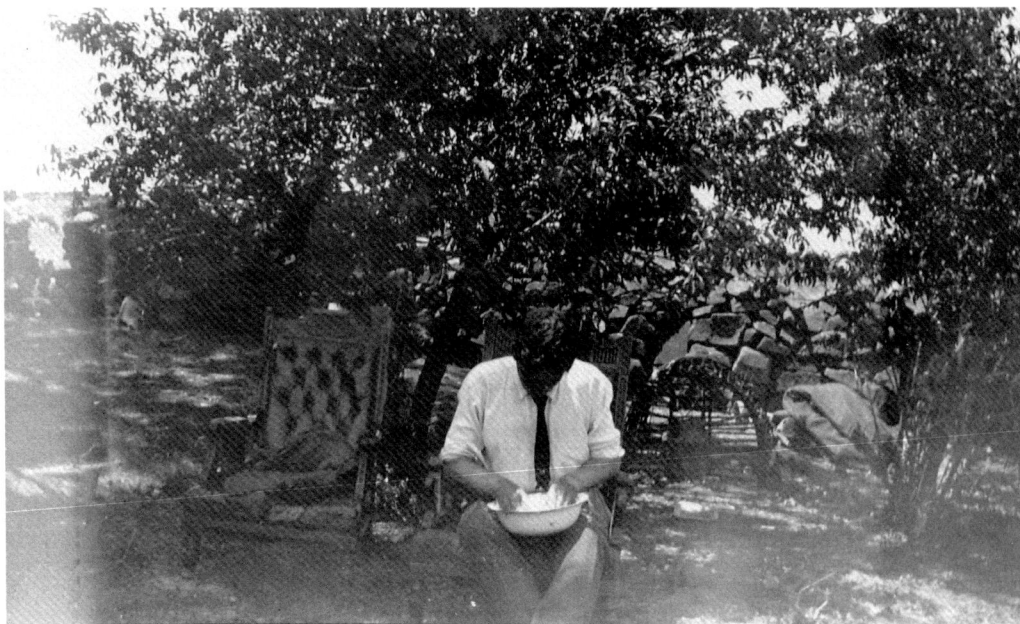

An SAC officer making bread. (*National Library of South Africa, Cape Town*)

Right: An SAC gravestone. (*National Library of South Africa, Cape Town*)

Below: SAC officers mount up. (*National Library of South Africa, Cape Town*)

SAC troopers on the veldt. (*National Library of South Africa, Cape Town*)

C Division's No. 9 Troop making their mark on the land. (*National Library of South Africa, Cape Town*)

Right: Medical orderlies Dewhurst and Shaw at an SAC hospital. (*National Library of South Africa, Cape Town*)

Below: SAC troopers making their grub. (*Anglo-Boer War Museum, Bloemfontein*)

Above: A squad from No. 19 Troop. (*Anglo-Boer War Museum, Bloemfontein*)

Below: An SAC troop. (*Anglo-Boer War Museum, Bloemfontein*)

A section from No. 19 Troop. (*Anglo-Boer War Museum, Bloemfontein*)

SAC HQ in Bloemfontein. (*Anglo-Boer War Museum, Bloemfontein*)

Left: Grub up at South African Jamboree 1936, East London. (*scoutwiki.scouts.org.za*)

Below: 2nd Muizenberg (Jewish) Troop at 1936 SA Jamboree. (*scoutwiki.scouts.org.za*)

Above: Baden-Powell trail in Camp Byng, British Columbia. (*Elizabeth Ross*)

Right: Camp Byng. (*Elizabeth Ross*)

Baden-Powell's inspector general SAC inspections coach being transported from Modderfontein to Gilwell Scouting Centre. (*Gilwell Scouting Centre, South Africa*)

The Scout patrol that restored the SAC inspector general's coach. (*Gilwell Scouting Centre, South Africa*)

More complex, however, was the case of the force's principal medical officer. Baden-Powell met Colonel Beevor on 18 January and told him he was not 'up to the job of PMO and we shall probably have to make a change'. Afterwards, he simply informed Milner that he had spoken to Beevor in such terms. It came about as a result of medical officers complaining about Beevor's managerial incompetence; but it went beyond that in that staff, pay, and control officers complained of his inconsistent dealings. It was not his professional competence that was at fault but his ability to manage the medical service. Baden-Powell wrote to Beevor telling him that his further enquiries confirmed his opinion against him and he should resign. Baden-Powell conceded that Beevor had worked hard and under difficult conditions; but administration was not for him. Beevor sent in his resignation on 16 February, but regretted that Baden-Powell should infer that his accounts were wrong and asked for a board of enquiry to examine them. Baden-Powell replied that Beevor had misread his letter, that he did not fault him on his honesty or zeal or his professional skill – but only in his administrative ability.

The army's PMO agreed to Baden-Powell's request to have Major Burtchaell RAMC as his replacement. Finally, Baden-Powell wrote a confidential letter to the officer commanding the Brigade of Guards explaining why Beevor was returning for duty with the Guards: 'not on account of any professional incapacity or want of zeal, but because the administration of so large a department as ours was beyond him.'

However effective the SAC had become they suffered some reverses. At the end of January, in the eastern Transvaal, the enemy carried out a clever operation that ended with the capture of three wagons carrying SAC supplies. Kitchener was displeased and telegraphed Major Fair (commanding C Division in the absence of Pilkington who had taken over E Division from Ridley on sick leave) and in traditional army fashion urged him to exercise personal supervision. That was not the answer though: the blockhouse line that 21 SAC Troops were manning extended for over 100 miles. With 10 per cent of the division on the sick list that meant there were about sixty men for every 5 miles to both patrol the country and do blockhouse duty. Hence personal supervision by the commanding officer would not have prevented what happened – they lacked manpower. What was needed was army support to cover the line; and that was what Baden-Powell urged upon Kitchener's chief of staff, Sir Ian Hamilton.

Next day he went to see for himself the site of the action and to learn what had happened from Captain Capell, who commanded that section of the line. He went by train in the inspector general's coach to Val and picked up Major Fair at Heidelberg. The site of the attack was at a point where the wagon track swung away from the line of blockhouses; and the commando planned it well: they split into three groups and lay concealed in dongas. They let the escort's advanced scouts through then they rushed the wagons. The SAC escort got into a kraal, split into two groups, one of which worked its way round to the enemy's flank. The firing brought out twelve men from two blockhouses nearby to support their comrades. At the cost of one man dead and five wounded the Boers got away with the wagons.

Again, the following week, the SAC suffered another reverse in the eastern Transvaal; and this time, Baden-Powell informed Milner, it was a fight, 'which was forced on us by Lord K.'s telegram'. It happened at Van Tonders Hock and it followed from a telegram Kitchener sent on 4 February to the officer commanding C Division:

> When do you propose moving forward your line? I don't think there has ever been anything in front to stop you. Certainly Wing [Colonel Wing who commanded a column in the eastern Transvaal] could not find them and now there should be little or nothing left behind. So I hope to hear you are moving.

However, Major Fair decided not to move until he had had the front reconnoitred and he sent Captain Capell with 130 men to do it. The reconnaissance force left at 3 am on 8 February. Capell expected the enemy to be in the area and he deployed his men in a semi-circular formation on the heights above Van Tonders Hock. The Boers were indeed there in force (a wounded prisoner later said there were about 800 in the commando) and at dawn Capell gave the order to open fire. The vastly superior commando put up a determined fight and by creeping up dongas until they were only a few yards away eventually turned the SAC left flank. Capell made the decision to withdraw for about 7 miles to the blockhouse line and sent an orderly with that message to Lieutenant Swinburne who was in charge of the advance party on the right. However, the orderly was shot and the message never got through. Capell and the main party withdrew but the advance party doggedly stuck to their post until nightfall, when they too got away.

That fight cost the SAC the death of nine men, including Lieutenant Abraham and Lieutenant Blackett, and twenty wounded; and it brought forth great courage and outstanding devotion to duty on the part of Surgeon Captain Martin-Leake, who,

> went up to a wounded man, and tended to him under a heavy fire from about 40 Boers at 100 yards range. He then went to the assistance of a wounded Officer, and, whilst trying to place him in a comfortable position, was shot three times, but would not give in till he rolled over thoroughly exhausted. All the eight men at this point were wounded, and while they were lying on the Veldt, Surgeon-Captain Martin-Leake refused water till everyone else had been served.[76]

For his valour Captain Martin-Leake was awarded the Victoria Cross. In time he would go on to become the first Briton to be awarded the Victoria Cross a second time – during the First World War.

Major Pack-Beresford, in the Orange River Colony, was moving along by the Vet River, a tributary of the Vaal River, in accordance with Kitchener's orders. However, at the beginning of February it was a slow business because heavy rains were making the roads impassable. Yet only weeks earlier there had been a drought that prevented him moving north of Boshof to the Vet River; he had to concentrate his force and go by known water places; and now he feared that the Boers could infiltrate the area taking livestock with them. In the staff diary Baden-Powell slips in a dig at the commander-in-chief – 'Lord K. should understand this.'

In his report Pack-Beresford said that his men were in excellent fighting trim and feared by the Boers. A Boer prisoner told them that the vice-commander-in-chief of the Boer commandos in the Orange River Colony, General Badenhorst, had told off special fighting Boers under Commandant Erasmus to watch the SAC. When Baden-Powell wrote to Sir Ian Hamilton, Kitchener's chief of staff, alerting him to Pack-Beresford's concerns about Boer infiltration, he also asked him to 'come and see how efficient and keen our men now are.'

The Boer commandos were not paid by their governments and they had to provide their own horses and weapons; they were not fed on a regular time scale like soldiers; they had to take their own victualling with them – all the more so because of the British policy of clearing farms and livestock.

Following Badenhorst's orders, Commandant Erasmus, it seems, kept a sharp look out for the SAC and on 24 January at Besters Kraal, his commando of between 250-300 men charged a detachment of twenty of Pack-Beresford's men who were driving off captured livestock. They captured nineteen of them and the livestock. However, Pack-Beresford had divided his force in two, one detachment about a mile apart from the other. At the shooting, the other detachment made a surprise attack on the commando and rescued their comrades and rounded up the livestock that consisted of 100 cattle and 600 sheep. The Boers had several wounded and four were captured; the SAC had four wounded.

A week later there was another action involving Pack-Beresford and Erasmus. It came about after two captured Boers agreed to act as guides to lead the SAC to Erasmus's laager near Baarters Rust, about 10 miles south-west of Hoopstad. Pack-Beresford carried out a night march of 30 miles, but on reaching the laager found that Erasmus and most of his commando had moved out leaving fifteen men behind. The SAC captured eight of them. However, Erasmus had not moved very far from the original laager and on the SAC's return march attacked them by charging up to them. The SAC's tactic was to stay firm against the charge rather than disperse and take cover. At that Erasmus's commando retreated from the scene, not wanting an all-out stand-off engagement. Five of them were seen to be wounded; they left 8 prisoners, 5 wagons, 52 trek oxen and 206 cattle. The SAC casualties were two wounded, two accidentally hurt and one captured and released.

At HQ Baden-Powell took a close look at the SAC's total casualties from its founding up to the first week of February 1902: 66 were killed, including 7 officers; and 148 wounded. At different times over the period 276 men had been captured and released. Each case was then examined by a board of officers and a decision made on the circumstance and whether punishment was appropriate.

He did a short analysis of deaths from all causes: the total from all causes was 267. Then he looked in detail at the previous six months: typhoid 55; dysentery 5; other diseases 16; wounds 46; accidents 10. Then he added in the number of discharges. There were 818 discharges – by purchase 80; for misconduct 52; medically unfit 328; time expired 205; miscellaneous 153. The total loss to the SAC from deaths from all causes and discharges came to 1,085. To off-set their losses, he wrote to Major McLaren, who was now in charge at the recruiting office in London, requesting that they increase the number of new recruits they were sending from 80 to 120 a month.

His programme of divisional inspections had to continue and his next tour of inspection was of A Division under Colonel Edwards in the western Transvaal. It was well-established and up to strength. Baden-Powell overlapped his inspection of the last two Troops of B Division by inspecting No. 16 Troop of A Division at Waterkloof. The inspector general found it, 'Very satisfactory in all points.' He saw though that many horses showed marks of old back sores and cautioned that care had to be taken to avoid a recurrence of these. He makes no reference to having staff officers or Colonel Edwards with him on this tour of inspection, and he adopted a slightly different pattern for recording his findings.

He inspected No. 18 Troop and No. 2 Troop at Witpoortje. No. 2 Troop was under the command of Captain Fowler and Lieutenant Higginbottom; there were ninety-two men and sixty-four horses; health, efficiency and conduct were very good. A complaint raised by several men – they wanted to purchase their discharge to take up work in South Africa. Baden-Powell told them to 'wait a bit'. No. 18 Troop, under Captain McLeod and Lieutenant Van Renen, consisted of eighty-two men and forty-nine horses. Health was fair; efficiency and conduct were very good; and there were no complaints.

Two Troops were stationed at Buffelsdoorn: No. 8 Troop under the command of Captain Williams and Lieutenant McFarlane had ninety-eight men and sixty-seven horses; No. 9 Troop under Captain Money and Lieutenant Robertson with eighty men and seventy-six horses. The inspector general was satisfied with both Troops; No. 8 Troop he assessed to be in very satisfactory condition; No. 9 Troop he placed in satisfactory condition.

The division's next move was intended to be to Hartbeesfontein, which was a known laager point for Boers, but it lacked transport to get there. The army, according to General Barker, commanding officer of the garrison at Klerksdorp, could not help with transport; and the SAC's inspector general lamented, 'our own is only sufficient to keep us fed from day to day.' On 7 February, to improve upon this hand-to-mouth situation, he did a deal with Colonel Sir R. Colleton the commander of the army garrison at Dompoort: Colleton would supply eight Troops of SAC up till 26 February in return for the loan of four Troops of SAC under the command of Captain Reynolds No. 5 Troop to assist the army clear their section of the country – Reynolds to command in the field.

Reynolds was soon in action with the support of 250 mounted infantry of Colonel Colleton's column near Bothaville. They captured two Boers and wounded three at no cost to their force.

Baden-Powell's assessment of A Division was that all Troops 'without exception' were in a very satisfactory state of efficiency – given the limited number of horses. It was a vindication of the SAC's devolved responsibility on to Troop commanders: 'This result is due to hard work, zeal and intelligence on the part of the officers, who deserve full credit for successfully developing their Troops under great difficulties.'

However, it was not so satisfactory further down the Troop: the squad system was not being used in the field as in quarters; there was a tendency to slip back into the old army drill of 'telling off, forming up as troops' which was not required if the squad system 'is properly employed'. Troop commanders needed to hold the squad commander responsible for everything in his squad: the state of their horses, 'sore backs', the duty roster of the men and how they worked in the field or in action. For this to work effectively, he wrote, 'squads must be kept intact', and he directed Troop commanders to 'Notes and Instructions for the SAC.'

Then in a passage he called 'Care of Horses', he recommended that on long patrols there should be a halt every 30 minutes or so 'when the saddles should be taken off and horses allowed to roll, and backs examined. This freshens the horses and prevents sore backs.' Then, not a recommendation but an order: 'I was sorry to notice in one or two cases the order is still neglected which directs that the moment a man halts he is to dismount without further orders. Sitting on the horse at the halt is never to be allowed.'

Describing the condition of the horses he found: 'it was very satisfactory throughout, but in one or two Troops there were several sore backs. Certain saddles were blamed in one Troop while in the next another kind of saddle was quoted as the cause of the backs.' He continued, 'As a matter of fact sore backs don't come so much from the saddle as from the ignorance or want of care on the part of the man using it. If the above instructions re off-saddling and also those given in the "Notes for the SAC" were explained and insisted on by OC Troop there would be no sore backs as was the case in many of the Troops where there were scarcely any.' Finally, he had a note on tethering horses: officers commanding Troops were to see that every mounted man had a means of tethering his horse rapidly so that he could dismount and leave his horse standing, to ensure it would not wander off or stampede. He suggested either a hook fixed to the stirrup iron or a strap hanging from the saddle or a 'plain rimpje' [from Afrikaans, a strip of worked leather] by which the horse's bit could be fixed to pull the head round to the side.

Not only the horses needed care and consideration, the lifestyle men had to live took its toll on their willingness to accept discipline. The inspector general sent a circular memorandum to all officers saying that they 'must pay proper attention to the wants of their men and show some encouragement and leniency when they are doing extra hard work.'

The circular was triggered by a case of insubordination in E Division. The proceedings of the subsequent court martial had come to the inspector general for confirmation. Twenty-three men had refused to march when ordered: their plea was that they would be unable to keep up with the wagons. They had fallen in, as ordered, but refused to march when ordered to. However, when Major Pack-Beresford came out and pointed out the gravity of their offence 'they marched'.

Sentencing varied from one year's imprisonment for the corporal. The 1st and 2nd class troopers were given prison sentences and the rest were let off with a warning owing to their inexperience. Commenting on it in an order, Baden-Powell took the view: there was no excuse for refusing to obey. Some men had claimed that they had had no rations; some that they were tired. Their proper course in such circumstance was to complain to their officers – hence the need for the circular to all officers.

Since Baden-Powell had returned to duty there had been very little face-to-face time with Milner. Orders, responses or discussion mostly took the form of memoranda from and to the military secretary. On 10 January, for example, Milner disapproved of the SAC's order for guns and directed that the order from Armstrong be cancelled. Baden-Powell wrote that he 'acquiesced' though he stated the reasons he wanted them in justification. By contrast though, Milner sanctioned the appointment of four chaplains to the SAC at 25 shillings a day cash. However, when the SAC applied to the senior army chaplain and the bishop of Pretoria neither could help. So instead, Baden-Powell wrote to Milner suggesting that each officer commanding a Division could make arrangements with local clergymen, 'giving them fees for attending our sick and holding services'. He proposed allocating £5 a week to each Division for fees for 'ministers of all religions'.

He also came up with a scheme for appointing officer cadets in the force. The military secretary responded that 'His excellency does not see advantage of proposed scheme.' That invited a well-reasoned response. Baden-Powell argued the RIC had something similar; that you got more and better trained officers without increasing the budget; that it did not follow that a good NCO would make a good officer; that instead 'you select a good gentleman from the ranks. He passes a qualifying exam in professional subjects and becomes a probationary officer.' He specified the exam subjects and concluded that it would, 'I think, produce the best trained officers in the world besides offering fuel inducement to good men to enlist, and to work well in the ranks.' However, he also sent the objections to the scheme from Pilkington and Edwards.

When Milner and Baden-Powell met for the second time it was on 13 February. The first item on the agenda was Colonel Ridley. Ridley was still on sick leave in the UK but, as Baden-Powell put it, 'having been Stellenbosched' by Kitchener [army slang for an officer side-lined to a position where his incompetence would be less obvious]; he had written accusing the SAC HQ of 'not adequately supplying him for the work required of him'. Baden-Powell reiterated why to Milner – the army had reneged on its undertaking that the SAC would be 'found' by the army, telling them to 'find' for themselves. Then Baden-Powell made plain to Milner, 'But we have no wish to keep Ridley owing to his sketchiness and want of method in running his Division.'

Ridley, however, followed up his complaint when he later met Lord Roberts in the UK on 11 April, the day before he was due to depart for South Africa. That prompted Roberts who wrote that same day to Kitchener outlining their discussion: Ridley had 'complained that scarcely over half the South African Constabulary are mounted, and when I asked him why he did not represent this strongly when he was in command, he said he did not like to give his Corps away. I told him I could not agree with him and that it was his duty not to leave a stone unturned in endeavouring to get his corps efficient.'[77] It is clear then that Kitchener had not been informing Roberts of the SAC's shortage of horses.

When Baden-Powell heard that Ridley was on his way out to South Africa, he telegraphed the military secretary to ask what were Milner's 'views with regard to him. We do not want him in SAC.' He cited some examples of Ridley's maladministration; and he ended with the example, 'No proper ledgers kept till Pilkington took over the Division.' The military secretary came back to him with the news that 'Col Ridley is to be provided for by C in C.'

The second item on the agenda with Milner when they met in February was Baden-Powell's idea of appointing cadets or cornets in the SAC. He reiterated what he had written to the military secretary: the advantages were that they would be able to select and train their own officers at 'scarcely any expense'.

Milner was more receptive now. Baden-Powell was instructed to prepare draft regulations for the appointment of cornets. His scheme proposed six cornets per Division for A, B and C Divisions and eight for E Division. They would be paid

15 shillings per day and they would be selected by the divisional commanding officer from among NCOs with at least one year's experience. Candidates would be required to pass a qualifying examination in drill and manoeuvre; care of horses; rifle shooting; interior economy; discipline regulations. If a man qualified he was appointed a cornet and carried out the functions of an officer on probation. After six months successful service the cornet could go for the examination to qualify as a second lieutenant. The syllabus for it consisted of the five subjects for the qualifying level at more depth, plus police law; official correspondence and boards; veterinary knowledge; reports.

Underpinning his scheme for cadets/cornets was Baden-Powell's faith in the recruitment and selection criteria for the SAC. However, he did not then know the political background to the assembling of the Canadian contingent until Colonel Sam Steele came to meet him in Pretoria on 5 March. The main purpose of their meeting was to talk over the organisation of B Division, the most recently formed. Sam Steele had been working hard at getting the division 'and especially his officers into shape'. He had all his officers undertake and pass a course of instruction given by the SAC's paymaster; its controller; and the veterinary officer. In this context of getting his officers into shape Sam Steele brought up the recruitment of the Canadian officers: according to Baden-Powell, Colonel Steele 'explained the errors of Lord Minto's selection of officers etc. for the Canadian contingent to SAC.'

Steele seems to have been a shrewd judge of men. He had objected to Major Wilberforce as his second in command and Baden-Powell agreed to transfer him to another Division. However, when he offered him to E Division they did not want him either. Baden-Powell then offered him to Major Fair of C Division and wrote to Wilberforce with the news telling him that although there was no complaint about his work no one could get on with him or work with him – 'a point that cannot be improved nor can it be ignored'.

There was also an element of give and take in the interaction between the inspector general and the commanding officer of B Division: when Baden-Powell recommended getting rid of Captain Lawrence, Sam Steele had gone ahead with it. That brought Captain Lawrence to request a meeting with the inspector general at which he explained that ever since he joined the SAC he had only been employed in temporary jobs in which he had to organise everything without assistance. What he wanted was another chance. The inspector general put it to Steele; since Steele had nothing against him, he agreed to it.

Then Sam Steele raised the issue of Surgeon Captain Vaux – whether 'he would be reinstated or whitewashed'. It will be recalled from Chapter 2 that the year before, when Baden-Powell replied to Lord Minto, governor general of Canada with regard to the arrival of the Canadian contingent, he said that he would have to get rid of Vaux who was inefficient as a medical officer and Captain Critchley who drank. Now, though, in response to Sam Steele, he agreed to inquire into the case of Vaux; and he included the following in the staff diary: 'The reasons for the nurses objecting to him was that one of them was immoral and he had tried to put a stop to it on board ship.' It would seem then that the phrase the inspector general used the year before – 'inefficient as a medical officer' – was a smoke screen that covered a multitude of sins. Now, following Steele's request, Baden-Powell wrote inviting Vaux to meet him.

When Vaux met Baden-Powell at SAC's HQ office, he told him that he gave up a successful medical practice in Canada as a result of being nominated by Lord Minto to come out to the SAC. There was no suggestion that he might be on probation; and he had expected to have the rank of major. On the outward voyage there was a lot of disease on board – 6 died on the ship – and Vaux found that he was overworked because the ship's doctor was a drunk, incapable of helping. The Canadian officers spent their nights drinking and playing cards. Vaux had no time to join them even if he had had the inclination. Then the nurses were 'made too much of by the officers' and he had to speak to them to get them to work. They repeated this to the officers; and a group of them sent him to Coventry. One of them, Captain Critchley, whose brother had been beaten for the post of surgeon with the contingent by Vaux, openly said that he would get Vaux turfed out. After he had been in the SAC a month the principal medical officer, Colonel Beevor, directed him to resign 'as he did not meet our requirements'. At the same time, according to Vaux, Beevor told him 'that he himself was satisfied with him in every way'. Vaux felt aggrieved: he had lost professional standing and his reputation in Canada would be affected. Could he be taken back into the SAC?

Baden-Powell's position was that several Canadian officers and nurses had said they would not remain in the corps if Vaux did:

> That was enough for me; even if I went into the whole case with court of inquiry etc., someone would have to go in the end. I could not have lion and lamb trying to get in to the same bed. I couldn't get rid of the whole of the Canadian officers and nurses so the lamb had to go.

He rationalised it further. Vaux had not lost out: the army had been keen to have him; and if it would help him in Canada, he, the inspector general, could give him a letter to that effect. He mulled further, 'I could not see why his reputation in Canada should suffer if the right version of the affair were given out there.' However, given that the affair had come about from among the Canadian contingent's officers and nurses, who would be returning home, that was surely wishful thinking – tales would be told in Canadian bar rooms and cafés about how, banding together in the SAC, they got rid of a killjoy doctor. Basic justice had not come into it. Now though, Baden-Powell would look at this tale of human weakness more closely: 'Meantime in response to Col Steele's request on his behalf and his own letters to me I am making inquiries among the Canadian officers for further light on the subject and will let him know result later.'

Certainly treatment of the sick and wounded was a high priority and the corps could not risk a haemorrhage of medical staff. Indeed the shortage of hospital beds meant that patients were discharged as soon as they were fit, but ideally discharge should be followed by convalescence and Baden-Powell felt that it was necessary to start a depot of convalescent men because the army hospitals were overfull and the SAC hospitals could not accommodate them. He decided to set one up at Zuurfontein. Colonel Nicholson, chief of staff, was among those convalescing but Baden-Powell sent him to Durban 'nominally to arrange our remount farm'.

Some, however, did not make it through to convalescence – in early March the SAC lost one of the men who had graced its laurels when Major Pack-Beresford died of typhoid in hospital in Bloemfontein. Writing to Sir Ian Hamilton, Baden-Powell said, 'Pack-Beresford is a great loss to us. I am greatly obliged for Lord Kitchener's kindly reference to him.'

All the while, the SAC was involved in actions thick and fast. In A Division Captain Money and 300 men were attached to Grenfell's column under Colonel Kekewich; and it was duly noted at the SAC's HQ: 'Both Kekewich and Grenfell have expressed very high opinion of our men's work in the field.' On 19 February Reynolds took 250 men from Bothaville towards Commando Drift and surprised a commando laager and captured eight Boers including the *Landdrost* of Bothaville and his staff. Then after a gallop of 5 miles they surprised and captured seven more of the enemy. Reynolds wanted to go on and attack a Boer convoy that was reported to be close by, but Colonel Colleton, with whom they were working, stopped him. Apart from their prisoners they had some carts and livestock: 10 mules, 30 horses, 60 cattle; and the report concludes that 800 sheep were destroyed.

Again on 22 February Reynolds with 250 men moved south from Bothaville. A little after dawn they came across a Boer laager and charged in, firing from the saddle. The Boers fled but the SAC pursued them for about 10 miles, when a second commando turned up and attacked them. The SAC beat them off but at the cost of four wounded and sixteen captured – men whose horses had stampeded.

Then Major Vaughan had four patrols out to the north of Hoopstad when one of them, along the Vaal, surprised a Boer laager on the opposite bank, but the river was swollen by heavy rain and impassable. They fired into the laager killing one Boer and wounding three who, according to report, were left on the ground by their comrades.

In late February a British army column under Colonel Von Donop was at Wolmaranstad and, on the 23rd, Von Donop sent an empty convoy of 130 wagons to Klerksdorp, a distance of about 50 miles. It had a strong escort for this was territory that General De la Rey's commando now roamed. The first two days all went well, then after a night of heavy rain, in the early light, the well-planned ambush was sprung. The convoy was destroyed and almost 200 soldiers lay dead.

Yet, despite the heavy enemy presence there were examples of individual acts of merit on the part of the SAC. Corporal Dale of No. 5 Troop A Division rode with a burgher guide from Bothaville to Wolmaranstad, some 48 miles, with important despatches for Von Donop; and two troopers, McCutcheon of No. 13 Troop and Steele of No. 5 Troop on the night of February 25, the day of the attack on the convoy, rode 40 miles in ten hours with important despatches for Von Donop. Baden-Powell flagged up the three self-reliant men in orders and recommended them for Kitchener's attention. He also commended in general orders, and to Kitchener, good work on the part of Corporal Hendry and Trooper Stewart of A Division. They rode on 28 February and again on 1 March from Bothaville with despatches to Colonel Kekewich at Wolmaranstad. They were driven back twice but got through the third time – only to find that the enemy occupied Wolmaranstad. They were pursued, 'but got on to Kekewich's spoor and safely joined him'.

On 27 February Captain McCartie with a patrol of fourteen men engaged a party of twenty-five Boers 10 miles south of Leeuwkraal in the Orange River

Colony. McCartie had his patrol off-saddled when the sentries he had posted spotted Boers in sight. McCartie opened fire on them with one squad, saddled up and pursued the enemy with the other squad until the Boers reached a farm and took cover in the farmhouse. When the SAC squad tried to rush the farmhouse McCartie, Manning and Noble were cut down. Then the Boers rushed out and galloped away. The patrol captured a wounded enemy and some rifles, saddles and eight horses. However, it was at the cost of McCartie and his two comrades who died of their wounds.

A larger force of SAC under Major Vaughan returned from Commando Drift to Hoopstad where he met Von Donop and Colleton. Vaughan's group had captured 12 Boers, 6 rifles, horses, oxen and 150 cattle. What Vaughan wanted to know now: should he continue with his blockhouse line to the Vaal River or should he remain as a field force. It was Kitchener who made the decision – he was to remain as a field force.

There were big issues at stake here in early March: the skilful and energetic Boer commando leader General De Wet had moved in from the east and he had with him President Steyn of the Orange Free State, now a fugitive in his own country, a president who, enduring the same hardships as his commando, was a moral support in their war against the usurper. The commando, De Wet tells in his memoir, had come to the blockhouse line that stretched from Kroonstad to the Vaal River and they rested for two days north of Bothaville.

On the night of March 12th we broke through the blockhouse line, some 5 miles to the west of Bothaville. When we were about fifty paces from the line, somebody to our left challenged us. 'Halt! Who goes there?' He challenged a second time, and then fired.[78]

No one was hit and the commando successfully cut through the wire.

De Wet was contemptuous of the blockhouse lines; they were ineffective – in his memoir he wrote 'having thus escaped from the last "White Elephant"' – but other commando leaders felt they were a serious threat.

Kitchener of course frequently reported in his despatches on the progression of the blockhouse lines and the role of the SAC: for example in his report on 25 March he stated that, 'Our blockhouse system continues slowly but surely to spread over the country, enclosing areas, which are gradually cleared by the mobile columns, and then occupied by a network of Constabulary posts.'[79]

In the eastern Transvaal, in C Division's area, Captain Capell reported in mid-March that thirty Boers tried to cross the SAC line from east to west on the Grootspruit and another five on Vaalbank, but both attempts were frustrated by the SAC's heavy firing at close range. Of those failed attempts Kitchener telegraphed, 'Am much pleased to see how successful you are in preventing crossing.'

However, Kitchener also wanted the SAC to evacuate a line of blockhouses and establish a new line. Baden-Powell felt an alternative was to break up the country into better sections to facilitate the forthcoming offensive. Then, on the Ides of March, he went on a daring tack: he suggested to Kitchener's chief of staff that Kitchener could make better use of the SAC:

> At the same time I am certain that if we changed places with the untrained yeomanry the SAC could do some good work in the field; if the yeomanry took over our blockhouses and we their horses – our men are well-organised, in small units, under first-rate officers and NCOs.

> They can ride and shoot and have experience of fighting in veldt life. They are now acclimatised. They are ready equipped – are very good shots (firing from the saddle) and are as keen as mustard. Among them we have Canadians – jolly good as scouts etc.

> At a juncture like the present I am certain that a force of 5000 of these men would give really effective help in the field.[80]

If Kitchener had simply said no and left it at that it would not have prolonged the exchange – however, he justified his decision by suggesting what he thought was best for the SAC in the future: he had his chief of staff write saying 'Lord K. much pleased with the work of SAC – but thought that to use them as mounted men would spoil them for Police work later.'

That of course prompted a response from Baden-Powell to the chief of staff:

> I don't think the future efficiency of the SAC as Police is likely to suffer through their being used as mounted troops in the field – quite the contrary. As a matter of fact we have found mounted columns work improves them all round.

Knowing he would get nowhere pursuing it he wrote at the bottom 'don't bother to answer this.'

Further attempts were made on successive nights to cross C Division's line and were foiled. However, as a result the division was under a lot of pressure, to the extent that the inspector general asked the chief of staff for Kitchener's agreement to his moving some Troops from B Division at Tafelkop. Again on 16 March C Division's line at Wildebeesfontein was heavily attacked, but the enemy were driven off with no casualties to the SAC. Then Major Fair reported that on 24 March two army columns one under Colonel Williams the other under Colonel Wing made a 'drive' from the east and north-east against the SAC line of blockhouses between Val and Standerton. One of the posts reported that the Boers had broken into smaller groups, then reformed and headed north-east of one of Colonel Wing's columns.

Omen might have alerted the sergeant major not to give the order – for it was 28 March, Good Friday, and word came in to the depot Troop during the church service that Boers had attacked native guards who were looking after cattle corralled in a protected area nearby and were driving them off. 'The sgt-maj turned out 13 mounted SAC men and rode off to the place without informing Maj Fair.' They drove off the Boers and followed them and predictably fell into an ambush. The sergeant major and another man were killed and two others mortally wounded.

In B Division friction between the SAC and the army developed at Irene, a village, at that time, south of Pretoria. The commander of the army camp, Colonel Pickford, began interfering and giving orders to the SAC detachment under the command of Captain Anderson to occupy blockhouses. The SAC's job there was to stop cattle raids; and as a result of Pickford's taking over, 'two cattle raids have taken place under their noses.' Sam Steele took a stand; he ordered Captain Anderson not to accept Pickford's orders. Baden-Powell agreed and wrote to both Steele and Anderson confirming it; and he added that if Pickford tried interfering again to write to Kitchener.

An interesting sequence of encounters between enemies took place in A Division when an SAC officer who had been captured and released by a Boer commando later returned to the laager where he had been held to discuss with his former captor terms for the commandos' surrender. It began at Spion Kop a hill about 1,400 metres high, which had been the site of a major battle two years earlier when the Boers were the victors. However, in those two years the type of warfare had changed: then it was armies and heavy weaponry, now it was hit and run commando raids. The Kop was the site of an SAC fort and it was under the command of Captain Rowe. On the night of 12 March at 11 pm about 100 Boers advanced up the Kop in heavy rain and mist and for fifteen minutes poured rifle fire at the fort; then the enemy retired to the foot and kept firing until 4.30 am. By the end of the engagement the known enemy casualties were one dead and two wounded; the SAC had no casualties.

Then, according to Captain Rowe's detailed account, intelligence reported a small number of enemy to the south of them. The captain took a party of men out to do a reconnaissance. The mist still clung to the hill and eventually Rowe and his advance scouts found themselves surrounded by small groups of the enemy. The Boers wore khaki and SAC hats (it will be recalled that a train with a consignment of Stetson hats for the SAC had been plundered in the western Transvaal) and were able to get very close before being spotted as enemy. Eventually, the two men with Rowe ran out of ammunition; four others by now had either been dismounted or had run out of ammunition and were captured. In all six SAC men were captured along with Rowe; and twelve men successfully withdrew and got back safely to the fort.

In the laager where he was being held Rowe had a long talk with Field Cornet Mears and was very civilly treated by him. Rowe began to form the view from their discussion that Mears was a realist about the war's outcome. Following the usual pattern – the commando could not feed their captives – the prisoners were duly released, but in small numbers. Finally two of them came back and said the Boers wanted to hear about terms of surrender. At that Captain Rowe proposed to go out himself, properly briefed on the military's policy. This he did and had a long talk again with Mears going over the terms by which the commando could surrender. Mears then consulted his leading men. When he returned he told Rowe that they had heard that their government had come to Pretoria and if their government 'gives them orders to surrender they will be glad of it; but if not they will carry on fighting for 10 years if necessary'.

To round off the sequence, the board of officers investigating Captain Rowe's capture and the attack on the Spion Kop post produced evidence of 'special gallantry in several instances' – Captain Rowe himself; Sergeant Saxby who with four men helped Captain Rowe in his fight and got back with two horses shot, remounted his men and went out again; Troop Sergeant Major McBeth, who took over command when Captain Rowe was captured; and Trooper Atkinson, who kept up his signalling while he was under close fire, turned his lamp on as a searchlight and played *Cock o' the north* on the mouth organ. Baden-Powell commended them all 'for specially good work and gallantry, and recommended them to notice of C in C'.

The C-in-C, however, had a lot on his mind and, under pressure, could be sensitive to criticism. For example, Colonel Pilkington reported to Baden-Powell that Kitchener was annoyed when it was pointed out to him that the SAC line along the Vet River was too weak to protect the large military convoys moving along it, because Major Vaughan and 800 men had been deployed to a column. The same day, 3 April, it was an officer in the SAC's A Division who was the focus of Kitchener's ire: Captain Money was under arrest on Kitchener's order to be tried by court martial – as Baden-Powell phrased it, '(presumably) for neglecting to come to assistance of Von Donop's convoy when reconnoitring in its neighbourhood'. It will be recalled that in late February Colonel Von Donop's convoy had suffered considerable loss of life when it was ambushed. If that was the charge that Kitchener ordered Money be tried on, and if he was looking for a whipping boy, he was in for a disappointment – three weeks later the court martial honourably acquitted Captain Money, and released him back to duty.

Within forty-eight hours of Kitchener ordering the arrest of Captain Money, Baden-Powell was naming and blaming. It arose from the report he had only then received of Captain Gaunt's fight with Van Berger's commando at Wegdraai in E Division's area on 15 March.

Captain Gaunt had taken out a patrol of sixty men. However, he had posted no rear look out; they were vulnerable. Van Berger's men may have had field glasses on them on earlier patrols – for the surprise assault was prepared. Suddenly, the SAC patrol was attacked by about 60-70 Boers who rushed them from the rear out of thorn bush country. One of the patrol was killed and Captain Gaunt and Captain Aldridge were wounded and captured along with nine men. However, Captain Palmer and six men covered the retreat of the rest of the patrol both 'skilfully and well'. The fight brought out great depth of reserves in Trooper Smith who would not give in though severely wounded. Baden-Powell sent out a circular expressing his dissatisfaction at the conduct of the fight, especially at the want of a lookout being kept to the rear. However, he commended Captain Palmer, those with him and Trooper Smith.

Carelessness on patrol, though, was the exception for the SAC had gained experience in intense actions on the veldt against a skilful foe; and its record of individual initiative and gallantry over the range of ranks speaks for itself.

A month after SAC HQ moved to accommodation in Johannesburg, to Government Square, the sub-manager of the dynamite factory came up with a useful device and a proposition for the SAC in their blockhouse lines – he brought specimens of two kinds of self-igniting flares to the inspector general and offered to make them for the cost price of the material if the inspector general would send him two carpenters to do preparatory work. To this Baden-Powell agreed; and he wrote in the staff diary, 'The whole cost will be under £30 and we shall have a very important addition to our blockhouse defences.'[81]

He also continued with the first round of his programme of inspections and he telegraphed chief of staff, Ian Hamilton, to say he intended inspecting C Division, commanded by Major Fair. This was approved the same day. (The inspector general had inspected E Division earlier in February but there is a gap in the archive from mid-February to the end of the month.)

Baden-Powell had Major Fair, PMO Major Burtchaell and Captain Keansley with him when he went by rail in the inspector general's coach from Johannesburg to Heidelberg. The usual pattern followed with the remount establishment and the hospital provision being inspected first. There was the inevitable grousing when the opportunity presented itself: three complaints, two against excessive punishment; and in one case a trooper who was a lay reader (the alternative arrangement for leading worship if there was no chaplain) wanted promotion to corporal and 'leave to wear plain clothes' – Baden-Powell 'gave him leave to resign lay readership'.

From Heidelberg he went by train to Val Station to begin the Troop inspections. The inspector general inspected thirteen Troops and fifty-seven blockhouses. The standard was generally very high. He judged No. 5 Troop, under Captain Capell and Lieutenant Swinburne to be first rate. It had ninety-seven men and seventy-eight horses and Baden-Powell noted the condition of both men and horses was very good. However, where there already had been failure of leadership at Troop level the damage took time to heal: No. 19 Troop had no captain and was commanded by Lieutenant Woodcock, who was on the sick list, and Baden-Powell wrote it 'went to pieces under Captain Orde (since dismissed) is now improving but wants a good captain.' It will be recalled that Orde was dismissed because of his heavy drinking.

Apart from sending a synthesis of his notes to Major Fair, Baden-Powell wrote a paper from his notes for officers and a general order for all ranks.

In his findings for officers he points out the quality of leadership:

> the general condition of C Division is most satisfactory and reflects great credit on the officers.

> Here, as in E Division, the amount of efficiency and willing work that the officers get out of their men varies almost exactly in relative proportion to the capability of the officer and the amount of interest that he takes in his Troop.

> I was very glad to see steps taken in almost every Troop to encourage the men with games and sports to relieve the monotony of their work on the blockhouse line.

However, more had to be done in regard to the welfare of the men:

> many of the men have told me that when they have a complaint to make they can not get a hearing – either the officer will not listen to them or the NCO will not introduce their case to him. This must be altered. The officer must be accessible to his men and he must hear them with patience.

Then there was a practice he discovered that had to be stopped. 'Also officers must put a stop to NCOs taking tips and bribes from young soldiers and troopers trying for promotion etc.'

In his general order for all ranks a tone comes through that, in the light of the world-wide movement that he was later to create, could be described as scoutmasterly:

> I have noted with great satisfaction the efficient condition of the Troops which reflects great credit on the officers, non-commissioned officers and men respectively.

> I was much pleased with the evident zeal and intelligence with which all have worked to carry out the instructions of the Commander in Chief

in the formation of a really effective line of blockhouses as well as with the good spirit in which they have carried out the uninteresting though useful work of garrisoning the line.

The smartness of the men in appearance was in many Troops conspicuous in spite of the difficulties of life on the veldt.

I noted too the steps taken in many of the Troops for practice in musketry, gymnastics and commend them to those that have not so far employed them.

But in carrying these out – especially gymnastics – it should be borne in mind 'little and often' together with plenty of competition is better than long lessons that are apt to become tedious.

More signalling should be learnt in the Division, each blockhouse might be able to communicate with the neighbour by semaphore signalling which is very easily learnt by any man. Diagrams are being printed for the purpose.

A little later on in his paper another note comes in – an inspector general committed to the welfare of the men.

I noted that in this Division there are fewer men depositing money in the Savings Bank than in other Divisions. A good many appear to send their money home by postal order instead. Some are evidently under an idea the Bank is devised with a view to the authorities getting a hold on their money. This is quite erroneous. I only want to see men putting by a bit now while they are drawing big pay with few expenses, ready for the time when they take their discharge and want to set themselves up in civil life. Our bank system is devised with a view to making this an easy and simple matter for them and to give them extra good interest on their money.

He also wanted to honour them in their death. He wrote to the military secretary asking that crosses for men's graves be included in the government allowance for funerals. 'I think it a very important point as regards the men and their relatives.' Iron crosses of a standard pattern he found could be got cheaply and would add only 30 shillings to the funeral allowance from government. In his budgeting, Baden-Powell had estimated for the following year that funeral costs would amount to £800 and that would include the cost of iron crosses.

That was a soldier's sentiment. However, the decision would not be made by a soldier but by a hard-nosed official with budgetary responsibility – Milner: and he in his reply gave the sentiment short shrift. In Baden-Powell's words, 'HE in reply to my application cannot sanction the principle of Govt paying for crosses on men's graves.'

The response did not faze the inspector general: he at once sent out a circular to all ranks of the SAC suggesting that all those who wished to honour the dead might subscribe up to one day's pay.

> This would enable a cross to be put up on every grave whether in a cemetery or on the veldt and the balance could be used at the end of the war to erect a big monument at each Divisional HQ.

In the field, in E Division, it seemed to the inspector general that part of the division's function in manning the blockhouse line was being seriously weakened by decisions taken elsewhere. Captain Kitson complained that his section of the line had been 'dangerously weakened by withdrawal of all mounted men to work with Col Rochfort's column and by the retention of 169 men at Bloemfontein'. Not only were they kept there but ninety-six of them were put on garrison duty by the garrison commander. The inspector general wrote to the chief of staff to know if this was on Kitchener's orders. Major Vaughan and part of a Troop had also been taken by Colonel Rochfort for his column on a three-day trek. They had captured a few prisoners and taken a lot of cattle; but they had two SAC men taken prisoner and then released.

Kitchener, however, was reporting to the War Office as the meritorious conduct of SAC men in the field continued – sometimes referring to actions months past: his despatch of 25 April referred to gallant actions in November, December 1901 and February 1902 – Corporal Plant for gallantry in November, with the additional note that he 'had been three times previously mentioned'. There were Troopers Medway and Wood for their conduct in December; and Captain Cornwall for gallantry at Ange Wert as recently as February.

A week earlier, 17 April, the inspector general went by rail to C Division and picked up Major Fair at Heidelberg; they reached Val Station at noon. From there they rode the 13 miles out to Captain Capell's post. What they found was that extra posts had been set up to make it more difficult for the Boers to break through the line; and they stayed there part of the night, until, as Baden-Powell put it, 'As moon set, 3am, we opened fire to wake them up.'

For the remainder of that day they travelled north but saw very few Boers – but the inspector general later learned that about 100 of the commandos had been gathering at Kromdraai. That night there was heavy rain and troops were opening up with bursts of fire periodically for enemy scouts were prodding for gaps in the line. Under cover of darkness they found that 'the left flank of the driving line was *en l'air*' and the inspector general later learned that about 700 had got through. That drive against the blockhouse and fort line had not been a winner.

The inspector general returned by rail first to Pretoria where he visited Captain Olliver who was in hospital with typhoid fever and pleurisy; and then he inspected the SAC hospital under Major Porter. He stayed on and inspected recruits for B Division; and he noted that twenty-five SAC were attached to the Town Police learning their duties; that one officer and several NCOs were going through a farrier's course and a course of control and pay accounting.

Death's arbitrariness this time claimed Captain Boyd who died of typhoid. Baden-Powell attended his funeral and wrote to Boyd's father.

Talk of peace, however, was already in the air. What Captain Rowe had caught snatches of when he had been a prisoner of Field Cornet Mears was now widespread; and on 24 April army headquarters put out a programme of the moves of the Boer commanders who were going about up until 15 May sounding out the commandos regarding peace.

Kitchener's changed approach to the SAC had its limits when it came down to the military budget. The SAC had lost eighty-four horses in military work and Baden-Powell asked him for replacements from the army. That Kitchener would not concede; he considered it all part of constabulary work. Baden-Powell, though, had heard something privately that merited a smile: the commanding officer of an army column took horses from his mounted infantry and gave them to the SAC 'because he finds them more useful'. However, Kitchener sanctioned the SAC to buy from army remounts up to the number that had been earlier agreed upon but never fulfilled.

There was continuing pressure to obtain remounts. Column commanders who had SAC Troops of A and E Divisions attached asked SAC HQ to supply remounts to replace losses. However, the SAC had none fit yet at Hill Crest; 'to send unfit walers [a riding horse from Australia, originally from New South Wales] into the field is to kill them,' Baden-Powell wrote. The force needed more horses and his hope now was that Milner would approve the purchase from army remounts of 250 fit horses to keep them efficient in the field. 'The SAC is certainly gaining thereby a very good name in the field, and also is putting a great deal of spirit and energy into all ranks which life in blockhouses for month after month is killing.'

On 25 April a consignment of 289 walers arrived at Durban from Australia; the horse trader that brought them was Willis. In addition there were thirty from another trader, Madden. SAC veterinary officer Lieutenant McKenzie reported that those received from Willis were in fair condition, but some were in a bad way; those from Madden were good in quality and condition.

At the same time an inter-organisational block threatened to prevent the sending of horses that were fit from Hill Crest Farm up country to the divisions: the railway company announced it was not willing to entrain horses as it would mean sending an empty train from Durban to Hill Crest to pick them up. Baden-Powell's response was to write privately and officially to the manager of the Natal Government Railway (NGR) asking for it to be remedied.

He followed it up by going to Durban on 30 April and interviewed the Traffic Manager of NGR and found the company had had a change of policy: the Traffic Manager proposed making a siding at Hill Crest station; and if the SAC sent their newly arrived remounts from Durban by train, the company would send the fresh and fit remounts from Hill Crest in the same trucks. At that though, Lieutenant McKenzie alerted Baden-Powell to another problem: the army's Assistant Director of railways did not allow SAC remounts to be entrained from Durban. So the next stop on the inter-organisational excursion was the office of the army's Assistant Director of railways. It was easy – 'after some talk he gave in' and also agreed that the SAC could have trucks for up to 500 remounts per month from Hill Crest.

Against the odds the run of luck continued: Baden-Powell heard that a number of Australian horse-traders had arrived in Durban; they had brought horses over on spec; but the army had stopped buying and these horses fetched very little on the open market. Hearing that, he delayed his departure and went down to look at some of the shipments. He thought one of the traders, Cotton, had about sixty cobs of the right size for SAC requirements and they were in good condition and broken to saddle. He authorised Lieutenant McKenzie to buy fifty at £28 and if Cotton agreed that price he would have Major Fair of C Division select them.

When two weeks later a ship with a consignment of horses was due to arrive at Durban, Baden-Powell was there to meet it. The SS *Orange Branch* came in sight of harbour on the night of 14 May, but it was too rough for the tug to take anyone out. Next morning Baden-Powell went on board at 7 am and inspected the horse decks. He left images that give an insight into the conditions in which horses lived during their long sea voyage:

> Found the two lower decks very hot and dank. The horses had been on board without changing out of their stalls for 40 days. Only 1 horse had died on the voyage, but 4 had in the last few days from the heat.

> We then disembarked the horses and found them of good class – small, substantial and well fed – but of course very stiff and soft after the voyage.

> But to send them up at once to the cold winds in the Transvaal in their present condition would be to kill them – so I telegraphed and arranged that they are to be kept a few days at Durban depot and then sent up to Hill Crest Farm.

> I bought from Ordnance 400 blankets for them.

The company that was responsible for landing the horses and taking them to the depot was efficient; it took time, though, before they were watered and fed. Baden-Powell went to see them in their kraals before nightfall when they were blanketed. It was the following day before he was able to assess them; and he picked out those that were unsound but the vast majority were very satisfactory. Whenever peace came the SAC's need for horses would increase, for it would assume the other main role it had been assigned to serve – that of mounted police.

Before that day came, however, SAC HQ answered to two masters, the civil and the military: the former controlled the budget; the other the deployment of the force. The question of the 'Stellenbosched' Colonel Ridley, resurfaced: he was still on the force's establishment and that prevented Major Fair, commander of C Division, from being paid as a colonel. Whatever triggered it, on 5 May Goold-Adams wrote privately to Baden-Powell 'to say he likes Ridley as a friend but prefers Pilkington as a Police Officer and thinks him very sound and efficient. Ridley has neither the health nor energy for the work.' Next day Baden-Powell met Milner to give an update on progress to date; and item one – 'That Lord K. says he has not arranged for employing Col. Ridley.' It would appear that information had not come directly from Kitchener for the following day, 7 May, Baden-Powell met Kitchener in Pretoria: 'I saw Lord Kitchener regarding Col Ridley. He says he will find some sort of employment for him – that is what he wants – to keep him going till the end of the war.' As we shall see later, there could have been ambiguity about the subject of 'wants'.

At any rate Baden-Powell reasoned that there needed to be more for the record – for two days later in the staff diary under the heading 'E Division Organisation' there is an entry:

> In reply to my letter Col Pilkington says the chief faults he noticed on taking over E Division were want of organisation especially in transport and remount department. Troop equipment and supply accounts were very inefficiently kept. There was a disregard and even resistance to orders from Head Quarters – admitted by Staff Officer.

In contrast to the early administration lapses of E Division under Ridley, the recently formed B Division under the efficient and effective Sam Steele was a hive of staff development. Thanks to the officer commanding's division having been directed in May to create a diary along the lines of that at HQ, Steele's divisional diary can be consulted. By 13 May several of his officers:

> Lts Humfrey, Currie, Steel, Trevor, Woolsted, Godson-Godson and Long Innes were going through a general course of instruction on Pay and Control, Instruction of Recruits, Police Duties etc. making good progress. Ordered Maj Steuart to see to the handing over of the Troops from 'C' Division.

> A class of 25 men have passed creditably a course of Police Duties in Pretoria and been sent to their Troops. 25 more men selected from the

Troops and put on duty. Lecture on parade to them by O.C. Division in each case.

Special orders to Troop officers not to be too ready to administer heavy fines to man on first offence.

Ordered reports upon points inspected for headquarter posts.

Board of officers convened to examine candidates for cornetcies on Wednesday next.

Transmitted copy of duties for Staff Captain laid down for Police to the O.C. Troops. Class of fifty men taking course of instruction in Dutch.

Orders sent to O.C. Troops yesterday to prepare classes in Dutch and directed that when men become pretty proficient they are to be spoken to in Dutch at stables and other places to keep them fresh in it.[82]

Following an inspection he then made of the division, Steele reported to Baden-Powell and commended to him the ability and improvement in Captain Sellar and Lieutenant Humfrey. He found a site that would be suitable for a new Divisional HQ; it had been earlier selected by the army for a barracks but was subsequently found to be too small. Baden-Powell's response was positive: to convene a group from HQ to check on its suitability and if it passed their scrutiny, he would put it to Milner to sanction it as the permanent site of B Division's HQ. He also flagged up in orders to all divisions as exemplary Steele's courses of instruction.

With a view to their peacetime presence in the land, Baden-Powell came up with the idea of a journal for the SAC; and on 10 April the first issue was ready for the printers. It contained a letter from Milner pointing up the value in every man's work in the force. Next Baden-Powell applied to the adjutant general for permission to publish. A week later the press censor refused to approve it because it gave disposition and numbers of the force – but that was as they were in March; they were no longer current. So Baden-Powell followed it up by meeting the press censor; and he agreed that the press censor could show it to Kitchener. Next day Baden-Powell saw Kitchener who 'seemed quite willing for the gazette to appear . . .' but would double-check with the press censor. Finally, Kitchener sanctioned publication with numbers and disposition details excised.

The staff culture that Baden-Powell wanted to promote in the force was one that was open and prepared to listen to grievance, so he took a dim view of receiving multi-signatory letters of complaint; and on 29 April he drafted the following order:

> that such 'round robins' are forbidden in the army and in most police forces – for two good reasons
>
> 1. They may very easily lapse into mutinous and seditious agitation.
> 2. They may lead to men being forced or induced to join in them against their inclination.
>
> But provided that these points are guarded against I am glad to hear general complaints as well as those of individuals.

Almost a year and a half after its founding the force continued to attract young men in Britain though there was little scope for the newspapers to make the 'Hero of Mafeking' perform derring-do from SAC HQ in Johannesburg. Entry standards for the force remained high. On 22 March, for example, Major McLaren who was responsible for recruitment in the UK sent in the recruit figures for February: the number of applicants was 1,425; those who attended for interview was 224; the number rejected as medical unfit 131; those finally accepted 85.

A week after those figures for February came in Baden-Powell noted in the staff diary an attempt to bend the entry rules. Seventeen Australians had arrived at Durban with the story that Captain Malcolm SAC, who was on leave in Australia, had promised them employment in the SAC in the Farmers Guard. Baden-Powell noted in brackets that Malcolm had no authority to make such a promise: the Farmers Guard was for local men only – 'otherwise all recruits will want to go for it'. So he replied that any men who wanted to join the SAC could do so on passing the usual tests. Only two of the seventeen were willing and competent; so he advised the rest to 'apply to Settlement Officers in ORC or Transvaal – as their main idea in coming over is to settle in the country'.

Be Prepared, the SAC motto, had to be taken to heart in the closing months of the war just as much as before. On 11 April, at the Battle of Rooiwal, SAC Troops of Nos. 2, 8, 9, 12, 16 and 18 Troops of A Division were commanded by Major Whiffen as part of Colonel Kekewich's column. The Boers made a determined attack and drove in the British advanced guard. At this some of the mounted yeomanry panicked and fled. The SAC were advancing in line behind them:

> The Boers then charged up to the SAC who, however, ran forward to gain the crest line of a rise, and poured a heavy fire into the enemy at 100 yards. The Boers turned off and retreated under fire leaving 43 dead and 34 wounded on the field.

So recorded Baden-Powell in the staff diary. What that early report did not contain was that the Boer commander General Potgieter lay 'sprawled thirty yards from the South African Constabulary line.'[83]

Actions continued in E Division's coverage. On 27 April Major Reynolds had a group of SAC in the Orange River Colony rounding up Boer horses when they were attacked by between 200 to 250 Boers. Lieutenant Stone's Troop was taking the horses and acted quickly and got them away. The commandos then made a rush through the bush to capture Major Reynolds's wagons; but he saw the move and ordered a Troop to head them off – which it did, checking the enemy with heavy fire and driving them off. However, the SAC lost Sergeant Lawrence killed and another man wounded. The report of the encounter specially commended Troop Sergeant Major Godson of No. 6 Troop for going back under heavy fire to rescue Trooper Jones. On the night of 3 May Field Cornet Van der Welt and his commando crossed E Division's line on the Vet River. Captain Malcolm followed them and after a fight captured eight Boers and some of their cattle; but the SAC lost two men killed and five wounded.

Into the last month of the war and up to the second last day of it action continued. In A Division, on the night of 7 May, Major Reynolds captured 6 Boers, their rifles, horses and 150 head of cattle at Bamboo Spruit near Bloemhof. Eight days later Major Lyon captured five Boers from Bester's commando; but this commando was exempt from attack during the peace negotiations and Kitchener ordered the five men to be released. Finally, the last engagement the SAC were engaged in took place in the Gatsrand on the night of 30 May: Captain Fowler had 250 SAC in column when they came across fresh spoor near Buffelsdoorn.

Their advanced guard were fired on from near a homestead. At that Captain Fowler arranged to surround the place – but in the heat of action plans often go awry; as the two wings of the encircling force closed to they mistook each other for the enemy and wasted some time in friendly fire. With that godsend of a diversion the Boers, estimated to be up to about 100, slipped through the cordon. The cost to the SAC was high: Trooper Woods was killed; Lieutenant Tredennick and Trooper Devireaux mortally wounded and three men wounded.

The following day, 31 May, the crucial decision was taken – the national representatives of the two republics, the South African Republic and the Orange Free State decided that they must accept the proposals of the British government. One of those representatives was General Christiaan De Wet. He wrote:

On the evening of the 31st May, 1902, the members of the Government of both Republics met Lord Kitchener and Lord Milner, in the former's house in Pretoria.

It was here that the Treaty of Peace – the British proposals which the National Representatives had accepted – was now to be signed.

It was a never-to-be-forgotten evening. In the space of a few short minutes that which was done could never be undone. A decision arrived at in a meeting could always be taken into reconsideration, but a document solemnly signed, as on that night, by two parties, bound them both for ever.

Every one of us who put his name to that document knew that he was honour bound to act in accordance with it. It was a bitter moment, but not so bitter as when, earlier on the same day, the National Representatives had come to the decision that the fatal step must be taken.[84]

Peace was declared on the first day of June. The following day SAC HQ received orders to send twenty men home to take part in the king's coronation. They had short notice – they had to be sent next day; however, the force would be represented at the grand parade in London.

Soon army regiments would be receiving orders to leave the country. Anticipating this, Sam Steele had contacted Baden-Powell a few days earlier with the request that he get about 100 men and one or two lieutenants from the 2nd Canadian Mounted Rifles before they were withdrawn to Canada: 'These are men who had intended to join the SAC under him but were stopped owing to sanction not being given in Canada.'

Baden-Powell responded, 'I approve the idea as we are still under establishment and we should be getting good and seasoned men without the cost of their voyage etc.' In addition to reaching establishment numbers, there were irregularities to be sorted out: one high on Baden-Powell's list was the business of Colonel Ridley; he was still on the SAC's establishment thus preventing Major Fair from being advanced in rank; and the force was short of a major. On 5 June the military secretary replied to the inspector general saying 'Lord Kitchener should be asked to give Ridley employment, and that Ridley's hospital bill should not be paid by SAC.'

Thus far the military and civil masters responsible for the SAC had turned a simple saga into a stage farce – with Lords Kitchener and Milner playing pass the parcel with Lord Roberts's protégé, while ventriloquizing through the military secretary.

The opener to the finalé began with Baden-Powell writing privately to Ridley asking when he was going to resign. Next day, 11 June, Ridley came to see him. He began with a surprising statement: he said that Milner 'told him he did not want him to resign but the military secretary suggested he did want him to'. Then Ridley pleaded his case: he had had insufficient equipment. Baden-Powell agreed that he had had those difficulties, but so had the other divisional commanders; and he listed the real problem – no system, no records kept and the results were unsatisfactory and he allowed his second in command to remain on staff work outside the SAC when he could have been of support to him. Then Ridley went on to say that in December 1901 the military secretary had told him he should resign as neither the C-in-C nor the inspector general SAC wanted him; that he heard from Milner in February suggesting that he could resign but not insisting on it. Whose was the forked tongue? The meeting with Baden-Powell closed with Ridley intending to go to military HQ 're a billet on Saturday'.

However, next day there was a message from the military secretary to say that only when Ridley left the SAC would they consider appointing him to an army billet. At that, Baden-Powell saw Ridley again to give the ultimatum that if he did not resign he, Baden-Powell, would write to Milner to sanction Ridley's transfer to the army. Ridley, preparing his ground for the HQ meeting on Saturday, said that he could not help it if the inspector general took such a course but he had never heard of the charges against him and he would afterwards demand an investigation. Baden-Powell summed up the case against him; and wrote to Milner.

Kitchener was not a man who delegated to subordinates; and so the curtain fell – according to Colonel Ridley's record: with effect from 24 June when he went on to half pay; in the line denoting regiment he was described as 'Unemployed on Active List'; and according to Baden-Powell in the staff diary on 24 June, 'Col Ridley left Bloemfontein for England on return to Army from SAC.'

Before the month would be out the SAC would come under the command of Milner; but before Kitchener returned to Britain he made a tour of SAC Divisions. A week before he inspected B Division he entertained the nursing Sister Superintendents of all the hospitals. Steele wrote, 'Sister Nicolson was present and all are charmed at their reception by Lord Kitchener.'

On 20 June Kitchener inspected and said farewell to the Troops of B Division on parade in Pretoria. Steele recorded the day in the divisional diary:

> Lord Kitchener inspected and said farewell to the Troops in camp here at 3.30. Paraded Nos. 2, 4 and 7 and Depot Troops for his inspection at 4.30.
>
> Received him with General Salute (Ported arms) then wheeled up in three sides of a square when Lord Kitchener addressed the SAC saying most complimentary things to the Corps for its gallantry and fortitude. He also said that he had never seen finer men than those on parade. In the course of his remarks he gave us some good advice as to our future conduct towards the inhabitants of the country. Some time afterwards Lord Kitchener saw me while I was riding back to quarters and specially complimented me on the turn out of the men, saying that they looked particularly well. In connection with the parade I may say that the appearance of the Command far surpassed anything that has been seen by me in this town from the beginning of the parades here nearly two years ago.[85]

However, there was an additional snippet that Steele did not put in the diary but told Baden-Powell about: after the formal proceedings Kitchener – with a penchant for the spoils of war just like the next soldier – 'asked him for the silver coat of arms off [President] Kruger's state carriage.'

Next morning Steele sent twenty-eight mounted men under Captain Hilliam and one lieutenant to act as 'an escort for the Commander-in-Chief on his departure from Pretoria for England. Was present myself at his departure which took place at 7 o'clock. Escort of SAC rode well and compared favourably with the cavalry and rode much better.'

The B Division to which Kitchener said farewell had already started its post-war training courses – early in May the training of cornets got underway. Steele encouraged a culture of staff development; in Divisional Order No. 2 he announced, 'It is notified for all ranks special qualifications of individuals are to be at disposal of OC Division – a lawyer should teach law – a Dutch scholar Dutch.'[86]

Kitchener left Pretoria with a mounted escort of SAC. Then on 23 June, as his tour of duty as commander-in-chief was drawing to an end Kitchener submitted his final despatch of the war; it contained the following paragraph:[87]

I have already, in a farewell order, expressed to Major-General Baden-Powell my deep appreciation of the services rendered by the South African Constabulary, but I am glad to have this opportunity to again testify to the good work rendered by this fine body of men.

Part III

Chapter Seven

Protectors of the People

When the young Winston Churchill was a newspaper correspondent he was captured by the Boer commando leader Louis Botha; and later, in his memoir, Churchill wrote of the viewpoint espoused by Lord Milner that the guerrilla war period would just fade away:

> This was an error destined to cost us dear. There were still many thousands of wild, fierce, dauntless men under leaders like Botha, De Wet, De la Rey, Smuts and Hertzog who now fought on in their vast country not for victory, but for honour.[88]

That being so, when the fighting ended how would the people from whom those principled warriors sprang respond to being policed by their enemy? In general, the response spanned from acquiescence to warm acceptance.

For example, the Pretoria based newspaper *Land en Volk*, whose editor tended to take a polemical stance, had an article on 7 November 1902, wrote Baden-Powell, that went, 'though they had no great love for their guardians they cannot deny that our mutual relations are good and promise well for effecting the permanent submission of the burghers.'[89] An affirmative community gesture towards the SAC took place in B Division in October: Trooper Meek of the SAC drowned accidentally in Middleburg district; and Colonel Steele said that the SAC detachment to which Meek belonged 'is very popular' among the people and '60 Boers attended Meek's funeral and provided a winding sheet for his body.'

Although formed in a time of war, implicit in the structuring of the SAC was its future police role. So argued Baden-Powell when it was put to him that the SAC was designed simply as a military force. 'Each patrol will consist of a squad of six men under its corporal',[90] he wrote – a key unit especially ideal in country areas where farms should be visited on a regular basis – there was also the smaller proportion of officers compared to army units which meant it was a good fit for the flatter hierarchy of the British police culture.

When he had been on sick leave in 1901, Baden-Powell got in touch with Colonel Neville Chamberlain the Inspector General of the Royal Irish Constabulary (RIC) and went to the RIC's HQ in Dublin. Chamberlain had been a colonel in the British army and was serving in South Africa when in 1900 he was appointed to the post. He had had no police experience; and so he and Baden-Powell were kindred inspector generals – appointed without police experience. Chamberlain gave him a copy of the RIC's Police Code and other papers.

Preparations for the transition of the SAC from military to a police role were going on as war was being waged. Baden-Powell envisaged the divisional structure continuing with districts and sub-districts. Initially he proposed that for the Transvaal there would be 540 duty squads; there would 56 townships and 172 centres. The townships would have 2 squads apiece and the centres 1; that totalled 284 squads earmarked. That left 256 squads that could be used for convoy duty, patrolling and escorting convoys during a transition period while the country settled after war. Divisions would have districts sub-divided into wards and magisterial wards.

That would be the basic structure but at this stage some thinking was provisional: it had been suggested that the divisions of the Transvaal could be arranged like E Division of the ORC which came under sub-divisional majors, but Baden-Powell thought it would increase expense without any real gain. He spent part of an office day mulling over structure options like that.

What there was no doubt about, though, was the personal integrity that each member of the force must aspire to have. In his notes for the circular on the SAC's police duties Baden-Powell wrote:

> In taking up the policing of the country they will be taking up a very responsible duty, because the inhabitants will deduce from their character and action what is the nature of the new government of this country, and will accordingly be prepared to acquiesce or to kick or plot against it.

> It is therefore of greatest importance for every member of the corps to devote himself to the loyal performance of his duty, to be well-disposed without being intimate, to be proof against cajolery, bribery or deceit and to maintain a personal dignity and absolute firmness in his dealings with the people.

The SAC squad system encouraged group culture to develop. The squad could be split into pairs; and two mounted troopers would visit a farm – the aim was that every farm should be visited regularly – and with the mandate all ranks had: 'I expect you to be "Handy Men" – ready to turn your hand to any kind of job'[91] – troopers helped families who were trying to cope with the shambles they found at the homes they returned to after the war.

When manual work was going on in the SAC the inspector general had a different principle on supervision compared with the army – he wrote '[N.B. – When this kind of work is in hand I do not like to see Officers and N.C.O.s with their coats on, merely looking on and superintending. Their business here, as elsewhere, is to lead the way.]'[92]

The patrol/squad also became the keystone for Baden-Powell when he framed *Scouting for Boys* six years later; he used the term patrol – 'I would strongly commend the "Patrol" system: that is small permanent groups, each under responsible charge of a leading boy, as the great step to success.'[93]

One of Britain's war aims was a speedy reopening of the gold-mining fields of the Transvaal: revenue from them would finance the reconstruction of the colonies. Policy makers decided that there would be three police forces: the Transvaal Town Police (TTP) which would police the Rand and Pretoria; the ORC Municipal Police for Bloemfontein; and the SAC would police the rest of the Transvaal and the Orange River Colony.[94] On 13 February Baden-Powell had a meeting with Milner and told him, 'we always wanted to police townships but Lord K. withdrew our men when we began to do so.' As a result, a month later, the military secretary, relaying Milner's instruction, directed that the SAC take over policing eight towns in the Transvaal by 1 May, and confirmed that in country districts they would come under the magistrate.

After the system had a few weeks to get settled down, Baden-Powell went to the town of Standerton to inspect the two squads of SAC at their police duties. First though, he met the magistrate Mr Orsmond. He was very pleased with the NCO and men: he said that they were a great improvement on the former police. Then the inspector general had a talk with the NCO in charge, Sergeant Carragher, about the duties and the behaviour of the men. He was pleased with them and he felt he would get good work out of them. The inspector general then talked separately with the men; and their only complaint was that Sergeant Carragher was over strict. So the inspector general spoke to him on his own: 'I told him to get the men to work well by encouraging them not by driving them; to make them comfortable and to give them responsibility; and to report confidentially upon them at inspections.'

Thus far Baden-Powell's plan for the SAC's police work was along the lines of the vast veldt counterpart of the bobby on the beat; and with his insisting on moral integrity as integral to their work, he was aspiring to the British culture of policing with the consent of the people.

However, there were the other duties of a police force – collecting intelligence and criminal investigation. A department in SAC HQ could be set up and a member of the force at the level of major might be suitable to run it. On 19 March Baden-Powell looked over the majors in the four Divisions; some SAC captains were qualified for promotion to major – and contingent on Colonel Ridley resigning, when Major Fair commanding C Division could be promoted to lieutenant colonel, there would a vacancy. He noted that there were two vacancies for major in B Division; and in running through the list of serving majors wrote, 'of these Walton [A Division] is employed on police work'. Walton had had police experience: he had been in the Burma Police and the Colonial Office cleared him for transfer to the SAC.[95] Baden-Powell also made a note that in C Division, 'Castello should be an exceptionally good police officer (possibly sub-divisional officer in E Division).'

Later that day Baden-Powell met Mr Showers, commissioner of police, and they talked over a system that might be created for police intelligence. One of the points that came up was whether the commissioner should head it or the SAC's inspector general should. At this stage Baden-Powell thought that Showers should be head for he already had criminal investigation as part of his remit. They should all be working towards the same end; the SAC could pass to Showers intelligence from the districts. As the discussion went on Baden-Powell mentioned that this was not the way it was done in Ireland where the RIC had both intelligence and CID departments. Perhaps the law department or the high commissioner should decide. Finally, Baden-Powell proposed that they have another meeting 'with some of our department officers present to talk it over and formulate ideas'.

On 24 March the next meeting on the police took place and it comprised Baden-Powell, the military secretary and Major Walton. The military secretary, having been briefed by Milner, told Baden-Powell that Mr Showers was merely responsible for Johannesburg and Pretoria – magistrates were appointed for the districts – so it could devolve to the SAC to have a department at HQ for criminal investigation and secret service intelligence. Major Walton was detailed to take this in hand and produce a scheme.

Two days later Baden-Powell met Milner who confirmed that the SAC should carry out the police intelligence and secret service. It was agreed that the department should be organised by a special officer (Major Walton was to be tried in it at first) who would be under the high commissioner and the inspector general SAC; he would be in a fairly independent position and in communication with the commissioner of police and the attorney general; the staff officer for police duties in each Division would be his assistant and collect information from the sub-divisions and district officers.

On 28 March Major Walton sent the inspector general and the military secretary a long essay giving his views on a police force. Baden-Powell noted that he omitted two important duties that the force should undertake: checking the spread of cattle and stock disease; and also suppressing locusts.

In addition though, Baden-Powell took issue with Walton who had compared the structure of the SAC with other police forces – he had not taken account of the population of the country: 'Boers and Natives will be armed which necessitates the police being organized also for military mobilisation.' Walton also claimed that the SAC did not conform to the requirements of a police force. Baden-Powell countered by stressing that the SAC had been structured from the start for the dual role – had it been formed solely as a military force it would have divided into regiments and squadrons and it would have had a higher proportion of officers.

By now Baden-Powell had reservations about Walton's suitability for the role of head of police intelligence; and in a letter to the military secretary he aired his unease: 'I am not sure of Walton. He was Edwards' selection, and all Edwards' swans are not invariably swans. He may be all right.'

What Baden-Powell wanted was the best advice from those who held similar positions in other police forces; and that was why he had consulted the inspector general of the RIC when he was on sick leave; now, at the beginning of April 1902, he took the train to Maritzburg to consult General Sir John Dartnell, head of the Natal Police. Dartnell was very experienced; he had been a British army officer and in 1874 had formed what was then the Natal Mounted Police (NMP). Baden-Powell in his notes of the meeting wrote, 'He urged decentralisation and approves our system. He also urged that Police Officers of Sub-districts should be JPs to be able to adjudge minor cases.' He also advised that the SAC executive police officer in a district should work in conjunction with the magistrate; the magistrate should not arrogate powers of the police officer.

Two days later, at SAC HQ in Johannesburg, Colonel Pilkington came to see him and talked about policing the ORC. Pilkington had been making progress on a number of points: he had met with the head of the Department of Administration and they agreed that the SAC should absorb the Municipal Police by July 1903. Pilkington had put some work in on the personnel required and he was anxious that Major Morris should be appointed sub-divisional officer; he wanted his help in organising police intelligence duties.

Later the same day Baden-Powell met the military secretary, the police commissioner, the attorney general and Major Walton. The attorney general for the Transvaal, a highly respected figure with a lot of experience, was Sir Richard Solomon. Baden-Powell outlined his scheme, which, he said was based along the lines of notes that Milner had given him: there would be a staff officer at SAC HQ who would have charge of police intelligence and secret service; he would be delegated the power to liaise with the commissioner of police and the attorney general if the need arose; there would be a staff officer in each divisional HQ for police intelligence; at each magisterial district there would be a captain as executive police officer for the intelligence remit; and in each district there would two or more officers in charge of sub-districts or wards. He said that he did not propose laying down hard and fast details – these were the general principles. A police code had to be drawn up and he had given Walton the RIC, the Natal and the Metropolitan Police code.

From his outline the police commissioner and the attorney were broadly satisfied. When Baden-Powell asked about police officers being JPs, the attorney general approved it as useful in cases of dispute resolution.

Now it was time to get responses to those general principles from the three Divisions in the Transvaal; and forty-eight hours later Major Fair came to see him and was in agreement with the proposed scheme. Colonel Steele sent in his notes on it. Greater clarity on the relationship between magistrates and police was essential, he argued. Baden-Powell replied and told him to come and see him. They met two days later, 7 April, along with Major Twyman (A Division) and Major Fair. All three were in agreement with the principles the inspector general drafted. Then Colonel Steele described the Canadian system where police officers were magistrates – very much against the advice of the law department to begin with – but it had worked effectively, so effectively, he said, that all magistrates were now police officers. Baden-Powell pondered on that and afterwards wrote, 'The system commends itself to a free-minded people like the Americans and Canadians and should be popular in this country also.'

Next day he sent a letter to Attorney-General Solomon putting the point about JPs and he wrote:

> The Police of NW Canada are the most advanced and most successful combination of military and police much on our own lines with a wide country. . . We are lucky in having Col Steele, their late chief, in the SAC.

Commissioner of Police Showers sent a draft of his instructions to his officers regarding police intelligence. Baden-Powell thought they were good and told him so; and then, thinking like a policeman, told him to watch informal meetings of Dutch clergymen and their parishioners where they might preach politics.

Before Walton drew up the Police Code he was detailed to draft, he produced a costing for police intelligence. It would have added an additional £25,000 to the SAC budget. Baden-Powell did not see the need to take on additional clerical staff for the work; and he produced a scaled-down projection. That was the beginning of two weeks of set-backs with the potential head of police intelligence at SAC HQ. It was settled as far as Baden-Powell was concerned when he received a private letter from Attorney-General Sir Richard Solomon saying that he did not think highly of Walton's abilities and would resist Walton's code. Milner had to be kept in the loop with that; and Baden-Powell, writing with information for Milner, added Sir Richard Solomon's opinion of Walton in the form of a postscript for the military secretary.

Whether it was a follow-on from Walton's unsuitability or whether he was simply looking for the chance to have a go at him Milner went for Baden-Powell over his method of selecting officers to the SAC; and he did it using his weapon of choice: the military secretary. It comes to light in Baden-Powell's response to the military secretary on 11 May; and it throws a glimmer on the way the great and the good at that time could lobby a commanding officer to accept their nominees as officers of an imperial force.

> I am very sorry indeed if HE thinks I have not selected SAC officers in a satisfactory manner.

In order to get the best results I endeavour to make the Commandants of Divisions really as fully responsible for the efficiency of their respective commands – but this I could not fairly do if I were to force upon them officers of my own nomination.

My rule therefore has been – either to let OC Divisions suggest to me candidates of whose qualifications they have personal knowledge, or for me to suggest for their acceptance (or refusal) candidates who have been specifically recommended to me.

Baden-Powell then outlined the main criteria: previous experience as officers; previous police work; the capability of taking over recruits and forming them into disciplined units. Then he turned to the large number of those rejected.

I cannot say offhand how many pressing recommendations I have had from Lord Roberts, Mr Brodrick [Secretary of State for War], MPs (by the dozen) and even from Royalty, but they amount to so many that had I taken them we should have been entirely officered by nominees.

But at the risk of offending these authorities I have put aside their recommendations in favouring candidates selected on their merits and it was only by doing so that we have obtained the efficient body of officers we now possess. I do not know where the corps should have been without them – certainly not in its present condition.

I have of course put Lord Milner's recommendations on a different footing and at least fifteen of those whose names he sent me have been admitted or applied for. This is in addition to the 31 sent from Canada.

I hope that HE will believe that I have done my best to meet his wishes and at the same time to get the force efficiently officered, but if there is a different course he would like me to adopt please let me know. Are there candidates he would like to be taken on trial if any further vacancies occur?

The number from Canada alludes to Lord Minto's selection that was far from Sam Steele's choice. Baden-Powell then goes on that he would have gone to see the military secretary or Milner himself but he had been in the Gatsrand to observe an SAC contingent under the command of Captain Money, part of a military column flushing out the enemy. However, he puts the ball back in Milner's court – 'if there is a different course'. One can assume this offer will not be taken up: His Excellency had taken a broad swipe at the inspector general – no specifics are adduced for he had no close knowledge of the generality of officers – the likelihood is he had been lobbied by an aggrieved sponsor of a rejected candidate; six months earlier he used non-attributable sources to wound the inspector general. Baden-Powell, though, held the professional and the moral high ground – but finishes on a personal note: 'Meanwhile, I feel it very much that my action regarding selection of officers should have been misunderstood.'

Leaving it at that, next day Baden-Powell visited the HQ of the Natal Police for a second time. This time it was to examine the details of their forms, patrol books and the processes that were involved in collating information. He also looked at their clothing and equipment. Then he visited the force's CID under Major Clarke. He felt that their returns and books 'do not beat our proposed ones' but the diary every detective was made to carry was a good institution. Though he would have preferred it had counterfoil and duplicates which could be sent in daily. Such was the attention to fine detail and ability to exercise an oversight he preferred.

He also went to see Sir Percy Girouard the Director of Imperial Military Railways (IMR). The first item Baden-Powell wanted to discuss was the SAC's request for a siding to be built at Potchefstroom. Girouard had made a strong impression on Kitchener with his development of the railway network, which had greatly helped Britain's military effectiveness; and in a despatch he described him as 'an officer of brilliant ability'.[96] However, Girouard said to Baden-Powell that it was necessary that the siding and its maintenance be paid for by the user – 'but he would do all he could to help us'. Then with a pointed flash of humour coming through in the formal record, Baden-Powell told him to read *The Octopus*, a novel by Frank Norris; the book, published only the year earlier, is set in California and centres on the conflicts between a railway company and the wheat growers; and it highlighted the power of the railway monopoly.

Baden-Powell then turned the discussion to the railway police and outlined what Dartnell, head of the Natal Police, had told him that there was a collection of various thieves from Europe waiting to go up country; some of them were able to buy a permit and travel up to the enticing prospects of the gold-rich areas. All

Dartnell's force could do about it was to inform the Johannesburg police, 'but the suspects are not such fools as to go there first'. Girouard, however, said that his police did not inquire into such details, 'they only see that people are not travelling without permits.' However, he would send his chief of police to see Baden-Powell in the hope that they could work something together.

The quality of the railway police came up again when Baden-Powell, checking on the policing of towns in the Transvaal, visited Heidelberg. He spoke to Mr Aitchison the magistrate, who was pleased with the SAC; he found them very helpful. Then the magistrate gave his views on the railway police. He found it frustrating that they were separate from the town police: the separateness was strongly adhered to by the railway police – to the extent that the town police had not been able to enter the railway station, and there was no check on the identity of those alighting or departing. He also said that the station refreshment bar was shielded by the railway police – allowing it to contravene licensing laws.

Back at the office in Johannesburg, awaiting Baden-Powell was the attorney general's heavily corrected copy of Walton's police material. There was a note from the attorney general to Baden-Powell saying that there were several points that they had to talk over. Baden-Powell read over the amendments the attorney general had made on the material and 'fully agreed with his remarks.'

He then telegraphed Major Fair, commanding C Division, asking for Major Castello to take temporary charge of the police intelligence department at SAC HQ. That same day Baden-Powell met Milner, gave him an update on the towns the SAC were policing and told him that 'Major Walton will not do for head of our Intelligence Department and that I propose to use Castello for the time being.' He also suggested that Scotland Yard send them a good man to help 'organise the department for a few months'.

Had Baden-Powell been prone to 'happy thoughts', as Milner claimed, instead of Scotland Yard he might have come up with the idea of buying in local consultancy to advise on the Intelligence Department – for he would refer to Conan Doyle several times in *Scouting for Boys*. Conan Doyle had already made his mark with 'Sherlock Holmes'; but he had earlier studied medicine at Edinburgh University; and during the war he worked as a doctor in a hospital at Bloemfontein where, in his free time, he wrote his chronicle of the war. In one section Conan Doyle describes the discovery, in the Vrede district, of General De Wet's hidden cave – and perhaps implies that in the case of De Wet's cave Holmes would have met his match: 'Halfway down a precipitous krantz [overhanging precipice], with its mouth covered by creepers, no writer of romance could have imagined a more fitting headquarters for a guerrilla chief.'[97]

However, there is no evidence of the SAC's inspector general taking a freewheeling style: he changed gear from the criminal investigation and intelligence roles to the emerging duties of town policing; he drafted orders for detachments in police stations; their responsibility to the inhabitants; their duty to obey both magistrates and their own officers; and the need to be smart in dress in the stations. He wrote to all divisional commanders instructing them to keep a personal diary like the one he used, and to post duplicates to him every two or three days.

He went to Pretoria to discuss town police matters with the attorney general; but first they discussed Major Walton's draft code. Baden-Powell agreed with Sir Richard Solomon that it was too wordy and not on the best lines. They decided that the inspector general should draft a fresh code and send it to Solomon; and they agreed that the diary sheet that the inspector general had drawn up had all the information needed in a police station and that it should be adopted:

> Daily occurrences
> Charges and arrests
> Property, lost, stolen, recovered
> Criminals, wanted or bad characters to be watched
> Arrivals or departures of civilians in area
> Patrols and beats
> Duty state
> Correspondence etc.

He also showed the attorney general the paragraph he had drafted to the SAC NCOs and men regarding their duties and their relation with the inhabitants. He flagged up the anomaly of the railway police having no requirement for checking on suspicious characters moving up country; and that he intended to discuss this with the railway police chief.

Police duties in addition to training courses were well underway in B Division: by 16 May Colonel Steele reported that the nominal roll of burghers in two districts had been completed. Next morning at 7 am he was present at morning drill session. He had arranged a riding class before breakfast for the clerks in the

Divisional Office. Three hours later he inspected the riding instruction of officers and cornets North of Daspoort.

Three days later Steele reported that Milner – though he referred to him as His Excellency – arrived. Steele gave Milner's bodyguard the loan of tents and provided their rations as well.

Progress in moving into the police role was progressing across the Transvaal and in A Division by 21 May the policing of Potchefstroom had been in place for several weeks.

Baden-Powell went and inspected the police station and the barracks; and he met the magistrate, who was very satisfied with their work. However, when the inspector general checked on the men they were not all from one SAC Troop – Major Twyman had selected likely men from several Troops. The inspector general ordered that this be altered: the dynamic and the bonding within squads were important in carrying out their work. The major had also left how they dressed in the magistrate's hands. Baden-Powell ordered that they dress uniformly.

Then it was on to Klerksdorp accompanied by Major Twyman. There the SAC men were under Corporal Brown; there were twenty-one in all including seven black constables. The inspector general's summation – 'all in good order'. Mr Grant the magistrate was very pleased with their work. The inspector general addressed the men and complimented them.

Back at SAC HQ Baden-Powell wrote a resumé of his findings to Twyman and dissatisfaction, stressing that the policing arrangements 'should be carried out entirely by squad system' – and he added an additional section on the NCOs' mess:

> Please tell NCOs that I am much disappointed to hear that their mess has degenerated into a common pothouse. I judge the NCOs, and equally the seniors, by their mess and its conduct, it is a great indicator of their self-respect and tone and largely affects their reputation and that of the SAC in the town, and consequently throughout the District.

Next day he went by train from Johannesburg to Bloemfontein where he saw Colonel Pilkington regarding the proposed distribution of police; and he inspected Captain Reading, staff officer for police in E Division, and his class of NCOs and men who were learning police duties. The inspector general was quite impressed: the course of training was comprehensive and practical. Captain Reading said that the men were keen and 'of good class'.

He then had an interview with Deputy Commissioner Goold-Adams of the Orange River Colony and Colonel Pilkington. The concord that Pilkington had established between the SAC and the Administration had become soured. This meeting opened with Goold-Adams showing a different attitude towards the SAC. However, it became clear it was formed from wrong assumption and false information. Goold-Adams assumed that the SAC had occupied buildings at Sydenham and did not mean to pay for them. A few days earlier he had sent for Pilkington and told him to clear out of Sydenham within three days; Pilkington let him cool off and later reasoned with him. Now at this interview Baden-Powell disabused him: the SAC fully expected to have to pay for them; they only wanted to hear how much.

High on Goold-Adams' agenda was the municipal police. He had had a despatch from the secretary of state for the colonies giving him the right to have a special municipal police (though the secretary of state thought the SAC were to patrol towns) on the assumption that Goold-Adams first consulted the military commander-in-chief and the SAC inspector general. Goold-Adams explained that he had not consulted the inspector general because 'the Municipal Police was an older institution than the SAC'; and also because Colonel Ridley in July 1901 (when he commanded E Division) had said 'the SAC were unable to do it.' When he wrote up his account of the meeting Baden-Powell went into a long aside in the staff diary – he could not understand it: Ridley had fully understood that the SAC would eventually police the towns and he was keen to do it; and yet he had not reported to SAC HQ what he had said to Goold-Adams.

However, at this point in the meeting Goold-Adams said that he had reconsidered the matter and now proposed gradually replacing the Municipal Police with the SAC – he had heard that Baden-Powell wanted it done suddenly; but the inspector general said that he had not expressed that view; in fact he agreed that it would be best done gradually.

Peace had fallen on both colonies and Sam Steele reported that the Boer generals, fresh from the negotiations at Vereeniging – except De la Rey and Botha – were still in town on 3 June at the Transvaal Hotel.

In that climate of peace a rare event took place in the annals of the SAC – Nursing Sister O'Donnell and Captain Douglas of the corps were married, Steele wrote in the Diary; he does not say whether he gave the bride away (a photograph which includes Sister O'Donnell and nursing sister colleagues with Colonel Steele appears in this book).

Of the divisional diaries only that of B Division was available for this work; it gives insight into the minutiae of commanding a Division and the range of areas an experienced commander had to deal with. For example, although a constabulary, there would be instances of drunkenness – if the offender did not reveal the source of his liquor supply, Steele directed, he should be charged with an offence.

The diary also reveals the major frustrations of a divisional commander being part of a bureaucratic system where seemingly arbitrary decisions are imposed from above – above the level of inspector general. In the particular case that irked Steele in early June the announcement came by telegram. It stated that SAC officers were not to keep statistical records. Steele felt that this would hamper them in their work:

> unless we are permitted to have records of our own quite separate from the Magistrates, of all people in the districts; our intelligence without this will be of very little avail. I am informed that some Military officers are to be magistrates in the districts. I hope not. If they want Magistrates who are not lawyers they can get them from us. I hope the IG will permit us to keep records of the people for our own information. This war was prolonged by the ignorance of our own people with regard to such matters. Now that we have full power we should know everything. We will have to patrol and see the people at all events and they will eventually be glad to see us, as the Corps is now with the people the favourite branch of the public service.

It was on 18 June that the change-over from serving two masters, the military and the civil authority, to serving one was symbolised when Baden-Powell received the chief of staff's telegram in which Kitchener expresses his warm appreciation of good conduct, endurance and gallantry which has distinguished the SAC. They have encountered their hardships with cheerful alacrity and have earned the affection and respect of the rest of the forces. The SAC now have the great task of acting as exponents to the inhabitants of the British character, and Lord Kitchener could not leave the work in better hands.

Two days later Colonel Sam Steele Commanding B Division reported that Lord Kitchener inspected and said farewell to the Troops in camp. He was received with a general salute. The Troops then wheeled up on three sides of a square. Kitchener, in Steele's words said 'most complimentary things to the Corps'. Steele thought that it surpassed anything he had seen since joining the SAC. That same day he received orders to parade 100 men for the 'ceremony of swearing in Lord Milner as Governor and Commander-in-Chief'.

On 21 June Lord Milner was sworn in as governor of the Transvaal at a ceremony in Pretoria. The SAC lined the entrance and stairway of the building. Taking great pride in his men, Steele recorded, 'the most favourable remarks upon their soldier-like bearing were made on all sides.' [98]

Next week Milner returned and asked to see the site selected for the division's barracks. It was an early morning ride out to the site and Milner returned at 9 am. He pronounced that he was pleased with it; and he asked Steele some questions about the division and its districts and outstations. Then Steele took command of the agenda,

> and said that I hoped the Native Commissioners could get to their stations and explain affairs to the Chiefs so as to prevent complications of any sort. His Lordship stated that the Commissioners would be sent out at once and are men of experience.

From as early as 13 June, a few days before repatriation officially began, Baden-Powell had got Milner's agreement to have the District Commandant (Commander) SAC on the Repatriation Boards – they would have a fuller insight into the people of their district 'and cause them to be looked on as benefactors rather than gaolers by the people'.

That added knowledge of the people who were returning to the land prompted the SAC to take the initiative in areas where departmental officials had either not foreseen need or lacked the transport to effect. For example, those returning families who were trying to get their homes back together had little time to provide home education for their children who were getting no schooling – Colonel Pilkington came up with the idea that the SAC could transport peripatetic teachers from the Education Department to the outlying farms in their two-wheel, four-seat Cape Carts.

In the Transvaal, in B Division Colonel Steele began issuing food to burghers who were in need; and he hoped it would become sanctioned wherever it was

necessary. Baden-Powell sought and got Milner's approval for it; and so he wrote
to all Divisions to issue rations to the inhabitants where there was need.

Milner wanted Baden-Powell 'to take a few burghers into the SAC: half
from the National Scouts and half from surrendered burghers'. Baden-Powell's
interpretation of that was to aim for a squad of burghers in each Troop – not to be
employed in their own area and National Scouts to be separate from surrendered
burghers. Milner agreed with his scheme

> and impressed on me that the present good spirit among the burghers
> generally should be fostered so as to effectively pervade the prisoners
> of war when they return, and this would be an important part in the
> work of the SAC.

Volunteers were slow to come forward – by the third week of peace all Divisions
reported that they had no burgher volunteers. Intending to begin an initiative,
Major Hoskins, who commanded the National Scouts, telegraphed Baden-Powell
that 'his burghers were a little shy of joining the SAC without their own officers;
he hopes therefore that we will take 2 or 3 of them.' Baden-Powell wrote back that
they could not take any officers, 'and his men had better make up their minds or
there would be no vacancies for them'.

In A Division in the western Transvaal, in the absence of Edwards on leave,
Major Twyman was in command; however, he had not been keeping up to date
with diary submissions to SAC HQ. The inspector general wrote to him, 'I have
not had your diary for a long time and so am not up in your progress, wants
etc. Could you post it say every other day (or as some do daily).' The inspector
general then went on to give some advice on how to use the burghers attached
to the division: as 'interpreters, guides and information collectors so they can be
distributed as you think best, but not in their own District and not in collision
between "hands-uppers" and ex prisoners of war'.

The SAC also lacked significant numbers of indigenous Africans in police
roles. In June the total complement of the force was 286 officers, 19 sister nurses,
9,130 NCOs and men, 653 Farmers Guard, under a Major Morris, and 2,193 black
Africans who were mainly in ancillary roles – with the emphasis switching to its
long-term police role that would have to change.

One or two options were floated at divisional level. Colonel Sam Steele sent
Baden-Powell a copy of Lieutenant Trevor's suggestion of raising a Troop of

Zulus – 10 per cent English speakers – but Baden-Powell said that he had already instructed Captain Gillsom to raise two Troops. In the meantime he thought that squads of native police would be required in each Troop.

The idea developed further as a result of the imperial takeover of Swaziland. Swaziland had been a protectorate of the South African Republic. On 11 June Baden-Powell met Sir Godfrey Lagden commissioner of native affairs in the Transvaal to discuss policing the border of Swaziland. Lagden intended sending F. Enraght-Moony there at the end of the month as native commissioner and he thought an SAC escort would be appropriate. 'The British have very little prestige among the Swazis, and as a Hut tax is to be enforced and the country occupied by us a strong force will be necessary.'

Lagden agreed with Baden-Powell's idea for three Troops of SAC, two of them with fifty natives in each, under Captain Gillsom. The composition of the two, Gillsom suggested, should be made up of Zulus and 25 per cent Swazis. However, to free up three Troops from C Division, Baden-Powell arranged with Fair that the Middleburg district be handed over to B Division; and he wanted Captain Capell to be in charge of the Swaziland district. Capell, apart from having had police experience, had been recommended for promotion to major and Baden-Powell thought highly of him. Milner suggested that a Troop of burghers might be raised for the Swaziland district.

Although Kitchener, in his valedictory message to the SAC, had referred to the affection and respect they had gained from the rest of the forces, that was in war – now there was the peacetime situation; there was still a military garrison force in the colonies; the SAC were better paid – that affection and respect may have worn thin. So found Colonel Sam Steele commanding B Division. On 26 June he wrote in the divisional diary: 'Our officers must be careful lest the extreme jealousy or dislike for the corps by the military gets them into scrapes.'[99] He wired all Troop commanders of the division,

> Reports come in of interference with people returning to farms or on business. It is your duty to protect all persons in their legitimate occupations, you must act at once in cases where there is danger of a breach of the peace and not on any account wait for orders from any central authority, exercise judgement, promptitude and tact.

In B Division they were getting into the swing of conventional police duties: investigating a case of murder; following up some natives who had looted cattle from local farms. The opening up of the gold fields and the mines brought an influx of all sorts; and a squad from No. 11 Troop, after a rapid march to Pilgrim's Rust, got there in time to take up a case of house-looting by miners. The remainder of the Troop followed as quickly as possible.

Their conduct in public befitted the role of police – so the chief of the CID in Pretoria confidentially informed Colonel Steele: he said that they were particularly well behaved in town; did 'not consort with low company' and kept 'clear of everything discreditable'. Relationship with the Town Police seemed to be quite good for Showers, commissioner for Johannesburg and Pretoria police, asked Baden-Powell if he could have 'two men (Davis and Stephenson) of B Division transferred to Town Police'. Baden-Powell wrote to Steele asking him if he could spare them for he had no objection. He also said to Steele that he agreed with his idea of adding CB (confined to barracks) as punishment in a case of drunkenness.

The division also had the prospect of 150 men and 2 officers transferring from the Canadian Mounted Rifles: their regiment was soon due to return home. Not only did Baden-Powell agree but hoped Steele could get them because the SAC was slightly under complement and they would not have to pay the transport costs of recruits from overseas. Within four days the deal was done: Sam Steele reported that the 150 'are being carefully selected'. The two officers transferring were taking a drop in rank: the adjutant Captain Mackie was coming as a lieutenant; Lieutenant McBeth ('another very good officer') was joining as second lieutenant. So there was some consolation for Steele after his frustration at the way the original contingent of recruits had been gathered in Canada. Captain Mackie knew what he wanted though and was strict – Steele wrote to the inspector general that there would only be eighty Canadians coming to the SAC: 'Mackie very exacting in selecting men resulted as above.'

There was still the legacy of the original consignment of Canadians to live with and Sam Steele did not hold back when he got a confidential report from Major Edwards who had inspected Nos. 14 and 17 Troops, both comprising Canadians, which stated they were 'not in as good a state of discipline as possible'. So on 4 July Steele wrote to the officers commanding directing them

to give their men to understand that as Canadians I expected them to be a credit to their country and the SAC and that any neglect to uphold the honour of the SAC and their place of birth will be severely dealt with. Officers who do not know them, even their own countrymen are timid. This cannot be tolerated.[100]

The case of surgeon-captain Vaux's experience in the SAC was left with Baden-Powell going to take soundings among the Canadian officers. He reported his findings on 30 June in a private letter to Steele:

> Dear Steele,
> Re Vaux.
> I have taken opinions confidentially from 7 or 8 Canadian SAC officers about him. Some are for and some against him – about equally divided. But two testify to his habit of taking morphia, which stands against him as a medical officer.
> The PMO's opinion I enclose (please return it). I propose therefore to write to Vaux as per enclosed draft. Have you any remarks to offer?

None of those papers: the PMO's opinion, Baden-Powell's draft or Steele's reply is available; but if we consult Vaux's record it is clear that he was not reinstated in the SAC. According to his record Vaux served with the SAC from 28 April 1901 to 10 July 1901; then with the 18th Bn. Imperial Yeomanry as medical officer from 11 July 1901 to 31 May 1902. However, his career did not suffer as he had feared: he remained with the Canadian military and attained the rank of major; and at the start of the First World War he was a lieutenant colonel.

The focus remained on B Division and the SAC's medical teams – Steele had written to the inspector general following the resignation of Nursing Sister Anderson; and Baden-Powell responded that it could be the time 'for Sister Richardson to join us if she wishes to. If you know her address could you tell her to apply if she wants to come.'

However, there was another request from someone who wanted a commission in the SAC and made the approach through the commanding officer of B Division: this was a member of the Scottish Horse who promised to gather volunteers from that regiment for the SAC on the condition that he was given a commission in the force. Steele passed this on to the inspector general; and the tone of Baden-Powell's response – which could be expected in the light of his stance in his disagreement with Milner over the way he chose officers – was that if men from the Scottish Horse wished to join they were free to do so, but to give a commission to their sponsor put that individual in the position of a 'tout for us and not for his personal merit and qualifications for the position of officer'. Then he went on say to Steele that the 'same applies to Lt Butler and Hoy whom you mention – and to loads of others who apply to me every day.'

Another approach seems to have come through B Division for Baden-Powell refers to it in the communication to Sam Steele: this was a burgher called Van der Merwe who tried to dictate the terms on which he would come to the force. The inspector general referred him to Major Leggett who 'is raising the burgher Troop for us'.

Steele, with his broad perspective on relationships between magistrates and police, reacted to a circular he received on the status of the SAC in the Districts. He noted that

> they are very much under the orders of the magistrates, much more so than in any part of the British possessions. The officers should certainly be trusted to inspect their own cells and to keep them as they ought to be. Certainly a good soldier should know better how to superintend such work than a civilian who has probably taken office for the first time. This is one of the things most likely to cause friction. Of course it may turn out differently and we will loyally support the magistrates.[101]

In their role as helpers of the people the SAC, when they had established the network of outposts and had their own mail service up and running, could help the post office deliver mail in Cape carts, pack horse or even by despatch riders as a temporary solution until the post office could make their own delivery arrangements. Baden-Powell suggested the idea to Steele for B Division were well advanced in creating a wide outreach in the northern Transvaal.

One month after the end of hostilities, there was a diversion from the post-war reconstruction of services for the colonies on 4 July when a ball was held in Zoo Hall. It was well attended, Sam Steele recorded, and there was a good representation of SAC officers and army officers: General Lyttelton and his family were there and so was the SAC Inspector General.

However, as far as some of the other ranks were concerned it was not socialising they wanted but the exit door. Steele wrote that Captain Jarvis came in from his post and told him that a lot of No. 14 Troop wanted their discharge; they had been told in Canada that they would be able to get their discharge by purchase whenever they liked. Steele's response was to tell Jarvis to inform them that they had signed 'their agreement with their eyes open and that they will get the same chance as the other troops'. The inspector general followed that up by supporting Steele, telling him that there was no promise made to men to purchase their discharge: 'It was stated to them that it would be possible to do so on the understanding that their services could be spared.'

There were others who thought they could beat the system – it comes to light in Baden-Powell's answer to Steele's query in early July: his response tells it all, 'The men who obtained 3 months furlough and then decline to re-engage in SAC will have to serve three months extra to make up their term of service – such leave not to count towards completion of engagement.'

Problems like these were time-consuming to deal with – but they could be dealt with in the interaction between HQ and Divisions. The real frustration came from being caught up in the corporate system of civil authority. An example comes from Hill Crest, the SAC up-country site for rehabilitating their imported horses. The site had been found, the inspector general had negotiated rental, a Troop was stationed there – but for some structural work the corps had to deal with the Works Department. The inspector general's report to CSO Nicholson runs as follows:

I am sorry to find there is too much red tape at work in the Works Department. I have for some time supposed something wrong from the slowness with which they are doing things e.g. HQ buildings at Johannesburg, Potchefstroom, Pretoria etc.

And now at Hill Crest the 'dip' was asked for 3 months ago and the drawing and estimates are still being made for a footling little thing that could easily be made in a week with unskilled labour for about £5 or £8 of material. Meantime for want of it disease has spread, all farriers have had their whole time taken up with hand-dressing instead of shoeing, and horse flesh has been wasted.

The doors of the stable at Hill Crest have not yet been filled up. This could have been done within a few days of my last visit when I pointed out that 2 cross battens (in addition to the existing one) were all that was needed for the iron (which is there already) to be nailed on to. But nothing has been done and horses meanwhile have been sickening with colds and losing condition.

I was told that even a bit of wire fencing wanted tightening and repairing but could not be done by the Works Department without authority for HQ, so the Troop set to work and did it themselves in their off time without charge.

This kind of system is exactly the reverse of what we want in SAC.

In the big things there seem to be months of preparation and no results; in the little things no ingenuity of quickness.

Unless this can be altered I don't see much use in having the department.

Much coming and going between Divisions and HQ was necessary at this time when the SAC was settling into its peacetime role. There had to be regard to tight internal discipline and Sam Steele had been proposing some measures that he wanted to run past the inspector general – one was drunkenness. In this Baden-Powell supported him, he wrote,

I quite agree that 'under the influence of drink' should be a crime and will consult CSO to how we can legislate for it. Meantime I should certainly support any officer who punished a man for it; and it is quite sufficient grounds for reducing a NCO as unsuitable.[102]

Steele also wrote about an inconsistency he had picked up – gambling was prohibited among men but there was no limit on the stakes that could pass between players of bridge. That led him to another difference that needed clearing up. A board set up to consider a case of two NCOs being drunk only fined them. Steele thought this was an insufficient deterrent and he intended that in future cases NCOs convicted of drunkenness would also be reduced to the ranks.[103]

Correct uniform was always an important indicator of group cohesion to the inspector general and he was dissatisfied with what he came across in several Troops in B Division in July. He wrote to Steele that some of the minor items of uniform were not satisfactory; there seemed to have been idiosyncratic selection of items such as hat badges, shoulder straps, spurs and boots; and he told Steele that it was a matter for Troop officers and the assistant controller to put to rights.

The range of concerns that a divisional commander had to cover in this vast country with the indigenous people and the Europeans who had settled there led to frustration at times even for a commander like Steele with his experience of the Canadian north-west. He wrote to the inspector general about some incident that had not gone well and Baden-Powell responded, 'I have passed on your information re the Natives being uppish.' The inspector general passed this information to the Native Commissioner.

However, there was one important area for the SAC that Colonel Steele thought should be resolved at policy level; he had raised the issue before and he wrote again on 22 July:

> I still wish to point out that the longer we are in existence the more necessary it seems to me that our officers, at least OC Troops, should be Justices of the Peace with power not only to issue warrants but to try cases of a petty nature and that if necessary two of them sitting together have the power of a magistrate. The distances are so great that the expense of bringing petty cases before the Resident Magistrate perhaps to be dismissed will be considerable and they can also be tried on the spot if necessary and the expense avoided. I think that this course will cause the natives and Boers to have a respect for us that they will never have with the present system. The officers of the Corps should also report all short comings on the part of all officers dealing with natives and will perform a great deal of the work now done by Native Commissioners. Will see the IG and talk over these matters with him.[104]

Even before the meeting took place the inspector general took action: he replied on 31 July that he agreed with Steele's proposition; not only did he agree with it but thought it was so clearly expressed that, 'I am having your notes typed for submission to Attorney General in support of my application to that effect.'

Steele's idea of having SAC officers doing the work of Native Commissioners, though, was not one the inspector general was going along with – at present. He thought that the interaction with the native community required great care: the present Native Commissioners 'are a specially selected lot of men – experts –

under a most capable and experienced chief and we have to work entirely with them.' Baden-Powell, though, proposed raising for B Division about 150 Native Police who would be under two of Steele's officers. These two officers 'would work in with the Native Commissioner' and be prepared to be guided by him when it came to the distribution and duties of the men 'for duty entirely in the Native Territory'.[105]

Following that up, Baden-Powell wrote to CSO Nicholson – money had to be found in the budget for 150 Native Police – and told him to cut down Native Scouts after a certain date and authorise raising Native Police for Native Commissioner from that date.

The content of B Division's diary entries for the second month of peace covered a comprehensive range of subjects. Steele had some information that, he thought, should go up the line; but this time it should reach the ears of Milner; he wrote an intriguing note.

> All the Boer farmers, some prominent leaders in and around Pietersburg are reported to be well satisfied with arrangements made for their repatriation etc. etc. It has leaked out that it is important that all such notes as these should be brought personally to Lord Milner otherwise he may not see them and that anything of this sort unless brought to him in that or some official way will escape him. This is of course more than confidential as it has come to my knowledge of course properly, but I have my doubts as to its being intended for publication.

Steele was also informed, and it seems to have been on the grapevine, that Milner did not wish burgher squads to be employed where there were large numbers of natives. Steele acknowledged 'I have held this opinion for some time that it would be better not to have them with large numbers of natives on account of the feeling.'

The Transvaal, as we saw earlier, as far as repatriation was concerned, was said to have been the more heavily centralised of the two colonies; and in his same Diary entry that day, Steele added that in the Executive Council most departments were represented and he thought so should the SAC inspector general; 'I hope he will agree with me and get appointed.'

On 31 July the inspector general wrote again to Steele; he saw in the newspapers that Milner was going to Delagoa Bay about 10 August; and he wanted the SAC to be on the lookout for any attempt on His Excellency's life along the railway. The inspector general also ordered the officer commanding B Division to find guards of honour at stopping places.

Keeping the force up to the mark, though, implied the continuation of the inspector general's inspection; and in July it was C Division's turn. The pattern was much the same with work on repatriation and establishing outstations. Now that Ridley had resigned, Major Fair as commanding officer became lieutenant colonel. The only comment from the inspection that was in the negative quadrant was that the outstations were not in good shape. C Division was also considerably short of horses; and the inspector general asked Nicholson to see if the Repatriation Board would loan SAC some horses not only for C but for other Divisions that were short of them.

Then there was another border issue to be looked at and this was in the west of the Transvaal. Major Madoc wrote to the inspector general in early August; he estimated that Derdepoort was a suitable position for the SAC to establish a post to stop infected cattle entering from Bechuanaland Protectorate. Madoc thought they could make a cattle-preventive line from there to Crocodile Pool. He found that the natives of Linchwe's tribe were very helpful. Baden-Powell noted, 'Linchwe can probably assist us with transport in supplying this Troop via Mochudi.' There was a lot of cross-border smuggling by traders going on. Madoc said that one suspect was a man named Ricketts, an agent for Vickerman, a storekeeper at Mochudi. What Madoc wanted was a few Basuto police under an SAC officer and not the native commissioner's police. Baden-Powell replied agreeing to the proposed posts and advising him to act in concert with the native commissioner in dealing with Linchwe; and he would follow up on the request for Basuto police.

In the Orange River Colony Colonel Pilkington, officer commanding E Division, was making good progress extending the work of the SAC across the colony. After British sovereignty was established in June, Milner was made governor of both the Transvaal and the Orange River Colony; and he appointed Goold-Adams lieutenant governor of the ORC. Hence Pilkington, as commander of the one SAC division in that colony, was closer to the upper level of the civil administration than his counterpart COs in the Transvaal. Over time Goold-Adams changed his attitude towards the SAC.

Baden-Powell arrived in Bloemfontein in the afternoon of 6 August; and he had a long talk with Pilkington. In the staff diary he summed up the extent of coverage – 'SAC are now well out all over ORC and doing good police work in all directions.' The colony was divided into 8 sub-divisions, 30 wards and 127 outstations. Each outstation had about 500 square miles to patrol and every farm was visited about once a week. That was the aim. The outstation was usually manned by an SAC squad of an NCO, and six men. In addition to policing the SAC ran mails in Cape carts or on pack horse. There was also a training programme at sub-divisional level; and there were four to five staff sergeants who acted as instructors – they had been carefully selected: ex-university or former solicitors' clerks. They trained NCOs and men in police duties as far as they could in the absence of a complete code.

However, a hindrance to effective police work in the ORC was the existence of the separate Municipal Police under Mr Gray, the commissioner. Gray was not answerable to Pilkington; and there were examples of bad feeling between SAC and Municipal Police: when a case was worked up at district level by an SAC staff sergeant it was handed over to the Municipal Police to take for trial. The SAC resented this: as Baden-Powell put it, 'The cream of the work was taken from them.' This led, at the level of petty politics in the colony, to an impression that the SAC were amateur police; whereas they had a leavening of ex-RIC, Canadian NW Police, BSAP (British South African Police) and Natal Police. Baden-Powell reflected that it was a great pity that Goold-Adams had not already sanctioned the amalgamation of the two forces, but it seems he had promised the Municipal Police they would remain until 1903.

During the time he had been working closer to the lieutenant governor Pilkington had taken the measure of the man and those round about him; and he told Baden-Powell that the impression in Bloemfontein was that a prominent burgher, Sir John Fraser, 'runs the ORC'. In June a legislative council had been established as a first step to self-government and Fraser and a number of other burghers were unofficially part of it. Fraser did not want the SAC to take over the Municipal Police; and he wanted the merger delayed – it seems, as the staff diary has it, that Fraser had a script that read the ORC had become the dumping ground for the Transvaal rubbish, and Pilkington was some of the rubbish.

Discussion that afternoon then turned to the colony's CID. The department had not yet been taken over by the SAC pending the appointment of a head. Goold-Adams had suggested a Major Bayne formerly of the RIC and now in the Royal Engineers. Baden-Powell told Pilkington to cable the inspector general of the RIC for details about him. The reason Goold-Adams had come up with an outsider was that the present man was not fit for it 'but Lt Gov does not want to hurt his feelings by putting a younger man over him'. The younger man was Lieutenant Bantrop SAC, who, Baden-Powell thought, was better fitted for the job and had come to the SAC from military intelligence and had been strongly recommended by Colonel Henderson for his knowledge of the people and the colony.

Next day, Baden-Powell was one of the lunch guests of the lieutenant governor; and after it the two had a meeting. Baden-Powell's note of it picks up what Pilkington had sensed:

> He is evidently much more favourable towards the SAC than he used to be. He is pleased with the work they are doing in carrying the mail in all districts of the colony. Wants them if possible to take passengers as well as mails between Winburg and Harrismith. I told him this is already being arranged for.

Baden-Powell brought up the question of who should head the CID for the ORC. He told the lieutenant governor that he had seen Major Bayne. However, he was lukewarm about him but he had cabled the inspector general of the RIC to ask about his qualifications; and if they were satisfactory he proposed appointing him on probation for six months.

Having already asked him in a letter to present Gallantry Badges to members of the SAC for gallantry in action, Baden-Powell brought it up again. At that Goold-Adams swithered – he was not sure of his position; he thought he would wait until Milner responded to an invitation to a similar ceremony in the Transvaal.

Next day Baden-Powell began the series of inspections and rode to Jagersfontein with his personal staff officer Captain Kearsley. He recorded the scenes of destruction, 'The town practically deserted, houses standing but furniture etc. smashed up and streets littered with rubbish.' There were diamond mines and their machinery was starting up, 'but nothing doing in the place yet'. Then he rode on to Fauresmith, 'County town of about 500 houses with church, market square, schools etc. Numerous well-to-do houses. At present deserted except for about 20 families. Houses all standing but with doors and furniture in many cases broken especially by native looting.' However, Fauresmith was being policed by one constable of the Municipal Police and seven SAC. A magistrate had recently arrived. He told Baden-Powell he was very pleased with the men and 'Capt Dawson who commands this District and knows everybody in it'. Baden-Powell inspected No. 5 Troop who were based there and covered four outstations and two centres in the district.

The following day he rode the 41 miles to Edenburg and inspected No. 21 Troop commanded by Captain Ponssetti. The Troop was camped there until they could get enough supplies to Jagersfontein. Thus far in his inspections Baden-Powell had come across none where there were reports of bad behaviour; but this one was the exception: there was a bad element in it. After discussing the details with Ponssetti, Baden-Powell told him to give him the names of the 'four worst men for dismissal'. Ponssetti was confident that would change the tone of the whole Troop 'who are otherwise good men (all Canadians) and who much resent the bad conduct of these four'.

Major Walton, relieved from the temporary post as acting head of Intelligence Department, had been appointed sub-divisional commanding officer; he made Edenburg the temporary HQ of the Riet River Sub-Division until they could get transport to move to Jagersfontein. Walton, equipped with previous police experience, had done a systematic job of having each ward defined and the areas within them delineated; and he had introduced a rota where each farm was visited once a week.

Baden-Powell visited six families:

> They are all very friendly and pleased with the SAC. They partly look on them as protectors against their own political opponents as well as against natives. Our men are behaving very well towards them and in some cases are helping them in rebuilding their houses, cutting water-furrows etc.

He also had an opinion of the magistrate at Fauresmith – 'very satisfactory as far as can be seen, but the one at Edenburg (Brand) wanting in decision and not much liked by either Boers or British.'

When he returned to Bloemfontein he met Goold-Adams and Pilkington. In the intervening days it would seem that Major Bayne had not passed muster for the post of head of the CID; and so another name came into the frame: a J.L. Bennet, chief of police at Gibraltar. Justice Fawkes had recommended him for he had 'a European reputation as a detective'. Baden-Powell proposed that he would be paid £900 out of the Civil Estimates for the CID for a year and then, if he was suitable, Baden-Powell would transfer him to the Transvaal and replace him with Lieutenant Bantrop, who was able but who had 'not sufficient professional standing at present' to be promoted over the serving lacklustre senior man. Goold-Adams agreed and Pilkington was delegated to cable the chief commissioner of the Metropolitan Police under whom Bennet had formerly served. The arrangement was finalised on 26 August when Goold-Adams met Baden-Powell in Johannesburg and agreed to take on Bennet as head of the colony's CID for a year after which he would be either transferred to the Transvaal or to SAC HQ; and two months later, Milner, pressed by Baden-Powell to have an experienced man create a CID for the Transvaal, agreed to apply for Bennet for a year. So it came about that chief inspector Bennet was seconded to South Africa for special service.

Continuing his inspection of SAC posts, Baden-Powell went by rail to Winburg. Major Lyon had made his HQ of the Zand River sub-division here. He reported that the area was settling down, 'although the Refugee Camp is almost as full as ever, a large number have gone from it to their farms'. The SAC policed the camp and the native locations; the Municipal Police policed the town. Although he was not a member of the Repatriation Board Major Lyon directed the repatriation by the SAC.

In her research on the concentration camps, Elizabeth van Heyningen found that repatriation in the ORC was less centralised than in the Transvaal; and she quoted the Quaker emissary Lawrence Richardson who wrote at the time, 'They depend less on issuing circulars of instruction and more on getting good men and giving them a free hand.'[106]

From the perspective of Winburg its resident magistrate put it another way when Baden-Powell met him on his tour of inspection: he told him that it was entirely thanks to the SAC that the repatriation was so far forward. Their discussion then turned to the situation in the native refuge locations – the natives were not willing to leave them. This was in part due to an expedient practice the British had connived. During the fighting, the magistrate explained, a large number of Africans were employed as scouts by the British; and 'as they could not be taken on the pay lists they were given horses and stock in return for their services – but in order to avoid future questions no permits were given with the stock.' The result was that some returning Boers recognised their own stock in the hands of Africans, who had no written authority for its possession; but the word was out that the stock was given as payment.

Baden-Powell's eight-day series of inspections in the Orange River Colony gives insight into the role the SAC played in re-establishing community and farm life in the aftermath of the war. He wrote that their conduct and their health were very good and they 'show great zeal in their work'. The work timetable included instruction in police duties and a good number were learning Dutch.

There was an arrangement the inspector general saw in the ORC that he brought to the attention of Colonel Sam Steele in the northern Transvaal. He found they sent 'tired cattle to a farmer to graze and rest. He is allowed to use them 2 hours a day for ploughing. SAC give him a few bags of seed. He gives SAC one half of the crop.'

The lack of that 'free hand' in the Transvaal that Lawrence Richardson wrote of was reiterated in B Division's diary where Colonel Steele gives an example. On 8 August he wrote that Captain Swift wired that the army at Warmbaths had 168 cattle for sale. So Steele saw the authorities; but the result was that he found the Repatriation Board had an arrangement which prevented the army from disposing of cattle to any other department. In despair Steele wrote, 'This Board seems to have grasped everything within its reach.'[107]

A general problem came out of the blue to affect the wellbeing of men in all Divisions of the SAC: Dickeson's company had to give up supplying the SAC hospitality arrangements – he was losing money over it. Baden-Powell wrote to the OCs Division giving the details of how much each Division owed the company. What was to be the replacement arrangement? In a communication to B Division the inspector general wrote,

> But I am as a rule averse to Troops running their own because it gives
> so much extra work to the officer if it is properly run – and if it isn't it
> opens the way to a lot of fraud on the part of the NCO in charge.

On 17 August, Baden-Powell met Milner who had returned to Johannesburg from Delagoa Bay. He agreed to the inspector general's request that he present Gallantry Badges on 28 August to members of the SAC for outstanding service in action. Later though, he had second thoughts on presenting the Gallantry Badges and he had the military secretary broach the subject, telling the inspector general that his excellency was 'doubtful about the advisability' of his presenting the badges. At that Baden-Powell postponed the ceremony. Then there was the follow-up: Milner met Baden-Powell and it was settled that the SAC's inspector general should present the awards. So Baden-Powell presented badges to about thirty SAC of all ranks for gallantry during the war.

Although vacillating on the awards, Milner was in decisive mode when he agreed the important policy development that SAC officers should be invested with plenary powers as JPs to handle minor offences. This decision was to further improve the SAC's relations with local communities.

Baden-Powell's inspection of the north-west Transvaal was to last seven days. He inspected seven Troops; and with his penchant for minute detail, he noted that he had covered 332 miles by rail in the inspector general's special coach and 234 on horseback.

There were two instances of discord between resident magistrate and SAC officer: in Pietersburg the magistrate tended to interfere with the SAC. The tale went round that the magistrate had told fellow passengers on a train journey that the SAC were no good, but unknown to him one of those passengers was an SAC officer in civvies. Colonel Steele, though, thought that there were probably faults on both sides.

In Middleburg the magistrate and the SAC captain were often at loggerheads; and Steele proposed replacing the captain – Baden-Powell agreed to it. As a result he drafted a confidential circular to officers which stressed that for the good of the country and the service it was important that there should be harmony between magistrates and SAC officers; and he ended with, 'Private feelings and petty ideas of departmental rivalry must be sunk, and tact and helpfulness displayed. Officers not acting up to this will be considered unfit for their position.'

A few days later, however, the Middleburg case took on a new light when SAC Captain Hussey Walsh wrote explaining the origins of the friction and the final outcome. He was in post before the appointment of the magistrate; and he discovered and reported corruption among some local court officials. However, when the magistrate arrived these men nobbled him and smeared Hussey Walsh. After a bit, however, the magistrate discovered the truth and sent a full apology ' – and now Hussey Walsh and he are on the best terms'.

There seemed to be a secondary element there – the assistant resident magistrate: Major Ousley told Sam Steele that he removed his colleague to Christiania because he was 'unfriendly to the SAC'. Steele wrote in the divisional diary that in fairness to himself Hussey Walsh wanted him to mention it to the inspector general.

When Baden-Powell arrived at Pietersburg to see the situation for himself he found that the resident magistrate was a Major Bolton. The RM told him that he had nothing to complain about except that he had no briefing from the attorney general on the relative roles of magistrate and police and he wanted advice, for example on accommodation for the SAC. Baden-Powell explained that the charge office and lock-up should be supplied to him by the Law Department but the usual practice was for the magistrate to find an office near his own for the SAC district commandant. Thereafter, it was up to the SAC to provide all other offices and barracks.

However, the magistrate had a general criticism: he felt that the administration in the Transvaal was over-centralised; and he saw that it hampered the repatriation process and the burghers were not happy about it. He wanted more SAC posts established but Baden-Powell told him it was impossible to feed the men; they found it impossible to feed more than the existing ones – there was insufficient transport.

This was the biggest drawback the SAC had to face: lack of transport. In A Division Colonel Edwards reported that 90 per cent of his posts were out in their places but the establishment of transport was insufficient to keep them supplied with food and clothing – and they were in a bad way for clothing. In C Division the situation was little better.

In his B Division inspection Baden-Powell came across an example of the heavy hand of centralism that the Pietersburg magistrate had cited: in a small settlement he discovered nineteen wagons belonging to the Repatriation Board standing idle; they would have been of great use to the SAC in setting up outstations and feeding the men. He telegraphed Nicholson at SAC HQ to ask for them on loan.

In the Fort Edward area there were a lot of settlements of black people; and they were friendly to the British; but they could not understand why the Boers were being allowed to return to their farms. Baden-Powell cited an example: he had a discussion with ex-pat Mrs Cooksley who had lived for thirty years in that part of the country. She felt that while her black tenants were much as before others in the area had changed since the war; and she described a talk with a local headman who became angry when he was told that his people were not going to have possession of Boer farms which was what they had expected.

When he inspected No. 17 Troop under Captain Moore and Lieutenant Steel he found that it was camped on the flats among the new government settlers but the ground they were on was wanted by the Land Board. The Troop had three outstations each within 30 miles and 'a squad at railway station'.

Baden-Powell wrote,

> this Troop is in the least satisfactory condition of any in B Division. The men and methods slack. Capt Moore, though willing, has not sufficient strength and initiative. Horses fair. Transport very bad oxen too poor to work. No site yet selected for making barracks. I rode round the neighbourhood with Capt Moore but could find no good site on government ground. Found a very suitable one on private farm on a ridge overlooking the flats and commanding the main Waterberg road.
>
> Good water about 600 feet below, in river, and a practicable road up to the spot.

He also had a separate paragraph on black and white relations. He noted that the main trouble was that 'the Natives decline to work for the Boers and in many cases have Boer cattle which they refuse to give up.' The Natives would not sell or rent out trek cattle 'which is badly needed by us and Repatriation'.

On 25 August the inspector general wrote up his summary of the tour including the condition of the SAC, which was generally satisfactory except for transport; but the men were healthy, working well and keen on their work. Their relations with townspeople and those in the districts were generally good; their police work in isolating diseased cattle by the Limpopo 'is praised by the Boers themselves'. He then handed his notes to Colonel Steele who came down 'by train from Pietersburg sick – with "mumps."'

Boer commandos, however, were no longer the enemy; instead there were signs of the enemy within: sniping; attempts to undermine leading officers. There was an example in the Orange River Colony administration; and in the staff diary entry of 26 August there is a cryptic entry – 'I heard of Col. S. failure and wrote to him accordingly.' No explanation or development follows; but the context becomes clear in a separate letter file. Two days later, 28 August, Baden-Powell wrote to Steele as follows:

> I am much distressed to have heard a report about yourself to the effect that you have lately been indulging in drink. I cannot tell you how

greatly I deplore this if it is true as I have looked upon you as my best informed and most practically-experienced Divisional Commander, and could ill afford to lose your valued assistance (which would have to be the result if it recurred, as we cannot otherwise keep the subordinate ranks up to the mark as regards sobriety and reliability). I hope I may have your assurance that there will be no recurrence in the future.

There is no record of the follow-up; no copy of Steele's reply; and from the existing record there is no indication of friction between Baden-Powell and Steele; and indeed the inspector general's high regard for Steele continued into the future – after Baden-Powell founded the Scout Movement, and it quickly caught on in Canada, Steele became Scout Commissioner of Manitoba.

As to any signs of supporting indicators that might lend credibility to the report there are none – in the B Division diary submitted by Steele the entries for the week before and after the communication show no indication of Steele as anything other than focused on his work and detailed in recording it. Indeed only a month earlier, 15 July, Steele recorded in the diary, in connection with a charge against Sergeant Mackay, that 'the time has come for the slightest symptoms of intoxication to be sufficient to cause a member of the Constabulary to be placed upon his trial.'[108] When Baden-Powell read those words three days later he responded to Steele:

I quite agree with you that 'under the influence of drink' should be a crime and will consult CSO as to how we can legislate for it. Meantime I should certainly support any officer who punishes a man for it; and it is quite sufficient grounds for reducing an NCO as unsuitable.

Then, only three days after he had challenged Steele with the report he had been given about him, he wrote to him again on 29 August in different terms.

Dear Steele

Currie asked me if it would be possible for him to be left in his present Troop – and I said I would speak to you about it.
Do you think it would be feasible?
He seems to have taken a great interest not only in his men and horses but also in preparing plans for making his barracks, garden, recreation

rooms etc. He has got to know that bit of the country and the natives as well as whites in it and if it should be possible to leave him there I think it would be for the good of the service and a reward to him. But you may have reasons that outweigh these for moving him – and I don't like therefore to interfere – I have gone much further than usual in suggesting it to you – but his keenness and ideas seemed to urge me to represent his case.

Baden-Powell did not allude to who gave him the 'report' about Steele. His record of meeting people on 26 August cites three: Milner, Goold-Adams and the director of army supplies. It is unlikely to have been earlier that he had heard it for he met Steele on 25 August and gave him some notes from his inspection. A possibility is that the source had a corrupted version of a story that emerged the year before of Steele drunk at a London banquet and that tale had traction that, Steele's biographer Rod Macleod tells us, persisted up until the First World War; and it brought forth a testimonial for Steele from Lord Strathcona refuting – and that story flowed not at the level of the scuttlebutts but circulated among the policy élite.[109]

Baden-Powell had written his letter to Steele on 28 August in a professional manner – and he had alluded briefly to the action he was to take on 26 August – yet there is no reference to any follow-up – but it existed on the record (though the inspector general put it in the past tense: 'I heard of the failure of Col S. and wrote to him accordingly.') Questions come to mind – what was the status of the talebearer? Would he have any knowledge of the inspector general's action? Interestingly on 4 August, in a communication to Sam Steele the inspector general wrote:

> I keep a diary similar to yours in which I keep all such remarks as would interest or be useful to HE are inserted and I send it to him every day and he reads it [underlined in original]. In this way he is in touch with all the SAC doings.

So one other pair of eyes would have read Baden-Powell's single sentence entry in the staff diary for 26 August.

Only four days after Baden-Powell wrote to Steele regarding the report he had heard about him he wrote in very different terms – with the information that he had recommended him and five other officers to Kitchener's notice for their good work, 'but he has apparently only published the names of those who distinguished themselves in the field'.

It would be a mistake, however, to assume that Baden-Powell was dead against drink. He wrote to Nicholson his chief staff officer letting him know that some Troop commanders had placed hotel bars out of bounds to their men; but he preferred that they should have the right to go into bars, provided they were not on duty. 'But in the first instance we must get the law altered to let SAC go into bars in uniform.' He then wrote to the attorney general who gave the ruling that hotel bars would be open to the SAC. Baden-Powell asked Nicholson to send a note to officers indicating that the inspector general was in favour of men having access to bars 'so long as they don't abuse the privilege'.

What he did come down heavily on was an NCO who was convicted of drunkenness: he wrote to Nicholson to put in orders that in such a case the individual should be reduced to the ranks, 'regardless of any other punishment he's given'. However, the inspector general was open to appeal and responsive if the circumstances warranted it. In November an instance arose in B Division. Colonel Steele had Lieutenant Agnew placed in arrest for having been drunk at the theatre in Pretoria. It was corroborated by two lieutenants and Agnew himself had admitted it. Baden-Powell had initially called on him to resign his appointment; but Sam Steele had a good report of his work from Major Birdwood and strongly recommended that he should not be dismissed: Agnew's condition at the theatre had not attracted attention; he had fallen asleep during the performance. Baden-Powell's decision was that he should be reprimanded.

In the difficult circumstances the SAC found themselves – as some of the photos in this book show – keeping the men up to the mark was essential for self-respect and unit morale. Steele proposed encouraging this by given the men lots of patrol work. The inspector general was in favour of this and told Steele so; but he also suggested that for the men on outposts it would be good to bring them in for 'polishing up and change of scene and climate'.

Steele had sent one of his officers, Logan, to survey the Mozambique border and the likely siting of the SAC posts. Logan's reply was unequivocal in suggesting a different line of posts; his report was passed on to the inspector general and Baden-Powell wrote to Steele asking if he would pass on his reply to Logan. He suggested to Steele that a better line, and more inland might be along the Pilgrims Rest range of mountains. The inspector general's reply to Logan ran:

Dear Logan

I am much obliged for the very clear and concise report you have sent in through Col Steele of the Portuguese [Mozambique] Frontier and its protection.

I propose taking immediate steps in the matter and your information will be of great value in guiding our arrangements.

Yours truly,

While access to drink was available to the SAC if they were based near a town, their food rations were in danger of shrinking. The army had had their rations of jam, bacon and cheese cut and it was proposed this cut should apply to the SAC as well. Baden-Powell refused and ordered the present ration to continue:

> our men are now worse off for food than they were during the war, and it is impossible to run canteens and shops in out-districts owing to want of transport and I consider it would be impossible just now to cut the ration.

Living on iron rations or foraging while at the same time being well paid was the anomaly many of the SAC lived with. In a letter to Major McLaren at the London recruiting on 26 August, Baden-Powell pointed out an indicator of their high pay: he wrote, 'Dear Boy (this was the nick name Baden-Powell had first given him years earlier when they served together) We have 3000 men with Saving Bank balances the total I think amounts to over £135,000. Besides family remittances sent home amounting to £67,000.'

However, he also came across a practice that worked to the detriment of relatives of a member of the corps who died with a balance of money in some bank 'other than the National Bank' but no trace of it could be found and as a result the next of kin suffered. Thus the inspector general drafted a memo to his CSO to put in orders:

> It is therefore advisable for men who have deposited money in other than the Corps Savings Bank to make some note to that effect or to inform their Troop officer so that in the event of their death the money may not be lost to their relatives.

Although there were restrictions the Force was adapting to its peacetime role; and that role was quite comprehensive: there was the disarming of natives to be completed, according to an ordinance, by certain dates. In the northern Transvaal SAC officers thought there was not enough time; native chiefs would hold an *indaba* [a general meeting] and sometimes deadlines would be missed; but a new date, 7 October, was fixed by the Native Commissioner. When a handing-in took place a chief might have 1,500 rifles plus ammunition turned in; and on 8 October in a big turnout Chief Maleboch and 1,700 men went to Pietersburg to surrender arms.

Earlier Baden-Powell had alerted Sam Steele to the possibility of native unrest because of a combination of the disarmament orders and the forthcoming collection of hut tax:

> It would be well to arrange for your Field Troops to be ready for mobilisation at any time – I suppose you would use the Australian and Canadian troops at Pretoria for such duty? If so please do get them completely ready in every way.

In the mining areas the SAC had to respond quickly – there was the rush of miners to peg out claims. With Sam Steele's past experience he could act competently. The Commissioner for Mines contacted Steele:

> he wished to know what arrangements were made for the prevention of a breach of the peace on the pegging day. I replied that the officer in command of the Pietersburg District had a sufficient force at his disposal to prevent, and in reply to Commissioner's request for twelve troopers and an NCO to act as temporary beacon inspectors, notified him and in same wire that I had ordered their selection and placed them in charge of an experienced man who had for years been employed upon such work. I selected Sgt-Maj Tweedy No. 6 Troop and ordered Maj Birdwood by wire to select the men and directed that they be the very best. [110]

The road and the gold fields were being patrolled by the SAC and it was reported that all was quiet; and as part of their duty the SAC kept a record of the prospectors. All was reported to be quiet.

All the while repatriation was continuing. Sam Steele reported that the £200 advanced to farmers in Zoutpansberg district, in the north-east of the Transvaal 'has done much good and been appreciated'. Interflowing with the movement of life to something like the way it had been before the war personalities of the new order surfaced. In Milner's case he intended visiting Pietersburg and he had his itinerary sent to Steele and he wished the details to be kept secret. However, before Steele received the communication the whole programme of Milner's visit was in the public domain and even mentioned in the newspapers.

Occasionally an officer in a district would pick up something and felt he should inform the OC Division. Captain Davie said that there was a Reverend Mr Kriel of the Dutch Reformed Church who refused the sacrament to an ex-National Scout because his blood was stained! Captain Davie thought that the Dutch Reformed Church were 'at the bottom of all ill feeling'.

The SAC had a good coverage of the colonies and repatriation was going well; it had made much progress in the two years since its inception; but it had been at a cost to its two most senior officers: Baden-Powell had been sent on sick leave to the UK and now his senior officer Colonel Nicholson, the man who had taken over the corps when Baden-Powell was ill, came down. He was diagnosed with an abscess of the jaw and being generally rundown. He was to be sent home on sick leave.

Below the senior level though the levels of ill health were improving: the inspector general wrote that on the week ending 3 October the sick list amounted to 2 officers and 242 men. These included 44 with typhoid; 14 dysentery; 7 of wounds. In the previous month, the inspector general wrote, there had been only 4 deaths among the almost 10,000 personnel: 1 was by lightning; 1 accidentally shot; and 'only two from sickness'.

Looking ahead, their inspector general thought it was time to change the divisional structure. Restructuring would be necessary: the original peacetime complement of the SAC was to have been 6,000 but was increased to 10,000 because of the war. At some point the order would come from London to reduce the complement. In addition, though, the inspector general proposed creating a number of mobile Troops to give greater flexibility; he suggested one for each half Division in the Transvaal and one for every two sub-Divisions in the ORC. They would be ready for mobilisation anywhere; serve as depots for training every man in military work. He sent his proposals to the divisions for their comment.

At the micro level a specific complaint had to be dealt with too.

Major Castello reported that he had, without an open inquiry, looked into complaints raised in an anonymous letter from a Troop in E Division. The complaint was against Captain Malcolm for favouring Australians when it came to promoting men. The inspector general had also received the anonymous letter but because it was not attributed to anyone he did not act on it. Castello found, in his preliminary inquiry, that there were certain grounds for the complaint. The inspector general told him to take such steps as he thought best, but to show the correspondence to Malcolm (who was on sick leave) and to tell him that apart from that complaint the inspector general had come to the view that Malcolm did 'not promise well as a police officer – although dashing in the field'.[111]

In B Division Captain Hussey Walsh was performing well in repatriation duties: he visited 107 farms by mid-October and in his report he reckoned that the presence of SAC officers on the Repatriation Board gave more clout to the SAC in the districts and it helped them in their relations with the Boers.

The division's area abutted the Mozambique frontier to the north-east and a unit called Steinaecker's Horse was deployed there. It was an unhealthy area and the unit had been specifically raised to operate there. There was the benefit of a light railway, the Selati railway, and Steinaecker's men were able to use it. Since the unit had been raised with short term guerrilla activities in mind it would be disbanded soon after hostilities were over. Baden-Powell wrote to Milner that the SAC could probably take over the railway when Steinaecker's Horse was disbanded. This brought a response from Colonel Lambton, military secretary, that His Excellency would like the matter referred to him before the SAC took any action.

Baden-Powell replied,

Major Steinaecker informed me that his Regiment find it necessary to use the Selati railway for the supply of their northern posts along the frontier. They have one engine and a few trucks.

It therefore seems desirable to have the use of this line if it can be arranged, but I am making inquiries as to the necessity for it in our case when Steinaecker's Horse vacate the district and will report for HE information.

The follow-up to this was a visit from the military secretary to hear about the inspector general's overall plans for policing the Portuguese border. So Baden-Powell detailed their thinking: the SAC were waiting until Steinaecker's Horse cleared out as they wanted its transport to supply the various posts. He also mentioned that they were awaiting a response from the Customs Department as to whether they would pay extra money to allow the SAC to take on some of Steinaecker's Horse – this produced the response that the SAC might do this whether or not the Customs Department paid. Then though, the military secretary – echoing his master's views or not – suggested the SAC could put the whole border under one special officer. Baden-Powell told him that this had been considered but the length of the border – 250 miles – spoke against: rather it should be divided into sections with a supporting Troop in more healthy country within 50 miles of it. He went on and explained to the military secretary that manned posts could do little without efficient detective work and that at present cross-boundary smuggling routes went round the flanks of Steinaecker's line.

This discussion would duly lead to another, possibly involving Milner since it dealt with cross-border issues; but in the meantime inter-departmental management difficulties had to be looked at and on 17 October the inspector general travelled to Durban and went first to the SAC's new transit office run by Lieutenant Williams, who had one clerk but felt he needed another. The problem was truckage: the railway had agreed that eight trucks a day would be sent upcountry to the SAC but this had not been achieved; and the inspector general reckoned that they were thirty trucks in arrears. He went to see Mr McConnochie the railway goods traffic manager, who was sympathetic and said he would do his best. However, he pointed out that the army and Repatriation Board had priority – but he admitted that the army often had too many trucks.

The second difficulty that had to be faced in Durban was the site where newly landed remounts for the SAC were kept in horse kraals; the site was the Show Ground; and the problem was that the Sanitary Board ordered the removal of the horse kraals. This was a serious problem for the SAC because they had no place to land the remounts. That led to meetings with the town clerk, the deputy mayor and the chairman of the Sanitary Board. Basically the officials were well disposed towards the SAC. The army had been using the ground and after they had no need for it the military allowed private dealers of horses and cattle to use it 'to the sanitary danger of the neighbourhood' was the slogan used; though Baden-Powell interpolated a comment in the diary in brackets – (there is not a house within 500 yards). On top of that the cricket club that were sub-tenants of the ground were charging stock owners a fee – and 'so making money under the Town Council's nose'.

Next day Baden-Powell met the mayor, Mr Browne, and pointed out the importance of the ground for the SAC; that the problem was not the SAC's doing; private importers had quarantined their stock there making the neighbourhood insanitary; but the SAC would have fewer than 300 horses there. At that the mayor said that he would put it to the Town Council; and Baden-Powell drafted a memorandum for the town clerk making the following points:

1. Being an Imperial Force SAC have a claim to the ground, which is primarily Imperial property.
2. We undertake to place only 260 horses per month there and not for more than 3 or 4 days at a time.
3. We clean up the ground after use. There are no dwellings within ¼ mile; no other site available; and Capt Wilcox is responsible local officer.

Such was the range of areas a SAC inspector general had to manage!

From the horse kraals of Durban the trail led to Hill Crest Remount establishment – but the inspector general went by train. Captain Wilcox, Lieutenant McKenzie, Vet Lieutenant Olliver and No. 1 Troop of B Division under Captain Trew were in the depot; the inspector general inspected it. There were 380 horses in the depot. They were 'not so good in class' as the first shipment the SAC received from Kreuse and Madden; but their general condition was very good the inspector general felt; so were stable management and feeding arrangements. So the management of Remounts was much improved.

On 21 October Milner and the military secretary met Baden-Powell. Having been briefed by military secretary Lambton, Milner wanted to hear first the inspector general's ideas for policing the border with the Portuguese territory of Mozambique. The border with Mozambique involved areas covered by both B and C Divisions. Initially Baden-Powell planned to have four posts in B Division's area and eight in C Division's. Milner, however, suggested scrapping a number of the posts by utilising 'a few good white agents with native spies along the frontier country, backed by an interior line of SAC posts on healthy ground'. He also agreed higher rates of pay for the officers and men – a 50 per cent increase in their pay while they were serving in these frontier posts; and the time they spent there would count double when it came to their discharge or pension rights.

It was decided that Baden-Powell would go to the area and look at it from the perspective that Milner had laid out and report back to him.

Then Milner turned to the reorganisation of the SAC structure; and the inspector general outlined that he had put the general principles to the divisions for them to work out schemes for reducing numbers that would suit the local requirements. He would get their plans within the following two weeks and would be able to send Milner an overall plan. Meanwhile recruiting at home had been cut by 75 per cent and the divisions were 'clearing out from the Corps all useless men'.[112]

It was at this meeting that Baden-Powell pointed out the need for a CID Department in the Transvaal under an experienced officer. Milner agreed to apply for Mr Bennet's services for a year.

Putting off no time that night Baden-Powell left by train for Swaziland. He and Major Wilberforce and Captain Kearsley arrived at Standerton at 5 am. From there they rode to Ermelo a distance of 55 miles – an open road with black soil, very heavy with rain Baden-Powell noted – and got there at 3 pm. At the SAC District HQ there the senior officer, Captain Cornwall, was away on a murder case in Pretoria and his staff officer, Lieutenant Hill, was in charge of the office and the inspector general found him able and well informed.

The town consisted of about sixty houses, entirely in ruins, Baden-Powell wrote. About half the inhabitants had returned and were trying to rebuild. The SAC had built themselves 'a very satisfactory camp of iron huts'. The inspector general inspected No. 13 Troop under Lieutenant Tuthill and found it all in good order. There were good barrack rooms, stables and stores – all put up by the men. There was a field hospital of twenty beds but there were only three patients. Then the inspector general had a discussion with the resident magistrate who wanted to bring to the inspector general's attention the good cooperation he received from Captain Cornwall and his colleagues. His grouse, however, was that he would prefer the District divided into five rather than four Sub-Districts. Colonel Fair was not in favour of it. Before the end of the day Baden-Powell telegraphed Colonel Fair suggesting he take it into consideration.

On 23 October the trio rode the 37 miles from Ermelo to Carolina. It was a good upland undulating road and on the way they called in at Breitenbath's farm. The inspector general also inspected two SAC outstations on the way which he found in good order; the men had built good stables and dwelling huts; and he also noted that the patrol books and diaries were 'in good order'.

When the trio came to Carolina they pulled up their mounts – it was a scene of complete devastation; about fifty houses almost flattened to the ground.

They carried on to the SAC post; No. 19 Troop was under Captain Conolly and Cornet Shackelton and they were under canvas; their horses in tin stables – but bad ones the inspector general thought; he wrote 'Troop fair – no style. 4 undesirable men still to be got rid of.' The post badly needed quarters and a mess for the men. Repatriation was slowly underway in this area. Baden-Powell saw a Mr Everard a local farmer who was on the Repatriation Board. The SAC carried out the repatriation supply to poor burghers for over six weeks.

It was 82 miles from Carolina to Embabane and the three men rode against a cold wind and driving rain all day. The inspector general inspected three outstations on the way and he inspected No. 5 Troop under Lieutenant Swinburne; the men were in tents but the horses were in the open – quarters were going to be built for them on the hill above them. There was also a hospital under Captain Perkin but at the time no one was on the sick list. The trio went to look at a building belonging to a tin mine; it was for sale at £250. Baden-Powell reckoned that it would provide material for good quarters for the men but he felt it was worth about £100 to the SAC.

When they got to Embabane they found a tiny settlement of four or five houses and a group of trees in a hollow by a stream surrounded by hills. A plateau further up on the hillside had been selected as a site for the SAC post; it seemed an ideal spot. Baden-Powell rode the 2 miles out to the house of the Native Commissioner in the area Mr Mooney. It was situated in a government group of buildings which included the magistrate's house, office and stable – all according to the SAC inspector general in very bad repair. Baden-Powell sketched out to the magistrate Milner's general ideas about SAC posts on the Swazi frontier and the utilisation of white agents north of it. The magistrate thought the scheme was a good idea. Then he put forward his priorities: although he wanted the SAC posts in the area he agreed that until the SAC men could be fed the present patrol system they had was a useful show of the constabulary's presence.

Next day it was on the 15 miles from Embabane to Forbes Reef and then the further 20 miles to Piggs Peak in cold wet weather along slippery mountain tracks guided by SAC orderlies who really knew the country, having to ride it in all weathers.

Piggs Peak was named after a French prospector called Guillaume Pigg who found gold here in 1884. Baden-Powell described Piggs Peak as a collection of mine buildings and a store high up on the mountain side. In this challenging setting SAC No. 3 Troop under Lieutenant Neville had been ordered to establish an outpost from Komati Poort (present day Komatipoort). An advance party had been already there for a few days but the rest of the Troop were unable to make it because their wagons were bogged down on the high wet slopes.

The inspector general inspected the detachment of men; they were healthy and well-conducted he found but their horses although well-fed were badly groomed and managed. The question of whether the SAC could establish a force of any size there would depend on transport and access; and Baden-Powell had a discussion with the manager of Piggs Peak Mine, Mr Cross. The mine manager was keen to get government support to improve access and he proposed a joint project: a road for steam traction transport; his company would pay half the cost if the government would pay the other and his company would carry the SAC's supplies here at low rates. Baden-Powell said he would put the proposal to His Excellency.

Baden-Powell saw Major Capell SAC and outlined the package that he and Milner had discussed of frontier posts and agents and 50 per cent increase in pay and improved conditions of service. Capell agreed with it and suggested that the SAC should try to get the best of Steinaecker's Horse for the posts.

Then it was on horseback again for the 75 miles from Piggs Peak to Komati Poort. The road was very steep and treacherous with the rain; there was a drop of perhaps 2,000–3,000 feet; it would be impossible for wagons if it were wet. Soon the three riders came across the first and then at stages of the way the other bogged down wagons of No. 3 Troop. It was obvious that the SAC men had worked really hard on this ascent: they had cut ramps to improve drifts but even with half loads it was impossible.

The last long part of the road was a contrast, it ran through undulating bush country. Here the trio met a patrol of two SAC men and a packhorse from No. 5 Troop who had been patrolling part of the way along the frontier of Portuguese territory and who were heading back to Embabane. Baden-Powell noted that the 'horses and men were in good condition'.

After they reached Komati Poort the inspector general inspected the SAC squad there under Trooper Buller. Huts were being built for them; and they had plenty of work there and were doing it well. The inspector general promised that he would consider their getting the 50 per cent increase in pay etc. as well.

Then Captain Shewan the district commandant met him. He too agreed to the proposed pay and conditions offer. Baden-Powell then asked him to see Major

Steinaecker to find out if some of his really good men would join the SAC at the enhanced pay rates and if he knew any good white agents who the SAC would pay a daily rate of 15 shillings to and if he could recommend some natives who would be suitable for detective work. The last part of Baden-Powell's agenda comes across as though it was a frontier trading post: would Shewan ask Steinaecker to give them some pack mules and saddles at once in anticipation of the SAC buying them and take them out to beleaguered No. 3 Troop on the road to Piggs Peak.

Baden-Powell then went on by train to Lourenco Marques (present day Maputo) on the north bank of Delagoa Bay in Portuguese territory – there he met the general manager of the railway company. The manager was leaving for Johannesburg that evening for talks with government officials about the increase of goods traffic from Delagoa Bay. Then in the final discussion with Constabulary personnel he talked over with Major Baldwin the scheme proposed for frontier posts; and he too was in favour.

Thereafter it was back to the office by train; but Baden-Powell stopped off at Komati Poort and there met Major Steinaecker. Steinaecker had a different background from most unit commanders who served on the British side in the war. He had been a lieutenant in the Prussian Army; he had come to South Africa and explored extensively in wild areas – and he commanded an irregular force that served Britain's war aims. He told Baden-Powell that his 'regiment' was not going to be disbanded: the War Office intended to keep it on at its present work. Baden-Powell wrote that Steinaecker said, 'If it should be broken up some of his good men would probably be willing to engage with us, to act as agents, but he did not think they would be taken on as troopers for post duty.'[113]

It was a hard and varied track that the SAC and its founder had covered thus far – the qualities of the men underpinned the wartime record; but the wide range of their potential flourished post-war; and a significant marker was approaching.

Chapter Eight

The Long Day's Task is Done

Back at the SAC HQ office in late October – two years now since the founding date of the corps – Baden-Powell might have reflected on the anniversary. He had not applied for the job of inspector general: Milner had selected him after consulting the C-in-C., having shrewdly assessed that Baden-Powell, from his record, unlike other military commanders in the campaign, was able to take a line of his own; and for the force he wanted he required a different leader, one who was not bound by military stereotype. However, although it had suited Milner then to appoint Baden-Powell the halo effect had stayed with the inspector general, eclipsing His Excellency's éclat. He had out-served his purpose and though he probably did not know it, Milner had a stab at getting rid of him from the post just ten months earlier. Now, however, Baden-Powell could be replaced – though from the political perspective not in an assassination-like manner – but with finesse.

Baden-Powell had indeed been reflecting on the past two years and the anniversary and in a communication to Nicholson a little earlier he wrote:

> Don't you think we might get up for the Johannesburg public and the betterment of our men some sports for SAC about 22 October in commemoration of the Corps being started.

> I should be inclined for the first occasion at any rate to make them more displays than competitions. For example, exhibitions of 'roping' wild horses, jumping, gun drawing, rides, mounted drama etc. etc.[114]

The immediate priority, however, was the waiting mail – two were of particular interest; the first was candidate for wider dissemination. It was from the Mines Department: the local Mines Inspector praised the work of the SAC on special duty for the gold rush at the Letaba gold fields. Baden-Powell included extracts from the letter in general orders to all ranks.

Next day he went to B Division for what was to be a short visit. Sam Steele met him at the station; they went to the Depot and the inspector general inspected the most recent batch of recruits. Then it was back to the office.

From the extent of the inspector general's correspondence with his CSO and the OCs Divisions, it can be seen that he did not operate on the army officer 'Carry on' style – he did more than 'monitor and inspect' – he engaged and shaped practice as the situation required. He wrote, for example, to Nicholson to put in orders for the whole Force:

> The IG has lately received numerous letters from people who have been asked to press upon him the claims of various members of the corps for promotion.

> The IG wishes it to be clearly understood that he goes entirely on the merits of the men themselves in judging their qualifications for promotion and not on the recommendations of outside friends.

He had also become aware that an army practice had been adopted, at least in some Divisions, where a Guard Room was set up in a camp. This the inspector general did not want. 'An ordinary Constable should be on duty, but not necessarily a whole guard.'

As the two recently annexed colonies of the Transvaal and Orange River Colony were being resettled and stabilised, at the great empire's centre on 9 August Edward VII was crowned king. The splendid cavalcade that followed his coach in London included a contingent of the SAC that prompted a letter from Secretary of State Joseph Chamberlain with 'praise of the coronation contingent SAC.' That was the second letter that caught the inspector general's close attention on his return from the frontier.

Going through the divisional diaries Baden-Powell summarized one incident from B Division that is similar to an example he drafted five years later in his first edition of *Scouting for Boys*: a crime took place and a man in No. 8 Troop was arrested for the theft of £300 from the office of the superintendent of a burgher camp – Corporal Smith detected the theft and tracked the man to camp by the peculiar marking on the soles of his boots. There were other sources too for the story Baden-Powell included in *Scouting for Boys*,[115] but the sharp-eyed training that he exhorted Scouts to practise was exemplified by the observant and tenacious Corporal Smith.

Since mid-May each officer commanding a Division submitted a diary (similar in format to the inspector general's) to SAC HQ. However, for this book only Colonel Steele's diary of B Division was available; and it provides a lot of information that is cogently and usually lucidly expressed; not only that but the District Officers' reports were going to HQ and the inspector general commented that these were excellent reports.

Other Divisions' submissions have to be inferred from the inspector general's response and reaction to what he received, for the SAC operated very much in the spider web image of organisations where information passed to and from the leader. The inspector general engaged with the divisions; his role was more than merely overseeing from a distance in a detached hands-off fashion – his style was closer to hands-on but without disempowering his divisional commanders.

For example, in the case of C Division, at one point, it was the lack of detail in Colonel Fair's diary that the inspector general commented on – he wrote on 23 September, 'I should like to have a little more diary from you.' That had an effect for three weeks later he wrote to Fair, 'Your diary is very satisfactory now and comforting to me.' In that same communication – from the information he is now getting – the inspector general points out a practice that should be changed: 'In your Divisional Orders, undated, probably 20 October. Tolger awards 7 days imprisonment to a man. We don't want these small imprisonments now. It has been in instructions that fines should take their place.'[116]

On 29 October he wrote to Colonel Fair and gave him a summary of his trip round the Swazi border that lay in C Division's area and gave him some pointers to work on for the future. As always his summaries featured the comfort of the men and the condition of their horses. The comfort of the men he felt was still being neglected; while the condition of the horses was generally good – except in No. 21 Troop where they 'lack condition, grooming and trimming up'.

There was also a development required in Ermelo that the inspector general felt could only have come from his discussion and observation on the ground: he told Fair that Native Police are wanted.

The range of his findings on the border trip ran from the general – and important policy development for the SAC – to the wishes of an individual: the inspector general found that 'It was not generally known even among officers that SAC had taken over Cattle Disease prevention since 1st October; and that I want all ranks to exert themselves to carry out the duty really well.' In the case of the individual it was to tell Fair that Trooper Paul wanted his discharge 'as soon as possible' in order to set up in business and that Paul had sent in his application form.

Among the difficulties in policing that border area with Swaziland was the quality of life for the men: the inspector general felt that if possible in these hot outstations they should be rotated every three months. He wrote, 'To keep good men we must make the life attractive as well as well paid.'

Then, turning to other topics which he has come on from Fair's submission of C Division's diary, he wrote 'Your diary (which by the way is now exactly what I wanted, gives me all information).' Fair had raised a question about the Controller's Department on a point that perplexed him – the IG told him that the object of that department was 'to equalise promotion' across the whole Corps. If it did not serve that purpose he would 'be inclined to cut off the Department to be managed Divisionally'.

The inspector general wrote up his report of his trip to the frontier, going over the day-to-day occurrences up until his meetings with Sir Arthur Lawley, Lieutenant-Governor of the Transvaal, and General Lyttelton at Pretoria. His conclusion for Milner was that their projected scheme for policing the area is the 'best applicable to the country and approved by all the local authorities'. Two caveats from Lawley who did not fully approve of paying detectives on the border for results – an inducement for 'got-up cases'. In General Lyttelton's opinion the War Office had not yet made a decision on Steinaecker's Horse. The inspector general's view was to leave part of the frontier to Steinaecker's Horse until the War Office decides on the unit's future. With his penchant for detail Baden-Powell totalled his day-to-day mileage and the method of covering it – over the seven days he and his colleagues had travelled 573 miles by rail; and 284 miles on horseback.

While relations between SAC and the populace were generally good there were hints of underlying resentment against the empire. In the ORC Pilkington regretted the delay in amalgamating the SAC and the Municipal Police. On 4 November the inspector general was in Bloemfontein and Pilkington told him that relations between the Municipal Police and the SAC were deteriorating – the Municipal Police in the outlying towns were out of direct supervision; and Pilkington felt that the sooner it was merged with SAC the better. However, it went beyond the level of police forces; and he cited a few examples. One instance that the inspector general flagged concerned resident magistrate Brand at Edenburg who openly told Major Walton that he disliked the SAC being in the country 'and would have nothing to do with them'. Pilkington had also heard that the wife of another Boer resident magistrate, Van Heerden, openly talked of the re-establishment of a Boer government. There were also instances of Repatriation officials dealing among each other with repatriation stock: 'a member of Council offered a £250 bribe to an SAC officer to get a sale of a farm to government arranged – and no notice so far taken of it.'[117]

When Colonel Fair told the inspector general there was an undercurrent of ill feeling among the Boers in his area, Baden-Powell's response was to tell him to try to get the names of the worst offenders and any evidence of their breathing sedition – though urging him to do it quietly in no hurry. However, the sense that sedition was brewing continued to come through to Colonel Fair. The inspector general urged him to have church councils attended by trustworthy burghers in plain clothes or 'by getting information by other means of what goes on'.

Discussions about restructuring the force were not premature: on 18 November instructions came from the secretary of state to reduce the establishment of the force to 6,000. SAC HQ had already reduced recruitment and the next step was to make purchasing discharge more readily available. The military secretary contacted Baden-Powell and confirmed that the SAC were to remain an imperial force under Milner and that the British South African Police (BSAP) would comprise another Division.

Two days later martial law was abolished and the police peace preservation act came into force. The ordinance gave an SAC officer the power to arrest without a warrant. However, Milner sent a memo to the inspector general asking that the power should only be used in extreme circumstances without authority from SAC HQ.

Baden-Powell reacted to insider information from No. 9 Troop in C Division. His informant, he told Colonel Fair, was Trooper Tragmar – a man who had come to the SAC 'with a special recommendation to me'. The information was that the Troop, or three-quarters of them, were a drunken crew and the captain who liked a good drink had been hopelessly drunk before the whole Troop twice recently. Trooper Tragmar had told the inspector general that he had no problem being in the Troop but thought it his duty to inform the inspector general who promised to keep his name out of it. In his letter to Fair the inspector general asked if he could investigate it quietly and suggested that Sergeant Franklin and Corporal Williams seemed to be the only two reliable NCOs to question on the tale. Baden-Powell apparently got a comprehensive report from Tragmar for he wrote 'The best men are buying their discharge, the worst are staying on.'

However, the report about No. 9 Troop may not have been accurate – indeed it may have been false. Baden-Powell, responding to later feedback from Fair who had followed up the information it contained, wrote again to him to say that he had set up a Board on the Troop so that they could get Tragmar 'to give evidence and then catch him out if he repeats what he told me. My sole evidence would not be sufficient to convict, and the information was given to me in confidence.'

The battles were over in the field, the commando raids were no more; but the victorious side was intent on dominating post-war life and future generations in the former republics. One of the main props of Milner's policy to dominate the Boers and their language in the long term was to control teaching in schools. Early on in the war he wrote to General Pretyman: 'My view is that any school relying upon aid from the State should not only teach English, but make English the medium of instruction in all but the elementary classes.'[118] In B Division in South Pretoria burghers were kicking against the pricks – Boers intending to oppose English schools for their children, 'and are intending to get Hollander teachers,' reported Sam Steele.

Schooling, regardless of language was a problem for people in some areas – Sam Steele refers to it specifically writing that Captain Currie thought that a school was much needed in Haenertsburg and that the people could not afford to pay for a boarding school. Currie thought that was the only practicable solution because of the large distances involved. Steele took the matter up, he felt that in a case like that boarding schooling should be provided free; and he sent a report to the Board of Education. Currie also felt that a doctor should be located in the area: the nearest was at Pietersburg 40 miles away. Again Steele took up the case and sent a complaint to the Board of Health.

However, in C Division there was a tremor that could shake the foundations of the empire: Colonel Fair reported that on 16 November an English clergyman in Heidelberg 'preached a diatribe' both against the government and against whites generally in their treatment of blacks, 'who should have equal rights and should be called mister'. In Baden-Powell's reporting it in the staff diary he coined the term 'Preachery' for it. The sequel to the sermon was the inspector general telling Fair: 'The parson has been reported for his folly.'

Colonel Lambton, military secretary, was spokesman for the hierarchy above the SAC; and on 19 November Baden-Powell saw him and he told the inspector general – not surprisingly – that Milner was going to make a tour of the ORC but did not require the inspector general on the tour. The inspector general suggested to the military secretary that His Excellency take Colonel Pilkington along so that he might hear some points about the Municipal Police and the local officials.[119]

In contrast to the presence of the SAC causing friction in the ORC in the northern Transvaal there was some evidence of a positive relationship between the SAC and the burghers. Sam Steele reported that 'there were good reports of men in outposts.'

> Prominent Boers who remember the disjointed state of other African Colonies after native wars say that our force has done more in six months than the Cape and other police did in five years towards the resettlement of the country and that our men are much better behaved than those of the other police or Constabulary Corps. Mr Trollope is one in particular, who with an English name is one of a large family of Boers and is a member of the Board of Health at Bogsburg and in other local boards, is one of those who spoke so highly of the SAC.[120]

However, for a divisional commander like Sam Steele there were frustrations with the law as it stood – there was a need to rewrite what Steele called the Brand Law:

> As it stands now we cannot even arrest a man who is in possession of cattle with another man's brand on it. The laws are ridiculous and it is to be hoped that we will soon have some on British lines.[121]

This was a topic he was to return to; he felt it was a frustration that could incite a crime:

> There is every day evidence that the law for brands should be passed and I venture to say that if it is not done soon there will be serious trouble, even murder if one can call it murder to shoot a cattle thief. I know from the best of authority that a large number of men who were serving in irregular Corps during the war are little better than highwaymen, even their officers were picked up on the veldt never having been selected at

home or in the Colonies. These officers are what we would call cattle rustlers.[122]

Steele was also in favour of streamlining the SAC's system when it came to working certain cases. Where a case had a cross-divisional connection he suggested putting in General Orders that the OC Division initiating the case have authority to liaise with the district commandant in the other Division.

A setback to SAC HQ was Nicholson, chief staff officer going off sick. It was not just a case of being under the weather for a few days: in a letter to McLaren in London Baden-Powell wrote, 'Poor Nick who is going home sick – overworked in the office I fear. But I hope that the change will quickly set him up.' However, Nicholson's condition deteriorated and by early November Baden-Powell was writing to 'Dear Boy' that 'Nick still too sick (with an open abscess) to start for home yet.' Then Baden-Powell added a last sentence, 'We are clearing out loads of our "wasters" now – mostly Canadians.'

However, the policy was not limited to nationality – a month later Baden-Powell was writing again to McLaren:

> We are dismissing all men unlikely to make good policemen and all undesirable characters. Consequently great howls in the press from those who are chucked out – but it does us good as it shows the public we are not tolerating any bad men. We are also passing a fair number into the SAC Reserve and a good number are purchasing their discharge.[123]

The buying-out process was straightforward according to the paperwork of the author's grandfather. Trooper Gray applied from Schweitzer-Reneke on 16 December to the officer commanding No. 9 Troop A Division:

> I have the honour to submit this my application for discharge by purchase from the South African Constabulary.
>
> The reason for my wishing to take my discharge is I have been promised employment at my trade, tailor, in England.
>
> Would you kindly recommend me for my discharge when forwarding this to Headquarters.

Two months later, 12 February 1903, the next step was a medical form stating that Gray had had no hospital admissions and was 'sound on discharge'; and the last step a single sheet of paper with 'Particulars of Discharge' confirming it was by purchase; rank 3/class trooper; character exemplary; length of service 1 year 323 days. It was signed at Potchefstroom on 16 February.

Where arrests were made instructions came from SAC HQ on the manner in which these should be carried out; Lieutenant Colonel R.S. Curtis, Chief Staff Officer in the absence of Nicholson on sick leave, sent the draft of 'Circular Memo No. 17'[124] to the Law Department of the Transvaal for opinion and observations. The section that covers 'Arrest' shows the methods of working that were to be followed.

> Unnecessary violence should be studiously avoided, as much because it will probably entail legal consequences, as provoke resistance. Care should be taken to make the arrest quietly, without attracting attention or inflicting any needless exposure on the prisoner.

As a follow-on to simplifying procedures Sam Steele wrote in his diary that he had given orders that the district commandant keep in touch with the Public Prosecutor from an early stage in order to prevent the frequent scenario of that official being brought in at a later stage and requesting detectives. Steele's view was that 'The whole of the police work should be done by the officers of the District and only in a case of emergency should he ask for detectives.'[125]

Another enterprising incident also took place in B Division; and here Baden-Powell appears to quote directly from Sam Steele's words using North American expressions: 'Lt Montgomery in the Lydenburg district "tracked up" a party of horse thieves and captured them complete outfit.'

The same day that Baden-Powell transcribed those words in the staff diary, he also wrote, 'Col Steele considers that neither the officers nor men of the Canadian Contingents are fair representatives of Canadians.'

Canada and family values had entered Sam Steele's life afresh when on 22 November his wife and family came out to the Transvaal to be with him. It had been over a year since they had been together.

However, Steele's assessment of the Canadian contingent may have rung a bell with Baden-Powell about the correspondence they had a year earlier for he followed it up a few weeks later when he was surveying the results of C Division's work along the Mozambique border. The border was notorious for smuggling; and yet in one area, Baden-Powell observed, he hadn't heard word of 'any captures of smugglers'. Whereas, in the Natal section of the border with that country smugglers were being apprehended; and he wrote to Colonel Fair, commanding C Division, 'Does Fall go about his district at all? And are there any trained police NCOs and men there besides Whelan?' This was Captain Fall's district – and it will be recalled he had a key role in recruiting the Canadian contingent. Baden-Powell continued in his letter to Colonel Fair, 'I begin to think Steele was right in declining to have Fall in B Division. I have no real case against him but straws and grains of dust tell which way the wind blows.'

Following the wind's direction Baden-Powell made more enquiries and came back to Colonel Fair some days later. He said that he had no definite information

> except every now and then rumours of smuggling . . . and only today I have received a kind of confirmation of my suspicions in a report (from Steele) who says that rumours have reached him of slacking on the part of Fall, especially as regards patrols in his district which go out 'in bunches' along the roads and back, and make parade to record so many miles done.

Baden-Powell also went on to say that Steele's servant is a sort of secretary who could get information that would be difficult to get otherwise.

The rumour mill turned out more – SAC men getting drunk in the town, involvement with African prostitutes. Steele would not reveal his source, but his informant also said 'Fall is such a fool he lets the resident magistrate deal with crime on the part of SAC men; he knows nothing of discipline or of anything else.' In response to all this Baden-Powell suggested to Fair that a plain-clothes agent could be brought into the area.

That would probably take a little while to come to a conclusion; and the day-to-day work of the SAC became ever more involved with the population. Structures were in place to oversee a range of social needs; and on 12 December the inspector general travelled to B Division to see Colonel Steele. He told Steele that he had recommended him as a member of the Council – he simply put it at that, nothing more specific – and Sam Steele was honoured but felt it should be the inspector general who should hold the position; 'his rank and reputation having more weight on matters of Constabulary . . .'[126]

While the Mozambique area in C Division's area was being closely monitored for a time the inspector general had other concerns. Nicholson, his chief staff officer, was on sick leave in the UK; Edwards, CO A Division, had been appointed assistant adjutant-general for volunteers in the Transvaal; Major Twyman, of A Division had resigned; and a 'good number' of men were purchasing their discharge.

In addition to discharge by purchase Baden-Powell wrote to the convalescing Nicholson – in his characteristic address to him, 'Dear Nick' – that they were 'chucking out wasters and undesirables at a great pace'. Then later he sent him an update:

> The papers are full of complaints from those whom we have chucked, but these are so obviously rotten that nobody takes much notice of them. In fact I should hope they will see that it means we are serving the people well by not allowing any wasters in the Corps.

Over the previous few months he had been alluding to the dichotomy that existed between the strictures required of recruits by the attestation of fitness forms and an element within the force that had become more apparent since the end of the war and was an embarrassment to the reputation of the SAC.

In a paragraph in his six-monthly report he refers to it and the reason: 'A certain proportion of unsuitable men were enlisted for us, chiefly through Army agencies, during the war, but the weeding out of these has now been almost completed.'

However, on 14 December his main news to Nicholson was that Secretary of State Chamberlain and his wife were coming out to South Africa: 'My Dear Nick, It's quite a calamity Chamberlain coming and you being at home – because you could have told him a great lot. But I'm very glad he's coming.'

However, there was more than the news of Chamberlain's forthcoming visit in the letter: Baden-Powell reported on the outcome of Milner's visit to the ORC – the one he was told he was not required for:

> HE has been away on a long trip through the ORC and is due back tomorrow. I had Pilkington go with him and I gather from Lambton that HE is favourably impressed with some SAC ideas and opposed to those of the government offices at Bloemfontein.[127]

This letter to Nicholson and his next one, written a week later, give some insight too into the way top management colleagues of the SAC interacted.

> So A Division is rather in need of HQ staff. Edwards wants Madoc put in but I'm not over confident about him. We are a little badly off all round for a Divisional Commandant.

> Scriven has not been too careful in his correspondence lately; Wilberforce would set the officers by the ears.

> Godley from Aldershot wanted lately to come to us; but I think with the reduced numbers one of our own majors should suffice to succeed to command. Castello has all the administrative ability but I don't know about his soldiering smartness.[128]

One week later on 21 December Baden-Powell wrote to Nick again following up the news about A Division. He went over again the shortcoming of Wilberforce (his unpopularity with officers) though conceding that 'he is much improved in that respect.' He also gave Milner's thoughts – relayed by military secretary Lambton – on a successor to Edwards: Madoc came to Milner's mind at once. Baden-Powell reflected on that and reconsidered Madoc: he had been doing 'very good police work'; he had the ability to get 'good stable management and military smartness in the Troops in his District and he has the confidence of all the officers'; and the inspector general ranged further: Madoc

> understands the natives and has established good relations with the RMs and civilians in A Division, so I believe he will be all right there. At any rate I propose only to put him in on probation for a few months trial to begin with.

Meanwhile it was necessary to have the SAC alerted to Chamberlain's itinerary; the inspector general wrote to Colonel Fair to make security arrangements for the Secretary of State's travel by rail to one of his scheduled stopping places – Heidelberg. Fine detail had to be considered as well – he suggested that Fair could have some of his Nursing Sisters meet Mrs Chamberlain; but he came back to the security issue: 'You will of course to have a guard on the train wherever it pulls up for the night, and I should suggest supply them with bullseye lanterns as small search lights.'

When it came to B Division's turn to be responsible for the Secretary of State for the Colonies Sam Steele concluded that the SAC escort for him on 5 January worked very well 'and excited favourable remarks.' It was an instance too where the SAC detectives and the town police had to work together and on this occasion it proved a success.

The SAC was already well on the way to fulfilling its task for its time; and Baden-Powell, looking forward to the return of his chief of staff had written, 'And then I shall have a try for the leave I've been wanting for years past.'

However, it was not to be. Chamberlain's visit to South Africa was the time to deliver the coup de grace on the SAC's inspector general; and it came in the best British tradition – the War Office sent Baden-Powell an invitation to accept the post of inspector general of cavalry. It would seem that he did not jump at the chance – he asked Milner for advice; and Milner urged him to accept.

It was unusual for a secretary of state to visit a newly acquired colony and Chamberlain's visit was regarded as a success. He toured the country quite widely; and he and his wife stayed with Milner for a spell. In his discussions with Milner the future of the SAC was one of the topics.

Later, Chamberlain, on his return to the UK addressed the House of Commons and part of his speech was concerned with the role of the SAC:

> I attach the utmost importance to the South African Constabulary, to the new Force as a great civilising and uniting influence. (Hear, hear) It may have been regarded in the past exclusively from its military capacity, and indeed during the war it distinguished itself under military command, and some of the most gallant little actions of the war conferred the greatest credit on the Force.

> When I had the opportunity of addressing them, I impressed on the men that this part of their work was over, and that we expected from them in peace greater services even than those which they had rendered in war. We regard them not as a garrison but as the protectors and friends of the people: and if the House will only consider the circumstances under which the Administration has been conducted in those immense spaces they will see what it is I mean. How can you bring a Central Government

into anything like personal touch with isolated farmers hundreds of miles away across the trackless veldt: the thing is impossible. Their complaints, if they have any, their grievances, if they exist, can never come under ordinary circumstances to the knowledge of the authorities. There is no close sympathy therefore between the Government and the individual members of the community whom it has to control. The South African Constabulary has already made its position. Again and again I found by entering into conversation with the men, and with the farmers also, that the former, learning the language of the country, were becoming the friends of the people, were welcomed at every farmhouse, were doing little jobs for the inhabitants, carrying their letters and parcels, giving information, and settling petty disputes. So much was that the case, that I have had a serious complaint from one Resident Magistrate that his duty has become almost a sinecure, in consequence of a sergeant in the South African Constabulary, who in settling all the difficulties without bringing them to him (Laughter) I can sympathise with the Resident Magistrate, but I am bound to say that I cannot help expressing my entire approval of the actions of the sergeant of the Constabulary.[129]

Baden-Powell did his round of farewell inspections of Divisions – on 10 February he went by train to B Division and met Sam Steele who wrote in his diary: 'IG came today at 9.30 to inspect the Depot and bid farewell to B Division. All very sorry to part with General who has been very kind and considerate if firm. He went away by 2.30 train.'[130]

A few days later Milner's formal letter on Baden-Powell's services was composed. Written in the third person the voice spoke through the persona of His Excellency.

The High Commissioner desires to place on record his sense of the invaluable services rendered by Major-General Baden-Powell in the office of Inspector General of the S. A. Constabulary, from which he is just retiring.

While congratulating General Baden-Powell to his appointment to a high post in the British Army, Lord Milner regrets the loss which the SAC and the two colonies suffer by his retirement.

The first Inspector General has created in the SAC in the space of little more than two years a splendid force which already ranks high among the military and police forces of the Empire.

His great previous achievements gave to that body from the outset a prestige which has since been firmly established by the good work the SAC have done during the past two years, both in the field and in the discharge of the more peaceful duties now incumbent upon them.

General Baden-Powell's untiring energy and devotion to duty, the interest he has taken in the welfare of his men, and the high standard which he has set them have been of inestimable value and will remain an inspiring influence after his departure.

The civil authorities, with whom General Baden-Powell has co-operated, will also remember with gratitude his readiness to help in every difficulty, and his genuine interest in the welfare and progress of the country. He leaves with the good-will and best wishes of all who have served with him and under him, and who will watch his future career with a sympathy and confidence due to their intimate knowledge of his great services in South Africa.

In reply to Milner's letter Baden-Powell wrote a gracious acknowledgement that began,

I cannot tell you how much I prize and value these expressions of your approval; and they form a reward for such troubles as I may have experienced during the past three years . . . In the early days of the South African Constabulary we had difficulties, when all the promises of assistance from the army fell to the ground, and we were practically left to work out our own salvation as best we could . . . And when at times the difficulties made one think it useless to try to go on, it was your steadfastness of purpose at the helm – under stress of far greater difficulties – that made one ashamed of one's weakness and inspired one to further effort . . . I shall always remember with gratitude the courtesy, patience, and helpful encouragement which you have invariably accorded to us, and which were really the keystone of our progress . . .

In 1900 when Milner first mooted with Commander-in-Chief Roberts the need for such a force he thought that it 'would not be beneath the dignity of a Major General at any rate to create'; and in a sense it was quite fitting for Baden-Powell to move on when he did – the SAC would have to meld or become a different entity when self-government came to the two colonies. Baden-Powell was to be replaced as inspector general by Colonel Nicholson, who, in turn would be succeeded by Colonel Curtis, in 1905, and Colonel Sam Steele would leave in 1905; and the SAC, in a changed political climate, would be disbanded in 1908.

Baden-Powell had formed the force, given it a unique structure and ethos; but after two and a half years it did not require his contribution any longer.

Part IV

Chapter Nine

Lodestar for the Scouts

In his farewell memorandum to all officers, nursing sisters, NCOs and men of the SAC on 15 February 1903 Baden-Powell acknowledged that he was leaving with the greatest of regret. He made the following observations:

> In all classes of society we find too little patriotism and unselfishness, and too much looking after 'No. 1' and inclination to 'grouse' when things go a little wrong. A man thinks more of getting a good billet for himself and of sitting down to enjoy it than of carrying out his ordinary every day work to the best of his ability for the good of the whole, and of helping his fellow-men whenever he can.

He finished the memorandum with these guidelines:

A. Keep improving yourself in efficiency and smartness in performance of your duties.
B. Avoid doing anything low or underhand or such as might lessen your personal respect for yourself.
C. Be guided by what you know to be your duty rather than by what is easiest or most pleasant to yourself.
D. Carry out your orders or tackle difficulties when they arise with willingness and cheerily.
E. Conceal nothing from your superior officers, and be loyal to them and to the corps.
F. Be helpful and courteous to all.

Then he left the SAC – but the SAC did not leave him: and five years later some explicit values and underpinning aims he had given it he gave afresh to a younger generation when, in 1908, he published *Scouting for Boys: A Handbook for Instruction in Good Citizenship*; it contained the Scout Law.[131]

1. A scout's honour is to be trusted.
2. A scout is loyal.
3. A scout's duty is to be useful and helpful to others.
4. A scout is a friend to all and a brother to every other scout no matter to what social class the other belongs.
5. A scout is courteous.
6. A scout is a friend to animals.
7. A scout obeys orders.
8. A scout smiles and whistles.
9. A scout is thrifty.

Thirty years after *Scouting for Boys* appeared Winston Churchill referred to the movement it inspired in his collection of essays *Great Contemporaries*. Churchill, at the time, was in the political wilderness for his views on the Nazi threat to Europe. Each of his essays is titled with the man's name – one of them, however, is simply entitled 'B-P'.

In his essay Churchill alludes to how fortunate it was that Baden-Powell had the chance to break the military mould when he became inspector general of the SAC and was able to rise to the challenge it presented. Churchill wrote,

The caprices of fortune are incalculable, her methods inscrutable. Sometimes when she scowls most spitefully, she is preparing her most dazzling gifts. How lucky for B-P that he was not in the early years of the century taken into the central swim of military affairs, and absorbed in all those arduous and secret preparations which ultimately enabled the British Expeditionary Army to deploy for battle at Mons!

How lucky for him and how lucky for us all! To this he owes his perennially revivifying fame, his opportunity for high personal service of the most enduring character; and to this we owe an institution and an inspiration, characteristic of the essence of British genius, and uniting in a bond of comradeship the youth not only of the English-speaking world, but of almost every land and people under the sun.

This institution and inspiration, he went on, 'appealed to all the sense of adventure and love of open-air life which is so strong in youth'. Churchill outlined the values it evoked; then he went on: 'Success was immediate and far-reaching. The simple uniform, khaki shorts and a shirt – within the reach of the poorest – was founded upon General Baden-Powell's old corps, the South African Constabulary.'[132]

More than uniform and motto came from the SAC to the Scout Movement. In his 'Notes and Instructions for the SAC' (see in the Appendix) Baden-Powell had written: 'Now, the following are not laid down in any regulation beyond the unwritten code of honour which I shall expect will guide the actions of every officer, NCO and man of the Constabulary.'[133]

Years later, writing in the American magazine *Boys' Life*, Baden-Powell came back to the ethos he had wanted for the SAC. The sense of discipline was to depend on a man's honour, 'from desire to do the right and not from fear of punishment'. The men were divided up into 'patrols' of six under a senior constable, and were posted in different parts of the country. They were taught to be on the lookout to render good turns on every possible occasion. They were taught of course to fend for themselves by being able to rig up shelters, to build their own police barracks, to cook their own grub, to find their way by day or night across country, and to care for their horses as well as themselves in sickness or health.[134]

There are two photos in this book showing SAC officers preparing 'their own grub' out in the veldt, examples of what Baden-Powell instructed in 'Notes and Instructions for the SAC' – 'When this kind of work is in hand I do not like to see Officers and N.C.O.s with their coats on, merely looking on and superintending. Their business here, as elsewhere, is to lead the way.'

The success of the Scout movement that Churchill described as 'immediate and far reaching' crossed the Atlantic and rapidly caught on in Canada. It is thought that in 1908 Scouts were established in the province of Manitoba; and within two years of the appearance of *Scouting for Boys* Colonel Sam Steele formerly commander of B Division SAC was Scout Commissioner of the province of Manitoba.[135] He and Baden-Powell had kept in touch; and in early 1911 Baden-Powell replied to a recent letter from him:

BOY SCOUTS HEADQUARTERS

116 Victoria Street
Westminster
London S. W.

January 11th 1911

My dear Steele

Thank you so much for your letter which I was delighted to get and I am very pleased to hear of the progress which is being made in the organising of the Boy Scouts in your Province. I have been having similar news from other Canadian centres as well and all seems to be going most satisfactorily there.

I was much amused at Seton Thompson's definition of the Boy Scout movement. I think he is a little bit cracked, for beyond having met him for half-an-hour in London once I have had nothing to do with him, except that I quoted some of his games (with acknowledgements) in the book 'Scouting for Boys'; but I do not think it is worth writing to contradict his statement.

I am so glad that Godley pleased you. He wrote to me most gratefully as regards all you did for him during his short stay in Winnipeg. It was awfully good of you to take so much trouble and he is a man who would thoroughly appreciate it.

I have just returned from Russia where the Scouts are also being organised in the direct interest of the Czar himself who invited me to a long and interesting interview on the subject. In Moscow there were 3000 Scouts. The whole country there was very much like Canada both in appearance and in its Winter climate.

With many thanks for your kind messages to my Mother and Sister who are both very well and flourishing,
Believe me, with kindest regards,

Yours very sincerely,

Robert Baden-Powell [136]

The reference to Godley visiting Canada is another link to SAC days – Godley had been in the frame when Baden-Powell was making up his list of potential divisional commanders.

From North America to Czarist Russia the Scout Movement developed within two years; and by a further year it came full cycle when a Scout troop was established at Modderfontein where the SAC's HQ was first established in the dynamite factory in Zuurfontein. The Scouts used some of the factory's buildings. Mr J.E. Coetzee was AECI Explosives and Chemicals Ltd's Production Director in September 1987 and he wrote to the Modderfontein Scout Group Committee enclosing a paper researched by Karl Köhler, who was responsible for looking after the factory's museum, enclosing a copy of the research.

Karl Köhler, with access to the company's records in its museum, researched those early years and he found that in the SAC's time,

> A rigorous training programme was instituted, which made full use of the buffer zones around the factory for training in horsemanship.

> Target practice and .303 inch musketry training was conducted at the old Boer 'Shooting Range Farm' just south-east of the Johannesburg gate.

He went further and found that the railway coach that Baden-Powell used on SAC divisional inspections had earlier been the Transvaal State Secretary's and was used by Dr Leyds and General Jan Smuts. Baden-Powell, however, getting the loan of 'a shell of a coach' and a locomotive, had not referred to the coach's history. In due course, though, it and the locomotive had to be returned to the dynamite factory. For some years after it was used to transport employees of the factory between Modderfontein and Kempton Park Station. Later its wheels were removed and it became a showpiece exhibit in the factory's domain.

Karl Köhler writes:

> Modderfontein has always been a keen centre of Scouting activity and can trace its history back to 1911 . . . At first the Scouts met in various company buildings, which included the upstairs hay-loft of the manager's riding horse stables . . . and the Church Hall at the corner of Main Street and Nobel Avenue.[137]

After the First World War Gilwell Park in England became a Scout training area; and the following year in South Africa two Scouters, one of whom had gone through a course at Gilwell, came across the former government mine training school that was dilapidated at Florida Lake, Roodepoort in the Gauteng. Scouting myth has it that they declared there and then it would be the Gilwell for the Transvaal – and that is what it became.

It made a difference to Scouting in South Africa; and Baden-Powell, in a document he called 'Scouting a Definite Help to Education', wrote:

> My recent visits to Scouts in different counties in England and in South Africa and in Sweden have made me realise that a big difference has been made in the past few years, mainly due to the teachings emanating from Gilwell.

> All over the country Scouting seems to have got on to a definite standard with a good grasp of the ideals and the proper methods for carrying them into practice, so that in the United Kingdom Camp Chiefs and Woodbadgers may congratulate themselves that the results of their work will now have a national value.

> So it is in South Africa. The Gilwell training has spread over there at the hands of the few men who have been able to get the training at first hand, and they have passed it on to their brother Scouters at the Training Camps which have since been established over there.[138]

The first South African Scout Jamboree was held in East London in 1936; and C.J. Knapman, who was Contingent Leader for the Rhodesians, wrote an account of the highlights of the great event. He tells us that the only foreign contingent was from Portuguese East Africa – Mozambique. As a compliment to them they led the march past. There were about 3,400 Scouts in that march. Baden-Powell was there – his 'address was delivered in a strong, firm voice, and the yell of welcome he received and the subsequent burst of cheering was broadcast throughout the Empire by the BBC'.[139]

As for the dynamite factory's coach, in 1959, half a century after it was used to take the SAC inspector general on inspection duty, the factory manager, 'who was also a keen Scout', got the permission of his board of directors to donate the coach to the Scouts. There is a photograph in the book of the coach, without wheels, being taken to Gilwell Scout Centre. A restoration process got underway; but after a while it tailed off. Later though, a warden of the centre began a fund-raising scheme that enabled the Scouts to restore it. 'Today it is the centre of attraction there and highly regarded.'[140] It has a brass plaque that tells the visitor its provenance both with officials of the South African Republic and the Inspector General of the South African Constabulary.

The motto of the SAC 'Be Prepared' perhaps came from the men of the corps but Baden-Powell gave it anew to the Scouts; and when Winston Churchill wrote his essay 'B-P' he gave 'Be Prepared' special mention: 'It speaks to every heart its message of duty and honour: "Be Prepared" to stand up faithfully for Right and Truth, however the winds may blow.'[141]

That original SAC motto in the Scout Movement still speaks today and vast numbers of young people across the globe hear its call.

Notes and Instructions for the South African Constabulary

Excerpt

Work

I should like to point out to everybody, both officers and men, that service in the SAC is very different from that in the Army. You get, here, three or four times the pay of the Army and a great deal more work is expected of you. You will get here less of drill and of useless work than the soldier, but you will get more of responsible duties and of useful work than they do; for this reason you receive additional pay.

I expect you to be 'Handy Men' – ready to turn your hand to any kind of job and to be at work all day and all night, if required – though on the other hand, you may be sure that no work will be given you that is not necessary. I have purposely made two days in the week, as far as can be managed, slack days, in order to give you a rest.

Discipline

In a force such as this the highest discipline and 'tone' are absolutely necessary. These are to be got, not so much by heavy punishments for misconduct, as by employing a high class of men who see the necessity and carry out the discipline for themselves. If all parts of the engine do not work exactly in their places the machine will not go. You must remember that as regards discipline every order from a superior must be at once obeyed without hesitation; and even if it should appear distasteful and unreasonable it must be obeyed at once and no objection may be made until after the order has been carried out. The Officer or NCO who gives the order and not you who execute is responsible for its effects; and you obey the badges of rank rather than the individual who wears them. If necessary protest may afterwards be made in the proper manner to the officer commanding the troop.

Complaints

I shall always be glad to listen to any reasonable representation or suggestion so made, with a view of absolute justice and good feeling being maintained right through the corps, but frivolous complaints or airing of grievances and grousing without bringing the complaint to the notice of the troop officer do not remedy the evil and only lead to further grumbling; for these reasons they will not be allowed and will be treated as acts of insubordination.

Anonymous complaints do no good, and the silly system of airing grievances in the press only brings discredit on the members of the force generally, and is liable to severest punishment.

It is to the advantage of the officers as well as of all the men that any grievance there may be should be set right, and therefore men need have no fear about bringing it to notice – in a proper manner.

With the class of men who will form the Constabulary, I do not anticipate that there will be any appreciable amount of military crime in the corps. Slight dereliction of duty will be met with fines; serious crimes, such as drunkenness, insubordination, etc., by imprisonment followed by expulsion from the force; greater breaches of discipline, such as serious insubordination, acceptance of bribes (however small), making away with government stores, etc., will be dealt with by court martial and the heaviest penalties inflicted, involving penal servitude, etc., followed of course by dismissal from the SAC.

The maintenance of the good name of the corps rests largely in the hands of the NCOs and men themselves. By making themselves and the corps respected throughout the Colony not only will their work bring about successful results easily, but civilian employers will the more willingly seek in the Constabulary for men of reliability for filling important situations in civil life.

So it is in the interest, as well as the duty, of each man to use his influence to keep his comrade up to the mark when he sees a chance of his lowering the good name of the force.

Obedience to Orders

It is often the case that orders are apparently neglected or disobeyed when, in reality, they have not been fully understood.

It is therefore the duty of every officer or NCO in giving an order to be most careful in its wording so that there can be no mistake. First of all, you must know yourself exactly what you want the man to do, and then give him instructions that can admit of no misunderstanding. Only give them in a nice way – not in a bullying or inconsistent manner. These are the secrets of getting your wishes satisfactorily carried out.

In investigating cases of disobedience or neglect of orders, officers should be careful to satisfy themselves that the officer responsible for the order gave it properly.

It also largely helps, when dealing with an intelligent class of men like ours, to explain the reason and object of an order, and they will probably carry it out all the more completely.

At the same time, subordinates on receiving an order must not merely listen to it, or read it roughly through, but you must see that you thoroughly understand it and then keep it in your mind. If you do not understand it, say so at once and get it more fully explained. It is better to risk being thought a little stupid than to be damned for a genuine fool afterwards.

It is no excuse for anyone, officer or man, to say that he did not know of an order on such or such a point. You must find for yourself what orders, if any, have been issued and in the absence of any, you must act for the best. If then you make a mistake, it will be condoned provided you had a reason. Napoleon truly said 'a man who never made a mistake, never made anything.'

Powers of Commanding Officers

Details of Crimes and Punishments are to be found in the proclamation above quoted, copies of which are to be kept in all headquarter offices. The powers of commanding officers are briefly: to carry out all regulations issued by the Inspector General relating to enlistment, discipline, training, arms and accoutrements, clothing and equipment of the force; and in the event of the contravention of any such regulations by a member of the force, to impose fines, imprison, with or without hard labour, suspend, degrade, dismiss from the corps and reduce in rank to the extent laid down in Proclamation No. 24 of the 22nd October 1900. A more complete outline of the 'Powers of Officers' is given in standing orders under 'Crimes and Punishments'.

The above remarks are merely printed for guidance, not as threats; for as I have before stated, I hope, with the class of men whom we shall have in the corps, the amount of crime will be very small indeed.

Now the following are not laid down in any regulations beyond the unwritten code of honour, which I expect will guide the actions of every officer, non-commissioned officer and man of the Constabulary.

I appeal to the British spirit already ingrained in you of 'playing the game', that is of doing your duty just as thoroughly when you are away from the eye of authority as when under it – not from fear of punishment for neglect to do it, but simply because it is 'the game' and is expected of you as a man of honour.

Recruited from every portion of the empire, ours is the first truly *Imperial* corps and once imbued with this spirit, it is going to be the finest corps in the world.

It takes the place of a force of police who were perhaps the most corrupt and contemptible that could be found.

Duties of Constabulary

While our duties, especially at first, will to a large extent, be military, we must not forget that in peacetime or in pacified districts, they will be those of police, which require both tact and courtesy to all.

We must therefore always do our best to assist both the Military Forces on the one hand, and the neighbouring Police Forces on the other, to help them in every way we can, and to pull together with them under all circumstances.

Our special work in disturbed districts is to hold securely certain points and to keep a watch on the inhabitants and report to Military authorities all hostile moves and gatherings, and to afford protection to the peacefully disposed.

In addition to these outside duties you will be expected to be ready to turn your hand to every kind of work that may be found necessary for promoting the comfort and efficiency of the corps: that is, you may be required to build defensive works, huts, or stables, latrines, or repair the same, erect telegraphs, lay mines, water courses, move baggage, or stores, etc., etc.

[N.B. – When this kind of work is in hand I do not like to see Officers and N.C.O.s with their coats on, merely looking on and superintending. Their business here, as elsewhere, is to lead the way.]

Our ultimate duties will be to maintain law and order in the country districts, to stop traffic in arms, and unlawful assemblages, to check cattle and other thefts, and to assist in the suppression of cattle diseases, to carry out inspection of licences, permits and natives' passes, to arrest criminals and investigate crimes etc. For these duties special instructions will be issued from time to time.

In the meantime, working from central stations, you will be acting in small patrols of two or three men throughout the country, and your conduct as individuals will be watched and criticised by the inhabitants, and from it they will draw their own impressions of what is the true character of the Force, and of the British Government as well; when they see that bribery and cajoling are of no avail with you, and that your actions are guided strictly by a strict sense of duty and of justice, they will gain a deep and lasting respect for you and for the government you represent. A real, instead of a surface pacification of the country will then result. Therefore each individual man of the Force, as well as every officer, has a really important responsibility before him.

You will often have to act without the immediate guidance of superiors, and you will have to think for yourselves; in all cases of doubt or of temptation to slackness, you must obey what you know to be your duty, and not merely what is easiest or most convenient, and I shall trust you, as men of honour, to do this.

You will have the satisfaction of knowing that in doing your duty thoroughly and honestly, you are not only establishing the good name of the corps, but you are taking a really important part individually in building up this new addition to the Empire.

Duties of Officers and NCOs

The Duties of Officer Commanding Division are, briefly: to administer the district and command the constabulary in his division. He will be responsible to the Inspector General for the efficiency of all ranks in every department, and that such efficiency is maintained.

O.C. Division

He will judge of his officers by results, and will classify them accordingly for promotion or appointments.

District Commandant

The duties of District Commandant include those of Civil Commissioner. He will be responsible for the

1. Civil Administration of his District.
2. Employment and duties of the Constabulary under his command.
3. He will exercise a thorough supervision to ensure the efficiency of Constabulary units under his orders.

Troop Commander

The duties of the officer commanding a Sub-District are to maintain his Constabulary in the highest state of efficiency, and have the inhabitants of his Sub-District well in hand, and generally to carry out the orders of the District Commandant. He is absolutely responsible for the health, training and efficiency of his men, horses, transport, etc., and for every detail of supply, equipment, and pay of his command.

Troop Officer

The duties of the Subaltern Officer of the troop are to command the headquarters of the troop, and to act as Adjutant and Quartermaster to the officer commanding the troop (Sub-District). He is responsible to the O.C. Troop for the discipline and efficiency of the men, the condition of the horses etc., at the Headquarters.

Medical Officers

The senior medical officer of division will, in addition to the management of the Divisional Headquarters Hospital, have charge of Hospital arrangements and sanitation in the division. He will personally inspect and ensure that arrangements for treatment of sick and wounded at Divisional and Sub-District Headquarters are in all respects sufficient and effective, and that the sanitation of barracks and stations is thoroughly good. He will render a report on these points monthly. He will prepare an estimate annually of medical stores and expenditures required for his Division, and will be responsible for their custody and issue. The junior medical officers will, in addition to their routine hospital duties, assist the S.M.O. in the above duties to their fullest ability.

Medical officers will be held responsible for the best economy being used in the expenditure of drugs, medical comforts, etc.

Medical officers will be required to attend the families of officers, NCOs and men of the force.

Veterinary Officers

The senior Veterinary Officer, in addition to being adviser to the O.C. Division on all measures regarding Stock diseases etc., will have the management of the sick lines at Divisional Headquarters, will also have charge of all sick lines, farriers' shops etc., in the division. He will be responsible for the training of Cattle Inspectors, Farriers, and of Officers and Troopers for promotion.

Superintendents

Duties of the Superintendents are to effect important arrests, to conduct criminal cases, to examine cattle for the detection of disease, carry out protective measures for prevention of disease and police efficiency of the troop.

NCOs

The duty of an NCO in charge of squad, for which he will be held responsible to his Troop Officer, is that his men carry out every detail of routine and duty thoroughly, both in quarters and in the field; that they are properly fed and housed; that horses are well cared for; that the arms, equipment, saddles, etc., are well kept and complete; that every precaution is taken to prevent surprise by rebels etc., and that all orders issued are known to every man in his squad.

Note

Theses instructions are purposely nothing more than indications of the duties of each grade of officer. I shall observe for myself the individual intelligence and energy displayed by the several Officers, Warrant Officers and NCOs in elaborating and carrying their particular share into effect. Officers will accordingly frame and issue their own orders on the above lines, avoiding as far as possible a too rigid or confusing code of regulations. Give your subordinates each his job, allowing him plenty of initiative, and hold him fully responsible for its performance.

Want of energy or efficiency among the men is generally strong evidence of similar defects existing on the part of the officers responsible, and I shall be guided accordingly in forming my opinion of the individual Officers.

Notes

Chapter One

1. A. Wessels, (ed.) *Lord Roberts and the War in South Africa 1899-1902* (Stroud, Sutton Publishing, 2000), p.107.
2. C. Headlam, (ed.) *The Milner Papers: South Africa 1899-1905*, Vol. II (London: Cassell & Co. Ltd, 1933), p.163.
3. Australian War Memorial, www.awm.gov.au.
4. D. Reitz, *Commando: A Boer Journal of the Boer War* (CruGuru, 2008), p.79.
5. Baden-Powell, *Lessons from the 'Varsity of Life* (Arthur Pearson, 1933), pp.216-7.
6. Baden-Powell Papers, (National Army Museum) 1 October 1900.
7. K.T. Surridge *Managing the South African War, 1899-1902: Politicians V. Generals* (The Royal Historical Society, The Boydell Press), p.110.
8. *The Milner Papers*, 28 October 1900, pp.167-8.
9. Baden-Powell Papers, (N.A.M.) 19 November 1900.
10. Hansard, 13 December 1900, Vol. 88, c675.
11. Bruce Peel Special Collections, quoted in Rod Macleod (endnote 10, p.355).
12. R. Macleod, *Sam Steele: A Biography* (University of Alberta Press, 2018), p.233.
13. Baden-Powell Papers, (N.A.M.) letter book, 24 November 1900.
14. R. S. Curtis, 'South African Constabulary' https://www.Angloboerwar.com/unit-information/south-african-units/2004-south-african-constabulary

Chapter Two

15. R. Sibbald, *The War Correspondents: The Boer War* (Stroud, Sutton Publishing, 1993), pp.130, 144.
16. Baden-Powell Papers, (N.A.M.) 28 February 1991.

17. R. Macleod, *Sam Steele: A Biography* (Edmonton, The University of Alberta Press 2018), p.235.
18. Baden-Powell Papers, (N.A.M.) 6 June 1991.
19. Bruce Peel Special Collections, quoted in R. Macleod, *Sam Steele: A Biography*, p.234.
20. J. Fourie, A. Grundlingh and M. Mariotti, (2017) 'Poor South Africa! Will no nice English people ever come out here?' – The South African Constabulary of the Anglo-Boer War, *The Journal of Imperial and Commonwealth History*, 45:4, 580–606, DOI: 10. 1080/03086534.2017.1332131.
21. D. Reitz, *Commando*, p.59.
22. C.R. De Wet, *Three Years' War* (New York, Charles Scribner's Sons, 1902), n.p.
23. J. Fourie, A. Grundlingh and M. Mariotti.
24. Ibid.
25. Elizabeth Van Heyningen, *The Concentration Camps of the Anglo-Boer War: A Social History* (Sunnyside, Johannesburg, 2013), p.58.

Chapter Three

26. Baden-Powell Papers, N.A.M., 20 November 1900.
27. Ibid, 7 December 1900.
28. Ibid, 13 February 1902.
29. Hansard, 18 February 1901, Vol. 89 cc292-3.
30. Donal Lowry (University of York), 'A Fellowship of Disaffection: Irish-South African Relations from the Anglo-Boer War to Pretoriastroika 1902–1991'. https://www.persee.fr/doc/irlan_0183-973x_1992_num_17_2_1086.
31. Sandra Swart, 'Horses in the South African War' (*Society and Animals* 18), 2010.
32. Baden-Powell, *Lessons from the 'Varsity of Life*, 1933, pp.221-2.

Chapter Four

33. Baden-Powell, 'Notes and Instructions for the South African Constabulary', Bloomfontein Archive.
34. S.B. Spies, *Methods of Barbarism?*, p.73.
35. Ibid., p.30.
36. Major-General Baden-Powell's official report on the Siege of Mafeking; *London Gazette*, Friday, 8 February 1901.

37. *The Scotsman*, 'Death of Mr Frank Whiteley', Thursday, 28 December 1933.
38. D. Lowry (University of York), 'A Fellowship of Disaffection: Irish-South African Relations from the Anglo-Boer War to the Pretoriastroika 1902-1991', https://www.persee.fr/doc/irlan_0183-973x_1992_num_17_2_1086.
39. *London Gazette*, 18 April 1902, p.2600.
40. Baden-Powell papers (N.A.M.), 30 January 1901.
41. Ibid.
42. D. Reitz, p.97.
43. Baden-Powell papers (N.A.M.), 8 March 1901.
44. Albert Grundlingh, 'Collaborators in Boer Society', in *The South African War: The Anglo-Boer War 1899-1902*, p.266.
45. Ibid., p.274.
46. Pakenham, p.499.
47. Quoted in Sibbald, p.221.
48. *The Times History of The War in South Africa 1899-1902*, edited by Erskine Childers, p.261.
49. *Lord Roberts and the War in South Africa 1899-1902*, edited by André Wessels, p.176.
50. R. Macleod, *Sam Steele: A Biography*, p.236.
51. Baden-Powell papers (N.A.M.), 15 June 1901.
52. St John Brodrick to Kitchener, 15 June 1901; quoted in Albert Grundlingh, 'Protectors and friends of the people', The South African Constabulary in the Transvaal and Orange River Colony, 1900-08; Chapter Ten of *Policing the Empire*, Anderson, D.M., Killingray, D. (eds).
53. Baden-Powell, *Lessons from the 'Varsity of Life*, p.236.
54. *Hansard*, 17 March 1902 Vol. 105 c162.

Chapter Five

55. S.B. Spies, 'Women and the War', in *The South African War: The Anglo-Boer War 1899-1902*, p.165.
56. De Wet, n.p.
57. NAUK, WO 30/57/20/1 Kitchener to Brodrick, 20 December 1900.
58. 'Notes and Instructions for the SAC', p.16; see Appendix to this work.
59. Elizabeth Van Heyningen, *Concentration Camps of the Anglo-Boer War* (Jacana Media (Pty) Ltd, 2013), p.203.

60. Thomas Pakenham, *The Boer War* (George Weidenfeld & Nicolson Ltd, 1979), p.494.
61. Emily Hobhouse, *Boer War Letters*, edited by Rykie Van Reenen, (Human & Rousseau, 1984), p.37.
62. Ibid., p.89.
63. Ibid., p.109.
64. *The Milner Papers: South Africa 1899-1905*, edited by Cecil Headlam, Vol. 2, p.164.
65. Elizabeth Van Heyningen, p.153.
66. *The Milner Papers: South Africa 1899-1905*, Vol. 2, pp.229-30.

Chapter Six

67. *London Gazette*, Tuesday August 20, 1901, p.5471.
68. André Wessels, (ed.) *Lord Roberts and the War in South Africa 1899-1902* (Sutton Publishing Ltd., for the Army Records Society, 2000), p.189.
69. *London Gazette*, 15 November, 1901, p.7391.
70. Ibid., 18 February, 1902, p.1036.
71. *Lord Roberts and the War in South Africa 1899-1902*, edited by André Wessels, p.222.
72. *London Gazette*, 25 April, 1902, p.2769.
73. Tim Jeal, *Baden-Powell* (Hutchinson, 1989), pp.336-7.
74. Rod Macleod, *Sam Steele: A Biography* (The University of Alberta Press, 2018), p.240.
75. Ibid., p.241.
76. *London Gazette*, 13 May, 1902, p.3176.
77. André Wessels, p.245.
78. De Wet, n.p.
79. *London Gazette*, 25 March 1902, p.2059.
80. N.A.M., 15 March 1902.
81. Ibid.
82. Bruce Peel Special Collections, University of Alberta.
83. Thomas Pakenham, *The Boer War* (Abacus edition, 1992), p.559.
84. De Wet, n.p.
85. Bruce Peel Special Collections, University of Alberta.
86. Ibid.
87. *London Gazette*, 29 July, 1902, p.4835.

Chapter Seven

88. W. Churchill, *My Early Life* (First published by Thornton Butterworth in 1930 and by Eland Publishing Ltd. in 2000), p.320.
89. N.A.M., 25 November 1902.
90. 'Notes and Instructions for the SAC', Appendix to this work.
91. Ibid.
92. Ibid.
93. Robert Baden-Powell, *Scouting for Boys: A Handbook for Instruction in Good Citizenship* (First published in 1908) p.5.
94. Scott C Spencer, *Scientia Militaria, South African Journal of Military Studies*, Vol. 41, p.98.
95. Ibid., p.101.
96. *London Gazette*, 29 July 1902, pp.4835–4836.
97. Arthur Conan Doyle, *The Great Boer War*, (Thomas Nelson & Sons, 1903) p.529.
98. S.B. Steele, *Confidential Diary; South African Constabulary – 1902-1906*, Bruce Peel Special Collections, University of Alberta.
99. Ibid.
100. Ibid.
101. Ibid.
102. N.A.M., 18 July 1902.
103. Bruce Peel Special Collections, University of Alberta.
104. Ibid.
105. N.A.M., 31 July 1902.
106. Elizabeth Van Heyningen, *The Concentration Camps of the Anglo–Boer War* (Jacana Media Ltd, 2013), p.290.
107. Bruce Peel Special Collections, University of Alberta.
108. Ibid.
109. Rod Macleod, *Sam Steele*, pp.274, 279.
110. Bruce Peel Special Collections, University of Alberta.
111. N.A.M., 12 October 1902.
112. Ibid, 21 October 1902.
113. Ibid, 28 October 1902.

Chapter Eight

114. N.A.M., August 1902.
115. *Scouting for Boys*, pp.28-9.

116. N.A.M., 31 October 1902.

117. Ibid, 4 November 1902.

118. Milner Papers, p.134.

119. N.A.M., 19 November 1902.

120. Bruce Peel Special Collections, University of Alberta.

121. Ibid.

122. Ibid.

123. N.A.M., 14 December 1902.

124. National Archives & Records Service of South Africa, 'South African Constabulary Instructions'.

125. Bruce Peel Special Collections.

126. Ibid.

127. N.A.M., 14 December 1902.

128. Ibid.

129. House of Commons 1903, cited in AngloBoerWar.com.

130. Bruce Peel Special Collections.

Chapter Nine

131. Robert Baden-Powell, *Scouting for Boys: A Handbook for Instruction in Good Citizenship* (Oxford University Press, 1908), pp.44-6.

132. Winston S. Churchill, *Great Contemporaries* (Macmillan & Co. Ltd, 1942), republished by Simon Publications (2001) pp.285-6.

133. 'Notes and Instructions for the SAC', p.16, and the Appendix.

134. Robert Baden-Powell, 'Where the Boy Scouts Partly Started', *Boys' Life* magazine.

135. Robert E Milks, *75 Years of Scouting in Canada*, Scouts Canada, (1981), p.21.

136. Bruce Peel Special Collections, University of Alberta.

137. Karl Köhler, 'Some Aspects of Lord Baden-Powell and the Scouts at Modderfontein,' The South African Military History Society, Military History Journal Vol.12 No.1 – June 2001.

138. The Scout Heritage Service (UK).

139. C. J. Knapman, 'https://scoutwiki.scouts.org.za/wik/SANJAMB_1936_Report

140. Karl Köhler.

141. Winston S. Churchill, p.287.

Bibliography

Baden-Powell, R., *Scouting for Boys: A Handbook for Instruction in Good Citizenship*, 1908 and (ed., with an Introduction and Notes by Elleke Boehmer) Oxford University Press, 2004.

Baden-Powell, R., *Lessons from the 'Varsity of Life* (Arthur Pearson Ltd, 1933).

Churchill, W.S., *My Early Life* (First published by Thornton Butterworth in 1930 and by Eland Publishing Ltd., 2000).

Churchill, W.S., *Great Contemporaries* (Macmillan and Co. Ltd, 1942 and republished by Simon Publications, 2001).

Conan Doyle, A., *The Great Boer War* (Thomas Nelson & Sons, 1903).

Curtis, R. S., 'South African Constabulary' https://www.Angloboerwar.com/unit-information/south-african-units/2004-south-african-constabulary.

De Wet, C.R., *Three Years' War* (New York: Charles Scribner's Sons, 1902).

Fourie, J., Grundlingh, A. and Mariotti, M., 'Poor South Africa! Will no nice English people ever come out here?' – *The South African Constabulary of the Second South African War*, Stellenbosch Economic Working Papers: 04/15.

Grundlingh A., 'Collaborators in Boer Society', in *The South African War: The Anglo-Boer War 1899-1902*.

Headlam, C. (ed.), *The Milner Papers (South Africa 1899-1905) Vol. II* (London: Cassell & Co. Ltd, 1933).

Hobhouse, E., *Boer War Letters*, R. Van Reenen (ed.) (Cape Town: Human & Rousseau, 1984).

Jeal, T., *Baden-Powell* (Hutchinson, 1989).

Köhler, K., 'Some Aspects of Lord Baden-Powell and the Scouts at Modderfontein,' The South African Military History Society, *Military History Journal* Vol.12, No.1 –June 2001.

London Gazette, No. 27282, Friday, February 8, 1901, 'Major-General Baden-Powell's official report on the Siege of Mafeking.'

Macleod, R., *Sam Steele: A Biography* (Edmonton: University of Alberta Press, 2018).

Meintjes, J., *General Louis Botha: A Biography* (Cassell, 1970).

Milks, R.E., *75 Years of Scouting in Canada* (Boy Scouts of Canada, 1982).

Pakenham, T., *The Boer War* (George Weidenfeld & Nicolson Ltd, 1979).

Reitz, D., *Commando: A Boer Journal of the Boer War* (CruGuru, 2008).

Sibbald, R., *The War Correspondents: The Boer War* (Stroud: Sutton Publishing Limited, 1993).

Spies, S.B., *Methods of Barbarism: Roberts and Kitchener and Civilians in the Boer Republics January 1900-May 1902* (Cape Town - Pretoria: Human & Rousseau, 1977).

Steyn, R., *Louis Botha: A Man Apart* (Jeppestown: Jonathan Ball, 2018).

Surridge, K.T., *Managing the South African War: Politicians v. Generals*, (The Royal Historical Society, The Boydell Press, 1998).

Swart, S., 'Horses in the South African War', *Society and Animals* 18, 2010.

Van Heyningen, E., *The Concentration Camps of the Anglo-Boer War: A Social History* (Sunnyside, Johannesburg, 2013).

Warwick, P. (gen. ed. and Spies, S.B. advisory ed.), *The South African War: The Anglo-Boer War 1899-1902* (Harlow: Longman, 1980).

Wessels, André (ed.), *Lord Roberts and the War in South Africa 1899-1902* (Stroud: Sutton Publishing Ltd, 2000).

Index